SHOT DOWN

Also by Marianne van Velzen

Call of the Outback: The remarkable story of Ernestine Hill, nomad, adventurer and trailblazer

Bomber Boys: The extraordinary adventures of a group of airmen who escaped the Japanese and became the RAAF's celebrated 18th Squadron

Missing in Action: Australia's World War I Grave Services, an astonishing story of misconduct, fraud and hoaxing

SHOT DOWN

THE POWERFUL STORY OF WHAT HAPPENED TO MH17 OVER UKRAINE AND THE LIVES OF THOSE WHO WERE ON BOARD

MARIANNE VAN VELZEN

ALLEN&UNWIN
SYDNEY • MELBOURNE • AUCKLAND • LONDON

First published in 2019

Allen & Unwin
83 Alexander Street
Crows Nest NSW 2065
Australia
Phone: (61 2) 8425 0100
Email: info@allenandunwin.com
Web: www.allenandunwin.com

NATIONAL LIBRARY OF AUSTRALIA

A catalogue record for this book is available from the National Library of Australia

ISBN 978 1 76087 558 9

Set in 11.5/18 pt Sabon by Midland Typesetters, Australia
Printed and bound in Australia by Griffin Press, part of Ovato

10 9 8 7 6 5 4 3 2 1

MIX
Paper from responsible sources
FSC® C009448
FSC www.fsc.org

The paper in this book is FSC® certified. FSC® promotes environmentally responsible, socially beneficial and economically viable management of the world's forests.

To Tom and Romy

There is a higher court than courts of justice, and that is the court of conscience. It supersedes all other courts.

Mahatma Gandhi

Contents

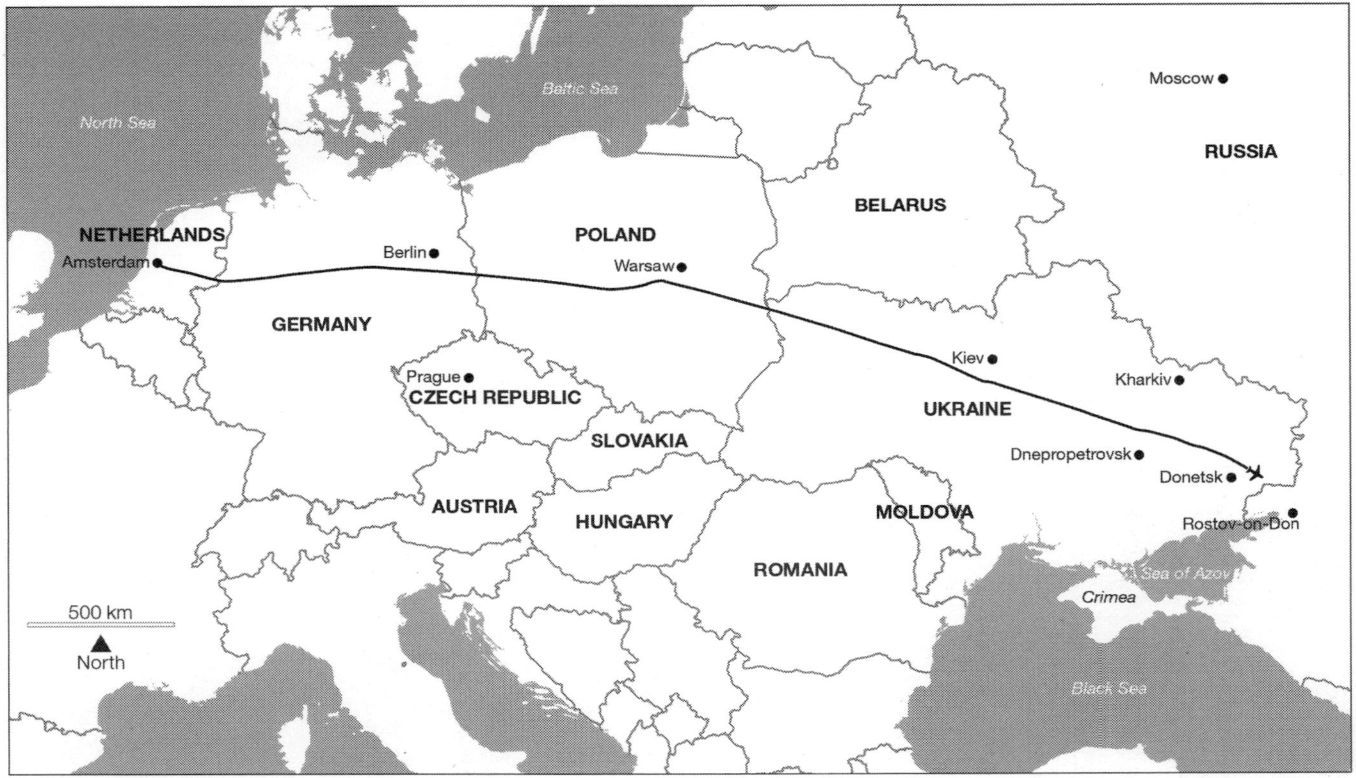

Route taken by MH17

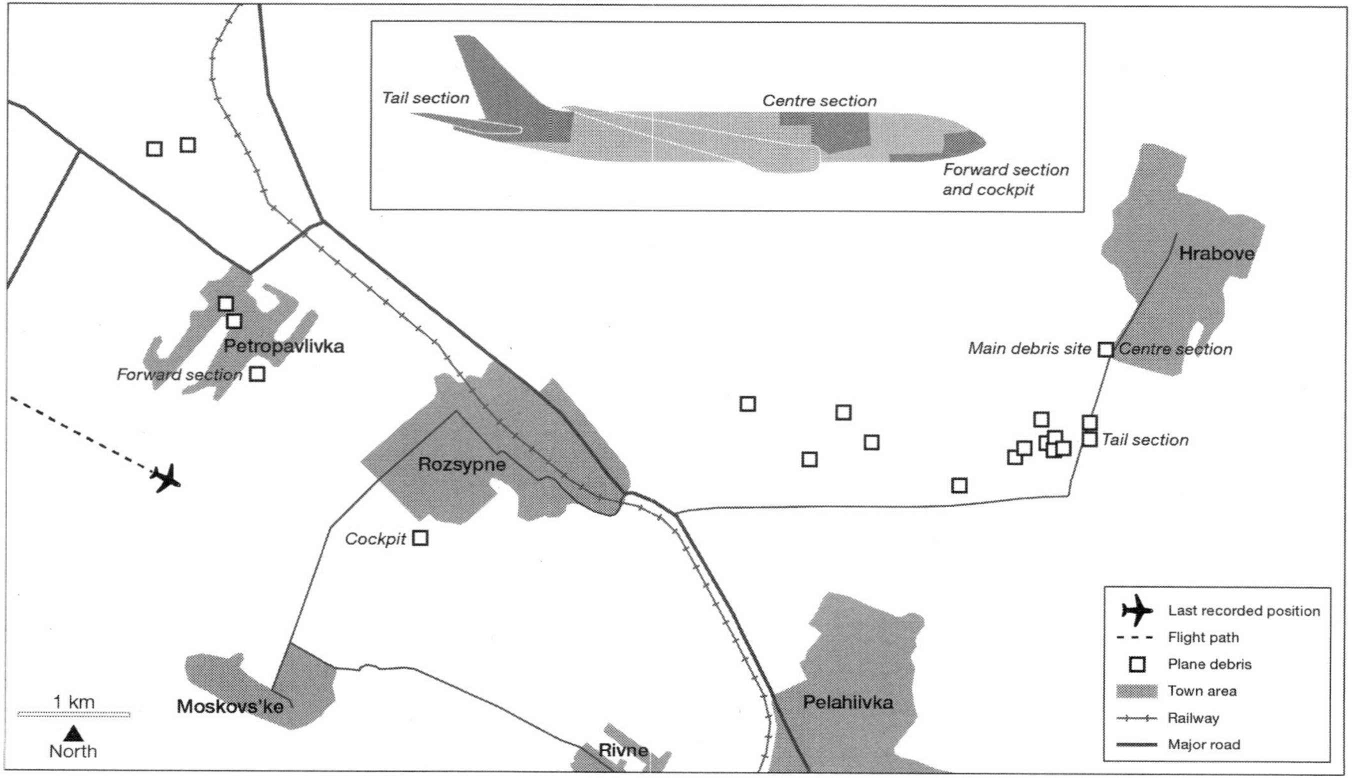

MH17 debris sites

Source: Dutch Safety Board

Chapter 1
Amsterdam, 17 July 2014

It was mid-summer, 17 July 2014, and the height of the school holidays in the Netherlands. Everyone in the country appeared to have booked a flight for today. There was a huge shortage of ground personnel at the airport, so it was all hands on deck to get the passengers through transfer, check-in and down to the gates on time to catch their planes.

Renuka Manisha Virangna Birbal had begun her shift earlier that morning at the transfer counter. She worked for one of the companies that helped dispatch passengers at the Netherlands' main airport, Schiphol. Appointed to various carriers, today she was working as ground staff for Malaysia Airlines Flight MH17. The night before Renuka had stayed up late, thinking that she would be able to sleep-in the next day. It was supposed to be her day off, but she awoke early in the morning to the sound of her phone. It was incredibly busy at Amsterdam's Schiphol airport and she had been rostered on at the last moment.

Despite having had only a few hours' sleep, Renuka didn't really mind: she would return to bed when she got back to her apartment later that day.

Although the job could be hectic, she loved it, especially when she was able to get the passengers seated according to their various wishes. She had made two football fanatics exceptionally happy after she managed to get them adjacent seats. One was already checked in and the other was still in transit, and they were openly grateful that she had them seated not only next to one another but had also given one of them a window seat.

Just after Renuka finished the transfers, colleagues at the check-in counter asked her for assistance. The passengers waiting patiently in line to be checked in were all dressed lightly. They were a mixed lot, as was the norm on the Amsterdam to Kuala Lumpur flights—mainly Dutch but also a large number of Australians, Malays, Indonesians and one or two New Zealanders.

It was a beautiful warm summer morning in Amsterdam. The Dutch so often complained about their weather but Renuka, born in Suriname (the former Dutch colony on the north-eastern coast of South America), never understood their whingeing. They quickly reverted to anxious remarks whenever there was even the slightest hint of rain or clouds, cold or damp; this appeared imbedded in the national character. Renuka had never come across a nation so obsessed with the weather as the Dutch were. This concern surprised her because summers in the small country were more often than not incredibly mild and warm, and also wonderfully bright and clear, quite different to the tropical weather of her homeland. She had come to love summer in the Netherlands.

A family of five with ten pieces of luggage thanked her for managing to get them all seated close to one another and she wished them a wonderful holiday. The youngest child seemed anxious about her suitcase as it disappeared through the transport hatch and she asked Renuka if she would get it back. Renuka smiled and assured the child that her luggage would be waiting for her when she arrived at Kuala Lumpur.

As the next passenger stepped up to the check-in counter, the plane's crew members waved to her as they rushed by to drop their bags off at the belt for odd-sized luggage. She waved back as the man next in line handed her his papers and passport. Asking him if he would like a window seat, the burly man nodded. The plane was so full that there were only a few single window seats left. The man smiled, telling her that he was off to Malaysia to start a new life. Her smile in return was sincere, and she wished him good luck as she handed him his boarding pass.

For Renuka the check-in seemed to take hours, but the long line in front of her desk had now almost disappeared and there was only a trickle of stragglers. When one final passenger rushed up to her counter, slightly out of breath, she checked him in quickly before he grabbed his boarding pass with a quick nod of his head and rushed towards the customs line.

The plane was obviously overbooked. For the moment she sent all of the passengers through because there were always 'no-shows'—passengers who missed their flight even after they had checked in. But just as she was getting ready to leave her booth, a group of about ten people rushed up. They were travelling together and Renuka immediately knew she would not be able to get such a large party onto the overfull flight. When she made this clear, their faces fell in dismay; one or two of them protested, but most of them just stood there in stunned disappointment.

Asking them to wait, she looked for a flight that could take them all. Emirates, leaving at half past two that afternoon, had enough empty seats to book them in. Because they were beginning to think that they might not be able to get on a flight until the next day, they were more than happy to wait just a couple of hours.

Renuka now headed for Gate 3, knowing there would be an overbooking problem awaiting her there. At the gate she discovered there were hardly any no-shows, and she discussed this with a colleague there. It was always a challenging task to be the staff member who informed checked in passengers that they would not be able to board the plane.

Asking for volunteers to be transferred to another flight was the first and easiest option. Those who did so received handsome compensation, but Renuka knew how difficult it was to persuade passengers to take a later flight. People were always eager to get home or start their holiday, or they had pressing business appointments to meet or urgent duties elsewhere; rarely were they willing to give up their seat on a flight they assumed they were booked onto. The always hard and thankless job of informing people that they would not be able to board the plane was the one part of her work she loathed, as passengers seldom endured their fate graciously. Some put up a fight, she knew from experience, but they usually backed down when the inevitable dawned on them.

Renuka always chose young and visibly fit passengers to be transferred onto a later flight. It was easier for the young to accept and adjust to the disruption of their travel plans than it was for older people or those travelling with children, for whom this was just one more issue to contend with. But first she would ask people to give up their place on the plane voluntarily and then, if the plane still had too many passengers, Renuka and her colleague would have to choose the unfortunates.

She scanned the rows of waiting passengers. An older man with three children had been on the phone for a while. The children pressed themselves against the huge window panes as they pointed at the various planes on the runway. It seemed no parents were accompanying the children, just a man who appeared to be their grandfather.

At the end of a row of passengers waiting at the gate, a boy of about sixteen or so was talking to his mother, his expression one of anxious anticipation. Noticing how his mother listened intently to what he was telling her, Renuka could read in her hand movements and reassuring smiles that she was trying to set her son's mind at ease. During her years of working at the airport she had learned to read facial expressions and body movements. It was part of her job.

A young man in his late twenties sitting next to the mother and son smiled cheekily at his phone, as he posted a message or maybe a photo into cyberspace; Renuka thought it was probably something silly he had sent to his friends at the last minute. As she stood behind her counter watching the passengers while they waited to board the plane, Renuka had no idea that she would never forget the faces of the people on this particular flight. She also had no idea that the choices she and her colleague would make in regard to who could board the plane and who could not, would later that day turn out to be the choice between life and death.

Not the young boy and his mother, she decided. He appeared nervous and apprehensive enough as it was. He had stopped talking to his mother now and looked to be observing the plane that was almost ready for the passengers. As he turned his head from the window, she glimpsed his face. His expression was one of fear, but also resignation. It wasn't hard for Renuka to guess what he might be thinking; she could almost hear the words in his mind: 'They've already lost one plane, so why can't they lose another?'

Just four and a half months before, Malaysia Airlines Flight MH370, a scheduled international passenger flight, had disappeared. It was 8 March 2014 and the plane vanished while flying from Kuala Lumpur International Airport, Malaysia, to its destination, Beijing Capital International Airport in China. The Boeing 777 operated by Malaysia Airlines had last made voice contact with air traffic control on 8 March as it was making its way over the South China Sea, just under an hour after take-off. The aircraft disappeared from air traffic controllers' radar screens but was still tracked by military radar as it swerved westwards from its planned flight path crossing the Malay Peninsula.

The radar lost track of the plane as it hovered over the Andaman Sea near north-western Malaysia. It was carrying twelve Malaysian crew members and 227 passengers from fifteen different nations.

A few days later Malaysia, working alongside foreign aviation authorities and experts, launched a joint investigation team to investigate the incident. Australia took charge of the search when there were indications that the plane may have gone down into the southern Indian Ocean. Different theories about the cause of the disappearance arose, even one that suggested that the plane had been hijacked and was standing somewhere in the desert in ISIS territory with all its passengers still on board. That was in fact the most comforting theory: it meant that people's loved ones were possibly alive and waiting somewhere to be found and released. It was also the most far-fetched of all the theories. Some researchers believed that it was a pilot's private suicide mission that had caused the plane to vanish, a difficult idea for Malaysia to accept with suicide a taboo.

Now, more than four months later, there was still no trace of the aircraft. Its disappearance remained a mystery. With no bodies to bury for the bereaved, all they had left were memories to cling to. There would be no closure for the families of MH370 for a long time to come, and everyone working for Malaysia Airlines had been devastated. Renuka realised that some of the passengers were inevitably asking themselves if their plane could go missing too. She also knew the odds were next to none. The disappearance was a freak incident, and the chances of something similar happening were likely to be one in a million.

As she tried to obliterate the horrible memory of all those missing people, she turned to her work.

Rather reluctantly, her colleague reminded her it was time to choose eight passengers to be transferred onto a later flight. Via the intercom they asked for volunteers. To their surprise, a man, his wife and three children rose from their seats and made their way to the desk. The flight with three children to Malaysia was very expensive and the man wanted to know how much compensation he would get and when the next flight was scheduled. When they told him, he smiled. The compensation was a very nice cut in costs and the family did not appear too worried about having to wait for the next flight.

They picked a young man travelling alone and a couple and called them all to the desk to inform them of the bad news. The couple weren't happy and tried to persuade Renuka to let them board anyway, but when she explained that the transfer to another flight was inevitable but that they would be compensated, they resigned to their fate. They weren't happy, but they didn't want to start this trip, a trip they had been looking forward to for so long, with an argument.

When Renuka checked the young man's papers she realised that his Dutch passport had almost expired—in fact, the expiry date was the next day. The fellow, in his late teens, became very upset when she told him that boarding was out of the question because his passport would expire before he landed in Malaysia. And before they could check him onto another flight, his passport would need to be renewed at the airport passport office. Irritated, the young man started directing his anger at Renuka, but after a while they managed to calm him and one of the Schiphol aides was called in to take him to the passport office. Around 11.30am peace returned to Gate 3 and they started the final check-in to board the passengers.

An elderly woman who had trouble walking was helped to board first by a crew member. A few people Renuka had helped at the baggage counter recognised her as they passed by her for the second time; there were smiles and a quick word.

Renuka noticed another familiar face in the boarding line, her colleague from the Malaysia Airlines ticket counter on his way home for a holiday with his wife and son. When she bade him a final good flight, he produced his boarding pass and said, 'See you soon,' as he disappeared into the passenger airbridge tunnel. When the last of the passengers had gone down the bridge and were seated, she heard the final clunk of plane doors closing, the sound hollow and dry as it echoed down the corridor. They were almost ready to remove the bridge.

Renuka was home by one. Tired from lack of sleep and the busy morning, she fell asleep almost at once only to be awoken a few hours later by her phone. It kept ringing incessantly and, when she peeked at it, the callers were colleagues. She turned it off; they probably wanted her to return to the airport, but she was tired and all she wanted now was to sleep. In a couple of hours she'd phone them back, she thought, as she blissfully slumbered back into that oblivious state of mind where bad things do happen, but only in dreams.

Chapter 2

Ukraine, November 2013

It was a cold Saturday morning and Viktor Yanukovych's breath was short and urgent, turning into small puffs of icy fog as he hurried down the steps to the presidential limousine waiting to take him to the airport. Weighing 110 kilos and over six feet tall, he had to squeeze himself through the limousine door, held open by one of his staff. His mission today was an important one: the president of Ukraine was on his way to meet the president of the Russian Federation, Vladimir Putin, in Moscow. To talk business.

The 63-year-old Yanukovych had been elected Ukrainian president three years prior on 25 February 2010. For the past decade he had loomed large on Ukraine's political scene. Holding a prominent position in the Ukrainian government wasn't new to him: from 2002 to 2005 he had been prime minister and from 2006 till 2007 he had served another term as PM.

Ukraine had been a Cossack republic that emerged and prospered during the seventeenth and eighteenth centuries, but its territory was eventually split between Poland and the Russian Empire, and finally merged fully into the Russian-dominated Soviet Union in the late 1940s as the Ukrainian Soviet Socialist Republic. It wasn't until 1991 and the end of the Cold War that Ukraine gained its independence from the Soviet Union.

Many still remembered the Holodomor, often talked about as the Ukrainian holocaust. The Holodomor, also known as the Great Famine, was a man-made famine in Soviet Ukraine in 1932 and 1933; it killed millions of Ukrainians. It was part of the wider Soviet famine, which affected the major grain-producing areas of the country. During the Holodomor, millions of inhabitants of Ukraine, the majority of whom were ethnic Ukrainians, died of starvation in a peacetime catastrophe unprecedented in the history of the country. When the famine started, Stalin exported almost two million tonnes of food out of Ukraine, thus removing the little people had to survive on. Then he barred the people who were hit the hardest from moving to any other part of the country. They had no food, and with no means of escape they could do nothing but wait for death. In response to the demographic collapse, the Soviet authorities ordered large-scale resettlements, with over 117,000 peasants from remote regions of the Soviet Union taking over the deserted farms in eastern Ukraine.

The elections held in late 2004 were the fourth presidential elections to take place in Ukraine following its independence from the Soviet Union in 1991. They were both dramatic and controversial. Ultimately, they became a contest between Viktor Yanukovych, the incumbent prime minister, and Viktor Yushchenko, who was at this time the opposition leader.

According to the results announced on 23 November, the run-off election had been won by Prime Minister Yanukovych, but the results were challenged by Yushchenko and his supporters, as well as by many international observers. They all claimed that the election, held in a highly charged political atmosphere, had been rigged and there were allegations of media bias, voter intimidation and even the poisoning of candidate Yushchenko with dioxin. The proceedings became a cause for national and international concern and in the end Yanukovych's victory was ruled fraudulent and annulled by the Ukrainian Supreme Court.

Under intense scrutiny by domestic and international observers, a second run-off was held and declared to be 'fair and free'. Yushchenko was declared the official winner and at his inauguration on 23 January 2005 in Kiev (also written as Kyiv), he nominated as his prime minister Yulia Tymoshenko, the first woman ever to be appointed prime minister of Ukraine. Her tightly braided blonde hair soon made her an internationally recognisable public figure. Yanukovych was left empty-handed and bitter, as he felt the court's ruling had been a great injustice. Political turmoil occupied the first few years of Yushchenko's presidency.

Even Yanukovych could never have predicted or foreseen that he would one day become such an important man. He liked to tell the press that he grew up barefoot and hungry. By the time he was in his teens he seemed destined to lead a life of crime when, just barely sixteen, he found himself on trial for robbery and assault and was sentenced to prison. The fiftieth anniversary of the Russian Revolution in 1967 saved him from a ruinous destiny; he was granted a pardon after serving eighteen months and released.

Thankful to the Russians for the pardon he had received, the young Yanukovych joined the Communist Party of the Soviet Union. He ultimately became the manager of a transport company, studied international law and became a professor of economics, although many were doubtful about the way in which he had acquired his degree.

In the region of Ukraine where he had grown up the main language was Russian, so he learned Ukrainian much later in life. Although he started studying the language after taking office in 2002, even as late as 2013 he still found it difficult to express himself in proficient Ukrainian and would switch to his native Russian when dealing with difficult subjects. Because of this, the opposition often found him a somewhat dim political candidate.

Before the 2004 elections Yanukovych's ego had been badly dented by what became known as the candidate's 'assassination by egg'. On a visit to a university, an egg was thrown at him by an activist and he had reacted dramatically, collapsing in the street, groaning and clutching his chest. Assuming someone had attempted to assassinate him, he was rushed to hospital and taken into intensive care. Just hours later he was discharged from hospital after the staff found nothing wrong with him, except for a soiled shirt front. He was the target of ridicule from the opposition for months afterwards.

In the six years that followed, Yanukovych perceived Yulia Tymoshenko, the woman who had taken the prime ministership from him, as his perpetual rival. She was ten years younger than the burly and somewhat coarse Yanukovych, and pretty to boot. Because of her resemblance to actress Carrie Fisher, she was nicknamed the 'Princess Leia of Ukrainian politics'. Not simply good-looking, she was also a practising economist and academic and, prior to her political career, she had been a successful, albeit controversial, businesswoman in the gas industry. This had made her one of the richest people in the country.

Before becoming Ukraine's first female prime minister in 2005, Tymoshenko became known as one of the initiators of the Orange Revolution in Ukraine. The Orange Revolution of 2004 had been aimed at stopping Yanukovych from becoming president after the election that was widely believed to have been rigged. After those elections Tymoshenko asked people to demonstrate wearing orange symbols, the colour of her party, in an effort to denounce Yanukovych's presidency. Tymoshenko called Kiev residents to gather on the square and asked people from other cities and towns to come to Kiev and stand for their choice and demand that the 'real' winner, Yushchenko, become the people's president.

On 22 November 2004, massive protests in favour of Yushchenko and Tymoshenko broke out in cities across Ukraine: the movement became known as the Orange Revolution. During the tumultuous months of the revolution, candidate Yushchenko suddenly became gravely ill, and was soon found by multiple independent physician groups to have been poisoned by TCDD dioxin. Yushchenko strongly suspected Russian involvement in his poisoning. But he and Tymoshenko had formed a pro-West pact and ultimately won the re-run of the elections that year.

A deep hatred of Russia had simmered among the ethnic peoples in northern and western Ukraine for eighty years now. They were the ones who wanted reform and the severance of ties with Russia. They wanted nothing more than to turn their hopes to the West, because this held a promise of better times if their country became a member of the European Union. They were the supporters of the pro-West Viktor Yushchenko and Yulia Tymoshenko.

But in the eastern part of the country the ethnic Russians and a large section of pro-Russian voters backed Yanukovych; he had promised to investigate all options that the European Union offered, but these voters felt assured that he would not turn his back on them. The nation was bitterly split.

Six years later in the first round of the 2010 presidential elections Yulia Tymoshenko ran against Yanukovych. She received 25 per cent of the votes and Yanukovych 35 per cent. Although she was behind, it was a surprise that Yulia Tymoshenko had managed to gather even this many votes. During Yushchenko's and Tymoshenko's reign, the country had been brought to the verge of bankruptcy as Russia implemented ever more sanctions in retaliation for the efforts of Ukraine to become part of the European Union. During the height of winter, Russia had tuned off the gas supply to Ukraine, and the fear of another Holodomor had left the older population anxious. Many of them turned to Yanukovych. In large parts of the country Yanukovych was admired because he had been a street kid, raised in a violent town by his grandmother, and had managed to achieve success by the force of his own willpower.

Nonetheless, Yanukovych's comeback against Tymoshenko in 2010 was not a convincing victory. Neither candidate managed to secure a clear majority in the preliminary voting and Yanukovych's victory in the run-off on 7 February 2010 was by a narrow 3.5 per cent. In the aftermath Tymoshenko refused to acknowledge the defeat, accusing her rival of having forged the outcome of the elections. It was only after Yanukovych managed to secure a parliamentary majority of five that Tymoshenko finally withdrew.

When Yanukovych had come to office in 2010 Ukraine was on the verge of bankruptcy, and because the Russians had turned off the gas supply, its population was freezing. After declaring its independence from the Soviet Union in 1991, the country had begun to forge relationships with its Western neighbours; this had caused relations with the Russians to become complicated and, when Vladimir Putin came to power in 2000, matters appeared to escalate. Russia shut down the Ukrainian gas supply in a dispute over debts in both 2006 and 2009; Putin also reportedly threatened Ukraine with nuclear attack in 2009 if it joined NATO and this threat pushed relations between the two countries to an all-time low.

At the start of 2009 Russia had refused to offer Ukraine a new gas contract because of a $2.4 billion debt that Ukraine had yet to pay for the gas it had received in 2008. On 1 January 2009, at 10am, Gazprom completely stopped pumping gas to

Ukraine, and on 4 January the Russian monopolist offered to pump gas back into the country for twice the amount Ukraine had once paid. Using their own gas reserves, the Ukrainian electricity generators were working to their utmost capacity but, due to sub-zero temperatures, demand was greater than the amount of gas available, so the entire housing and public utilities sectors were soon on the verge of collapse due to unworkable and unliveable conditions. Just before the 2010 elections, the country was suffering terribly and in turmoil.

Shortly after Yanukovych won the elections in 2010, the Ukrainian prosecutor general's office launched a number of criminal cases against Yulia Tymochenko, among others, for abuse of office concerning a natural gas imports contract signed with Russia in January 2009. These legal proceedings prevented her from normal political activity and from international travel to her allies in the West.

On 11 October 2011 she was officially convicted of embezzlement and abuse of power, sentenced to seven years in prison and ordered to pay the state $188 million. The prosecution and conviction were viewed as politically motivated by many governments. It was evident that for Yanukovych, Tymoshenko remained his pain in the rear end. Forever critical of his actions and intentions, Tymoshenko accused her rival of harbouring plans to sell out to Russia.

On 30 December 2011, Tymoshenko was transferred to the Kachanivska penal colony in the city of Kharkiv. For two years she went on a number of hunger strikes intended as a protest against her incarceration. Even hidden away in such a place, she managed to be an irritant. When Yanukovych went to the EU to propose a business deal, they had demanded that he release her from prison and that she be allowed to travel to Germany before they would consider accepting his proposal.

Most Ukrainians agreed that she should be released, though many were also suspicious as to how she had amassed her wealth. Yanukovych disliked her immensely and when he was asked if he would be inclined to release her, he told the press that Tymoshenko had never once acknowledged his legitimacy as president and had furthermore refused to ask him for forgiveness, thus making it impossible for him to pardon her.

When the stout man headed for the airport on that Saturday morning in November 2013, his rival was still in Kharkiv doing time. But he himself had come a long way from being the barefoot boy once imprisoned and destined for a life of theft and abuse, and he had not forgotten to reward himself handsomely for his ascent.

Just after his presidential victory in 2010, Yanukovych had bought himself a small house in Mezhyhirya, about twenty kilometres from Ukraine's capital, Kiev. The purchase appeared modest for a president, but the land that came with the small house was anything but paltry. The tiny structure was set on 140 hectares of stunningly beautiful countryside. As soon as Yanukovych managed to secure the property, he started turning the grounds into his own private 'Neverland'.

The modest home was replaced by a massive three-storey mansion as well as a wooden chalet. The guesthouse, intended to receive presidents and members of state, counted five storeys and was built in a typical Russian style. To amuse his visitors and himself, he built a golf course, a private zoo and saunas. Majestic bridges traversed the river that ran through the estate.

Not many people knew of Yanukovych's exorbitantly luxurious country home and he was very intent on keeping it that way. Only special guests and friends were invited to his private residence. Realising all too well that his wealth would not go down well with his fellow citizens, who were faced with shortages and poverty on an everyday basis, he did not flaunt his possessions and, for the time being, voters trusted him, hoping their new president would follow the democratic path the country was delicately tiptoeing along.

Yanukovych in fact appeared in no way hostile towards the European Union. To prove this, just after he was elected, he had made his way to Brussels to talk to the then EU president, Herman van Rompuy. But Yanukovych returned from this visit without having signed a European treaty. Estimates indicated that he would need US$160 billion over three years to make up for the trade Ukraine stood to lose with Russia if he turned to the West. The billions would also be useful in cushioning the pain from reforms the EU was demanding. But the EU regarded this sum to be exaggerated and unjustified, and it refused to ask its members to cough up these billions. The US$550 million that Europe had offered Yanukovych, to protect him from the wrath of Moscow, was a slap in the face for the Ukrainian president. The EU trade agreement they had offered would be worth nothing if Putin once again turned off Ukraine's gas supply.

Moscow had been systematically blocking sales of Ukrainian-produced meat, cheese and confectionery for a number of years. Yanukovych demanded sufficient protection from Europe against any Russian sanctions before he signed anything and was disappointed by what had been offered. Van Rompuy told him that any sanctions from the Soviets would be deemed unacceptable, but Moscow, as a warning, had already started tightening the thumbscrews during the Yushchenko administration. Yanukovych did not think that the EU would be able to do anything about Moscow's vengeance if it became thoroughly aggravated.

On the other hand, because of his humble roots, Yanukovych liked to be treated with respect and as an equal. During a meeting with the Party of Regions, the biggest pro-Russia political party in Ukraine, he had made it clear that he disliked Russia's approach to Ukraine and felt he was being treated as a second-rate participant in negotiations. He resented being patronised.

In Brussels, by contrast, he had been treated well by EU officials. In the eyes of Europe, Yanukovych appeared to be the perfect man to persuade Ukraine's pro-Russian eastern regions to strike up business deals with the West. The EU officials acted as if they would do anything to get him on their side, but they also showed they had reservations about a man whose reputation was considered at least dubious, and at times very questionable.

It was evident that the president of Ukraine was caught between a rock and a hard place. He feared that any treaty with the EU would enrage the Russians, so breaking from their tight grip was no small matter. Ukraine and Russia had much in common; the two countries had been economically, culturally and historically connected for decades. But his people craved democracy and wealth; they wanted clean air and water, safe food and a decent education for their children. Yanukovych knew most of his countrymen were pro-Europe and would not be happy if he did not turn to the West, but he somehow had to also deal with an angry neighbour in the east.

Russia was still considered to be the motherland by many Ukrainians living on the eastern borders with Russia. They were in no way keen to sever their ties; they still spoke Russian and were loyal to Moscow. The Ukrainian southern peninsula of Crimea had, not so long ago, been a part of the Soviet Union and it was home to more than a million ethnic Russians. Crimea had been gifted to Ukraine in 1954 by former leader of the Soviet Union Nikita Khrushchev. Russia still treated it as part of its empire and, although it officially belonged to Ukraine, the peninsula had its own parliament and its own government controlling its agriculture, public infrastructure and tourism. As Yanukovych made his way to speak to the Russian president, no one could have predicted that the February 2010 elections would be the last Ukrainian election that Crimea participated in as part of the local elections for their own parliament.

In the east of Ukraine, where Yanukovych had been born and bred, the Russian language had long dominated in government and the media, and when Ukraine became independent there were no Ukrainian-language schools in Donetsk. During the 2010 elections, voters in both the eastern and southern provinces of Ukraine had strongly supported Yanukovych. Two years after his election he had rewarded those voters when his government enacted a law decreeing that any local language spoken by at least 10 per cent of the population to be declared an official regional language within that area. Within weeks, Russian was declared a regional language in several southern and eastern provinces and cities. The law allowed the use of minority languages in courts, schools and other government institutions in areas of Ukraine and was used mostly in Ukraine's southern and eastern regions.

Little could Yanukovych have known as he headed to Moscow that what he was about to do would eventually lead to disaster in more ways than one. Within the year, a small village called Hrabove near Donetsk, very close to his birthplace, would become the scene of one of the worst civilian airline incidents in postwar Europe.

Chapter 3
17 July 2014

The flight's fifteen crew members—two pilots, two copilots and eleven flight attendants—had made their way past Renuka earlier that morning. As they hurried by and entered the airbridge, a couple of them had quickly waved their farewells to her. Most of the Muslim Malaysia Airlines staff were heading home to celebrate Eid with their families. An important religious holiday observed by Muslims worldwide, Eid al-Fitr marks the end of Ramadan, the Islamic holy month of fasting.

Flight attendant Sanjid Singh Sandhu wasn't supposed to be on Flight MH17 but had managed to swap shifts with a colleague at the last minute. Shifts were often exchanged for various reasons and it was quite a common practice among air crew members. It did not go against airline guidelines and, as long as the required number of crew were on board to assist, nobody minded.

Sanjid was looking forward to spending time with his wife and their seven-year-old son, Hans. He had been in Amsterdam for three days and his mother had promised to cook his favourite dishes to celebrate the end of Ramadan. No one called Sanjid by his birth name; everyone called him Bobby. The name had been given to him by his childhood nanny who loved Bollywood movies, especially one called *Bobby*. The name had stuck throughout his life.

Bobby took his job very seriously. Airlines look for friendly people who can memorise a lot of information and keep a cool head under pressure. His day began before the first passenger boarded the plane and would continue throughout the entire flight. To get a position with an airline, potential flight attendants must interview for the job, pass a medical exam, and work their way through a rigorous schedule of instruction and performance reviews. Bobby had done just that, but he was well aware that there were many more flight attendant applicants than positions. Only a select few made it through the entire process and were hired by the airline, but it was worth all the hard work because the job offered unique benefits. His family could fly domestically and internationally at minimal cost, so long as seats were available. Also, it wasn't a five-day, nine-to-five schedule, and this made it possible to synchronise his flights with his wife, who also worked for the airline.

Bobby's wife, Tan Bee Geok, was a flight attendant, but she was not on MH17 today. The couple had had a narrow escape four months earlier when Tan had swapped shifts on Malaysia Flight MH370. When that plane disappeared from the skies with everyone on board, Tan had been devastated, but at the same time she had felt very fortunate at the twist of fate. It had been a close call and had brought home to both of them how perilous the airline business could be. But Bobby was flying home in the knowledge that his wife was safe and waiting in Malaysia for her husband to arrive.

The senior captain on MH17 was Chinese-born Eugene Choo Jin Leong, who lived in Seremban with his family. After he stepped on board that morning he had gone through his checklist. It contained the details of the flight, and so far the procedures had been standard.

After Captain Choo and his crew boarded the plane, he'd gone through his checklist again with his first officer. It included flight details such as the weather, the number of passengers on board and the list of other crew members he'd be working with that day. His first officer then performed a general inspection of the aircraft inside and out to make sure everything was in good order. The walk-around outside was done before each flight to check for leaks, bird strikes or anything else unusual. The ramp area was busy with tugs, baggage carts, fuel trucks and belt loaders. It could be a hazardous place, particularly with bags and freight going up the belt loader and into the holds. But it was a standard procedure, and after this walk-through the pilots met up in the cockpit again and made sure all the instruments and controls were working properly. When they were finished, they had waited for the 'all clear to proceed' order to come in. The take-off had been fifteen minutes late but otherwise it had been smooth sailing.

Choo's wife, Ivy Loi, and his two sons, Melvic and Scott, thirteen and eleven years old, were waiting for him to arrive home. He was flying the first part of the twelve-hour trip together with his first officer and copilot, 26-year-old Muhamad Firdaus Bin Abdul Rahim. During the second part of the flight, Captain Wan Amran Bin Wan Hussin and his first officer, Ahmad Hakimi Bin Hanapi, were scheduled to take over.

The primary reason for having two captains on every long-haul flight is safety. Obviously, if something were to happen to the captain, the plane must have another captain who can step in. Additionally, the second captain provides another opinion on important decisions, keeping pilot error to a minimum. Long-haul flights are simply too arduous for a single captain to fly the whole route, so all major airlines provide a double cockpit crew.

In keeping with his usual routine, Captain Wan Amran had messaged his wife shortly before take-off. He had been piloting Boeing aircraft for more than twenty years and knew that his wife liked to know when he was leaving.

Wan Amran had big plans for this coming year. He was making preparations to perform the hajj, the symbolic pilgrimage to Mecca made by millions of Muslims of different ethnic groups and cultures from across the world to praise Allah and ask for forgiveness for their sins. Performing the hajj is a mandatory religious duty for Muslims and must be carried out at least once in their lifetime. He was already forty-nine years old and would turn fifty in September, so he had decided he could not wait much longer to perform this sacred duty; he must go before he was too old. And after Malaysia Airlines Flight MH370 disappeared, he had realised just how short life could be. Flight MH370's captain, Zaharie Amad Shah, was Wan Amran's best friend, and Wan had been devastated by the news.

After enjoying three days' leave in Amsterdam, Wan Amran was now returning to his kampung near the town of Kuala Kangsar and was quite eager to get back to his wife, Miriam, and his two sons, who were nine and seven. Celebrating the end of Ramadan was a festive and very family-oriented event, and he looked forward to it.

Neither Amran or Choo were overly worried about their flight path and where it would take them. Although civilian airlines had been warned since March 2014 to avoid flying over certain parts of Ukraine, those warnings were mainly for the area around the Crimea peninsula because there were ongoing hostilities between Ukraine and the Russian Federation about the annexation of the peninsula by Moscow. Some operators had diverted their routes to the north or south of Crimea, which took them to flight paths above either Turkey or eastern Ukraine. From 19 April British Airways was no longer flying over Ukraine, with the exception of its once-a-day flight to the capital Kiev, but British Virgin Atlantic continued to fly over the country.

Australia's Qantas had also stopped flying over Ukraine, shifting its London–Dubai route 645 kilometres to the south to avoid Crimea. Etihad claimed it did not fly over Ukraine but Emirates did; there were conflicting reports, although both airlines were certainly flying over dangerous areas such as Iraq. The American airlines United and Delta were no longer flying over the country; Delta had rerouted on 10 March, avoiding Crimea and taking a flight path further south, while United had followed suit on 14 July.

There were no specific guidelines and it wasn't exceptional to fly over dangerous countries; it was almost the norm. What could happen at 33,000 feet up in the air, so far away from any hostilities? None of MH17's fifteen crew members were concerned about flying over Ukraine. Although rebels were fighting the Ukrainian government on the ground, no union members had raised concerns about flying through the airspace above the war-torn country although a Notice to Airmen (NOTAM) had been issued days before, which stated that civilian aircraft were advised to fly only at high altitude to ensure international flight safety. 'Due to combat actions on the territory of Ukraine near the state border with the Russian Federation and the fact of firing from the territory of Ukraine towards the territory of the Russian Federation'. On 14 July 2014 a new NOTAM was issued specific to the Dnipropetrovsk region. In that NOTAM the eastern edge of Ukrainian airspace was marked as off limits, but the NOTAM also was only applicable for FL260–FL320, which meant commercial aircraft should fly above 32,000 feet.

The International Civil Aviation Organization had given the green light for aircraft to fly over the area, as long as their flight path was in the designated air zone. The troubled region of eastern Ukraine took ten minutes to cross for a passenger aircraft, and other airlines were sending their planes across its airspace on a daily basis without giving it a second thought. Although pilots could refuse to fly over a war zone, they seldom did. It did not win you any popularity points with airlines and, in the worst-case scenario, it could even get you fired.

Malaysia Airlines had flown this route repeatedly during the past several weeks without incident, as had many other carriers. And the rules when flying an aircraft were very similar to driving a car: if the road was open, you assumed that it was safe. If it was closed, you would find an alternative route. In any case, being forced to fly around Ukraine would be a major pain. The country was right in the middle of a common direct route between Europe and Southeast Asia. Longer routes meant more fuel and more chances for delays; delays and higher airfares caused irritation to passengers. War zone or not, airlines would generally fly the shortest route unless it was deemed too risky. With this flight it was no different.

Malaysia Airlines First Officer Muhamad Firdaus Bin Abdul Rahim was one of the younger members of the air crew. Only twenty-six years old, he was soon to become a father. His wife, Nur Zarith Zaaba, a nurse at University Kebangsaan Malaysia Hospital, was two months into her pregnancy. They had been high school sweethearts and had tied the knot just over a year ago. Muhamad was destined to become a pilot. His family included six aviators, with a few of his cousins still too young but waiting patiently in line, eager to take up piloting careers.

First Officer Ahmad Hakimi Bin Hanapi was also one of the younger men on board: he had recently started a family. Kimi, as he was known to friends and family, was married to the beautiful and intelligent Sharifah Asma'a Syed Alwi Al Junied. Their son, Abderrahman, was their only child, and their pride and joy. Kimi was a doting father who tried to spend as much time as possible with his son. Whenever he was home, the first thing he did each morning was take his son for a walk. Never in a stroller, but always carrying his precious child close to his heart. Taking care of his parents, as well as his wife and son, was an important part of his life.

Months before, Ahmad had experienced the same narrow escape as Bobby's wife, Tan Bee Geok, after he had been scheduled to copilot the ill-fated MH370, but he had swapped shifts with First Officer Fariq Abdul Hamid. The MH370 disaster had made Kimi and his wife realise how precious life was. The incident had also brought home that it was time to make changes in their lives, and they had started putting plans in place to move to Dubai. When they visited the United Arab Emirates on their honeymoon in 2011, its capital stole their hearts. Recently visiting Dubai again, they began seriously contemplating a move, searching for houses and visiting a school that young Abderrahman could attend. If they did move, Ahmad would have to leave Malaysia Airlines, but he hoped to be able to find a similar job with Emirates.

At fifty-four, Mohd Ghafar Bin Abu Bakar was the oldest crew member. He was the inflight supervisor, which made him the highest-ranked cabin crew member on board and responsible for the passengers' and crew's comfort and safety. He was there to ensure that no passenger presented a risk to others on board and he was responsible for informing the pilot of any problems within the cabin and to assist the pilot in any way. The inflight supervisor was also responsible for the safe embarkation and disembarkation of passengers. Although Mohd Ghafar had never experienced an emergency, if one did occur he would be the person responsible for getting everyone out of the plane on the emergency slides. He took his job very seriously and, together with the chief stewardess, he saw to it that the passengers were as safe and as comfortable as possible.

Flight MH17's chief stewardess was Dora Shahila Binti Kassim, a 47-year-old single mother. A long time ago she promised to take her fifteen-year-old daughter, Diyana Yazeera, on a holiday to visit the Dutch capital. The plan was that her daughter would accompany Dora on the next flight back to Amsterdam, where they would spend a week or so together.

Dora Shahila's main aim was to ensure that her only child led a successful and happy life. Working long hours at high altitudes helped pay for Diyana's schooling, and it also paid for everything else a young teenager needed. As a single mother, Dora knew all too well how important schooling was, especially for women. She wanted her daughter to be independent and able to take care of herself later in life.

Azrina Binti Yacob was the other chief stewardess on board MH17, as larger long-haul aircraft like the Boeing 777 often had double cabin crew to meet their passengers' needs. The chief steward or stewardess supervises and coordinates the cabin crew.

Azrina had been with Malaysia Airlines for twenty years and had gradually worked her way up the ladder. In a cabinet in her living room she proudly kept a model aircraft from the Malaysia fleet. Looking forward to being reunited with her three-year-old daughter Arisha when she got home, Azrina knew the rest of her family had been busy making plans to celebrate Eid together with her. A big and wonderful family meal would mark the end of the fasting period.

Forty-two-year-old flight attendant Lee Hui Pin had made sure all the overhead luggage compartments were closed as the plane readied for take-off that morning. Born in Kelantan, Malaysia, Hui Pin was a keen swimmer, but her greatest passion was cooking Kelantanese dishes. Following the disappearance of Flight MH370, she had considered quitting her much-loved job. But she had wanted to be a flight attendant and had worked for Malaysia Airlines since she was nineteen; she had no idea what else she would do or if she would ever find a job she enjoyed as much.

Although she knew that the chances of such an event happening again were minimal, the disappearance of Flight MH370 had brought home to her that the job was not without risk. However, the salary was excellent, and she had responsibilities at home—three of them. Together with her husband, Wong Kin Wah, Hui Pin had three young children to maintain. Her eldest, Wong Rui Qi, was thirteen, Hong Kai was ten, and Shen Kai only two. Her much-loved steady job provided for everything they needed. She couldn't just quit. So for the time being she had to set aside the idea of looking for a change of career.

———

Forty-year-old stewardess Mastura Binti Mustafa was from the town of Seremban south of Kuala Lumpur. She too was devoted to her job and, like Hui Pin, Mastura was mother to a ten-year-old son, Mukhriz, and had worked for the airline company for almost twenty years. Mastura was also a keen cook. When she was on any of the long-haul flights like this one, she would be away from home for four or five days, so she would cook her son's meals in advance to make sure he ate properly. Mastura's brother, who worked for Malaysia Airlines as an engineer, and his wife were taking care of Mukhriz. Just before she had boarded the plane that morning she messaged her sister-in-law to let her know that she was on her way home.

———

Forty-year-old Chong Yee Pheng had been brought up as a Christian and was the youngest in a large family. Her parents and some of her brothers and sisters lived in Ipoh in the north of Malaysia. Eighteen years ago, at the age of twenty-two, her dream to see the world came true when she was taken on as a flight attendant by Malaysia Airlines. In her two decades of working for the airline, the attractive flight attendant had just about seen it all and posed at all the famous landmarks around the world. But she always loved to go home again, to smell familiar smells and indulge in family feasts and gossip. The plane had taken off and home was just fourteen hours away.

Steward Shaikh Mohd Noor Bin Mahmood was aged forty-four and married to Madiani Mahdi, two years his junior. Years earlier they had met on this same flight route, from Kuala Lumpur to Amsterdam. His wife was also a Malaysia Airlines flight attendant and she had been impressed by Noor and his romantic notions. Their love blossomed after that flight and they had always tried to arrange their schedules so they could fly together, swapping with colleagues whenever they could.

Two years after they met on the Amsterdam–Kuala Lumpur route, the couple were married. Noor already had three children—aged six, eleven and thirteen from a previous marriage—but still the couple wanted a child together and Madiani soon became pregnant. Their daughter, Siti Darwysha Zulaika, was now two years old. After Zulaika was born, the couple frantically tried to swap with other flight attendants, but now their objective was not to get matching flights but to arrange alternate shifts, so they could take turns to look after their child.

Like so many others working for Malaysia Airlines, flight stewardess Hamfazlin Sham Binti Mohamedarfin was shocked after the disappearance of MH370. Her father had asked her to quit the job, deeming it too dangerous, but she loved her work and, like so many others, she thought the odds of something similar happening again were next to none. Her two sons, eight-year-old Haiqal and Hazim, who was two, were too young to understand that a plane had suddenly gone missing and did not realise that only fate had spared their mother that day.

Hamfazlin herself knew all too well what a close call it had been—she could have easily been rostered on the doomed flight. Since the MH370's disappearance, she phoned her husband, Ahmad, each time before she boarded a plane to tell him that she loved him. She had done the same on 17 July.

It had been Nur Shazana Binti Mohamed Salleh's childhood dream to become a flight attendant and she had applied for a job at Malaysia Airlines more than once before she was finally taken on. She had worked with them for nine years now. A single woman, born in Penang and the eldest of four children, her parents' dream was to see her married, but their daughter loved to travel, and building a relationship was difficult when you were in a different country nearly every other day.

She was thirty-one years old, loved football and loved her life. She was in no rush. Her father had asked her to quit the job because he was afraid something might happen to her, but she had refused. Even pedestrians could die, she told him.

Being a flight attendant was Angeline Premila Radjandaran's first and only job; she had been taken on straight after finishing university. Only twenty years old at the time, she had never looked back. For ten years now the flight attendant had worked for Malaysia Airlines and she often graced the airline's inflight magazine. Her good looks were also the reason she was frequently called on to promote the company at events.

Often away from her two younger brothers and parents, who lived in Klang, a city one hour south-west of the capital, Kuala Lumpur, Angeline would keep in touch through social networks; the whole family often joined in 'group chats'. Being born just one year before her younger brother, Murphy, they had gone to the same schools, had mutual friends and were close. The only creature Angeline was closer to was her newly adopted four-month-old beagle, Lexi. She loved him to bits. Before take-off she had texted Murphy to please take good care of Lexi until she got back. He promised her he would.

Chapter 4
Ukraine, November–December 2013

Viktor Yanukovych's meeting with Russian president Vladimir Putin on Saturday 9 November 2013 was held in utmost secrecy. For six years Ukraine had been constructing an Association Agreement with the EU and it was to be signed at the end of November at a special summit in Lithuania. The summit was considered a critical juncture and signing the agreement would show that Ukraine under Yanukovych's leadership would rather opt for further integration with the EU than join a Russia-centred Eurasian customs union.

What was discussed in Moscow on that day in November remains a secret, but it is likely that Yanukovych's mind was made up by the time he left Putin's chambers. Some said later that he was blackmailed by the Russians and was offered a deal he couldn't refuse; others accused the EU and the International Monetary Fund (IMF) of leaving the Ukrainian leader with no other option than to seal his fate with Putin. The IMF had presented very stiff terms for loans to the penniless Ukraine, and Kiev felt the conditions it demanded were simply impossible to fulfil.

On 21 November, a week before Yanukovych was expected to make his way to the summit in Lithuania, he informed the EU that he would not be signing the agreement. He said Ukraine could not afford to sacrifice its trade with Russia. It was a well-known fact that Russia was very much opposed to the EU treaty and had already threatened Ukraine with sanctions if it were to sign. Nonetheless, the EU was stunned. For the past six years the members of the European parliament had worked hard to establish a Brussels–Kiev pact, only to see it now dropped at the last moment.

At home, many Ukrainians were as much in shock as the astonished Euro parliamentarians. Was this the same man who had argued in favour of deepening trade with the European Union? Many voters felt betrayed by Yanukovych. They had been so sure that their president would, like his predecessors, look to the West for help in building a democracy. Now he was embracing the Russians and their president, Putin. Many voters felt Yanukovych's sell-out to Russia was an act of betrayal; they could not come to terms with the U-turn their leader had suddenly taken. As the people of Ukraine poured onto the streets in protest, their chants of 'He tricked us' said it all.

But certainly not everyone in Ukraine felt that way. The peoples of western and eastern Ukraine appeared almost to be living in totally different worlds, and their views on why and how Yanukovych suddenly changed his course were as contrasting as their backgrounds. Some argued that Yanukovych's initial desire to forge closer links with the EU may well have been genuine but that he became dismayed and discouraged when he felt the EU failed to acknowledge the scale of the financial difficulties he would face if he chose Brussels over Moscow. Offended when he discovered that Kiev would not be offered the firm prospect of full membership of the EU, he began to believe that Ukraine was being treated by the West as a country lesser 'even to Poland', its next-door neighbour, which was a full member of the EU. Yanukovych feared that Ukraine in the end would be left standing at the gateway to Europe, neither totally welcomed nor embraced in the way Poland had been by the EU.

There would be a cost whichever way Yanukovych turned, and Russia was now more than eager to offer help to its needy neighbour. Ukraine's 46 million people occupied a strategic position between Europe and Russia. Although Brussels realised it was losing its 'tug of love' over Ukraine, now that this strategically important country was suddenly striking up a deal with Moscow it was surprisingly slow to respond. Perhaps it believed that Yanukovych would eventually turn around. The Russians, however, moved in quickly and generously promised to invest US$15 billion in the government's debt and to reduce the price of its gas to Ukraine by a third.

Yanukovych's volte-face sent a thunderbolt through the country. People felt that their president had sacrificed the hopes and wishes of most of his countrymen on the altar of Russian money and contracts. That same night, 21 November, several hundred people came to central Kiev in protest. The protests took place in Kiev's central square, Maidan Nezalezhnosti (Independence Square), the same square that had been the focus of the 2004 Orange Revolution.

From her prison cell, Yulia Tymoshenko announced a hunger strike in protest at Kiev's decision. Her release and departure to Germany, refused by the president, had become a central demand by Europe for the pact with the EU to go ahead, but Tymoshenko let Yanukovych know that she would renounce that right if he signed the EU agreement. 'This is the only chance for you to survive as a politician,' she pleaded with Yanukovych. 'Because now, when you are killing the agreement, you are making the biggest mistake of your life.'

All through the week protesters set up camp in Maidan. The date of the protest was almost symbolic: it was exactly nine years from the days of the Orange Revolution, which had defeated what some voters believed was Yanukovych's attempt to steal a presidential election. People busied themselves putting up tents and making fires in Kiev's central square. Others brought in warm clothes and food for those who came to the Maidan from all over Ukraine. The cold night air was filled with the sound of voices singing Ukraine's melancholic national anthem. To avoid trouble, alcohol was quickly banned. To keep warm, people danced or played football.

On Saturday 30 November 2013, around 2000 protesters gathered in Maidan to express their discontent. Over the next few days protests grew, with thousands of protesters arriving at the beginning of December. As the crowd increased, so did their desire to express their disappointment more forcibly. A small group tried to enter government buildings but was dispersed by the police. In the end students managed to occupy several municipal buildings, turning the city hall into their 'revolutionary headquarters'.

That same day at about 4.30am, Ukraine's riot police, the Berkut, moved into the square. They came to restore order, they warned the protesters; when the activists refused to leave Maidan, the police pummelled them with truncheons and sprayed them with tear gas. When many students fled, the Berkut chased them and beat them when they were caught.

Never in its twenty-two years as an independent country had Ukraine witnessed such acts of violence against their own people. The public response to the attack was momentous. Parents were not going to stand by passively and watch their children being beaten. Later that day over ten thousand people, including parents and many elderly Ukrainians, poured into Maidan.

As the situation heated up, Ukrainian citizens from all over the north and west made their way to Kiev; it was estimated that some hundred thousand people were marching into the city, heading for the square. To give those who had travelled from other cities and the countryside a sleeping place, tents were erected not only in the square but along the streets leading to it. Barricades were put up to keep the Berkut at bay. The square's Christmas tree was dismantled and used as a barricade; Ukrainian flags and anti-government slogans decorated its toppled carcass.

A large stage was raised on the square and every day after work hours, people gathered to hear the speeches of community activists and politicians who supported the movement. Musicians and other artists kept the masses entertained, bringing some cheer to the crowds who spent the night braving the bitter cold. On Sunday the number of people pouring into Maidan doubled or tripled, driving their numbers into the hundreds of thousands. Throughout those first days, police tried in vain to disperse the crowds, but to no avail.

Two days later, 3 December, Yanukovych flew to China, where he was going to sign a deal which he claimed would bring in a US$8 billion investment to Ukraine. In the meantime, at home, his cabinet barely survived a no-confidence vote in parliament. The protesters were now less focused on the EU agreement; their focal point had shifted to ridding the country of its corrupt leaders. The crowds, united in their common goal to free Ukraine of decades of political corruption, demanded the resignation of President Yanukovych.

To show their solidarity with the Ukrainian protesters, the Dutch minister of foreign affairs, Frans Timmermans, and two liberal members of the European parliament, Hans van Baalen and Guy Verhofstadt, rushed to Kiev on 4 December. Timmermans stressed in an interview, after he posted a photo of himself speaking to people at Maidan on Facebook, that he wasn't there to pick sides. The Russians, however, were not amused by the visit of the EU members; Russian prime minister Dmitry Medvedev condemned their action, explaining that it was alright for foreign politicians to speak with Ukrainian leaders, but to take part in the protests and meet with the opposition was considered an interference in internal affairs. Even in Europe leaders raised eyebrows, considering the rushed and rash visit an inflammatory move.

In 1991, Ukraine had become an independent country without a drop of blood being shed or a bullet being fired. The hope of its people at the time, that this would result in an honest political system being established, in which those elected would modernise the country and build institutions, had been quickly shattered. As its elites looted the country's resources, leaving its people vulnerable and disillusioned, a younger generation had been introduced to greener pastures beyond the Ukrainian borders: thanks to travel and the bountiful and abundant prairies of the World Wide Web, they had been able to see how the other half lived. Young Ukrainians acted and felt European; they were the initiators of the protests and they were willing to fight and risk their lives, if need be, in an effort to change the entire political system and shake off the old post-Soviet legacy.

As the calls for Yanukovych to step down became louder, the president, who was still in China, let the protesters know that he was prepared to negotiate only if the activists were willing to stop blockading government buildings. At home the statement was considered one-sided and it largely ignored any of the protesters' demands.

Although his country was in a state of great turmoil, Yanukovych continued with his state visit. He viewed a collection of ancient artefacts, met with the government chairman in Shaanxi province, toured a factory of the Aviation Industry Corporation of China and flew on to Beijing for a business conference.

China had helped Ukraine in the past and Yanukovych knew that China could provide an alternative source of financing. At home things were bad, but business was business and Yanukovych let his countrymen wait.

On 6 December, Yanukovych left China and headed straight for Russia, almost in denial of any crisis taking place in his country. As he engaged in unannounced talks in Sochi with Putin on a 'strategic partnership', the people in Ukraine became furious. On 8 December more than a hundred thousand people rallied in Kiev and, in a collective act of fury, destroyed Lenin's statue, which had stood for decades in the city centre, hacking it to pieces in their rage.

The people on Maidan, still entering Kiev from all over the country, became ever more determined not to go home without having achieved something. The defiant mood was boosted when veterans of the Afghan war, clerics and pop stars joined in the protest. But everyone knew the backlash would inevitably come. Many protesters hoped, against all odds, that Yanukovych, awed by the number of people demanding his resignation, would rethink his position and step down. Most of them, however, were sceptical and some had armed themselves as they held their breaths in anticipation and fear of what would happen next. They didn't have to wait for long.

On 11 December, as temperatures fell to minus thirteen Celsius during the coldest night of that winter, columns of riot police entered the protest camp. Shortly after 1am battalions of police began to dismantle the makeshift barricades. The protesters, not planning to surrender what they had managed to achieve, put up a fight. Somebody brought in a tractor, trying to ram it into a police line. Petro Poroshenko, a politician and billionaire who actively supported the protest and would later become president of Ukraine, climbed on top of the tractor, speaking to his enraged countrymen, trying to calm the horde in an effort to prevent any violence, but it was too late. Rage took over as masked provocateurs started to hurl stones and wield chains at the police. As the pent-up anger on both sides began to explode, what had begun days before as a peaceful demonstration rapidly turned very ugly and spun out of control.

The fiercest battle came on the north side of the square, where hundreds of black-helmeted riot police struggled for several hours against lines of protesters wearing orange helmets distributed by organisers, in scenes that threatened to descend into an all-out pitched battle. There were no figures on injuries, but it was said that several protesters had been hurt, while police said at least ten of their officers had suffered serious injuries in the scuffles. People later reported that many more protesters had been injured during the clashes, their numbers climbing as the days passed. Miraculously nobody died that night.

The US secretary of state, John Kerry, released a strongly worded statement on the events: 'The United States expresses its disgust with the decision of Ukrainian authorities to meet the peaceful protest in Kiev's Maidan Square with riot police, bulldozers and batons, rather than with respect for democratic rights and human dignity. This response is neither acceptable nor does it befit a democracy.'

On 15 December the people, in no way defeated, returned to Maidan, rallying once again in the city centre. By now even Yanukovych's own government was losing faith in the president. High-profile opposition politicians, such as boxer Vitali Klitschko, started leading the protests, and a number of Yanukovych's supporters, including many MPs and his chief of administration, quit their jobs and surprisingly joined the opposition. Opposition leaders were calling for a nationwide strike, demanding that Yanukovych and his government resign.

Two days later, Yanukovych set out to make yet another visit to Moscow to talk to Putin. Several hundred protesters stood along the route as he headed to the airport, holding signs that read: 'Turn the plane round to Europe!' In the subsequent TV news footage, Ukrainians witnessed how Putin appeared relaxed and somewhat uninterested before the meeting, slouching in his chair, while Yanukovych sat tensely bolt upright, speaking slowly, leaving long thoughtful pauses between sentences.

Day after day the protesters continued to fill Maidan. In scuffles with the police, people fell wounded on both sides. Sometimes police were trapped behind protester lines during the scuffles, but the demonstrators would set them free and even hand them back their shields; moments later both sides would once more be involved in fights.

One evening a priest brandishing a cross walked towards the police lines, but he was pulled back by protesters. Protest leaders announced from the main stage that theirs was a peaceful demonstration, pleading with police for a stop to the crackdown. By now hordes of people were paralysing the centre of Kiev daily.

When Christmas came, there was a noticeable dwindling appetite for protest. Pro-Yanukovych politicians thought the protest had finally reached its peak, but they soon realised they were wrong. As the New Year arrived, protesters returned and the talk in Kiev was not whether blood would be spilt but how much of it would eventually flow through the capital's streets.

Chapter 5
17 July 2014

Samira Calehr had seen two of her sons off at Schiphol airport earlier that morning. All three of Samira's children would be going to Bali to visit their grandmother, Yasmine, who lived in Houston but had a bungalow in the mountains there; the boys were looking forward to their annual trip. Shaka, nineteen, and his little eleven-year-old brother Miguel had boarded Flight MH17 to Kuala Lumpur that day. Samira's middle son, Mika, had not been able to get a ticket on this flight, so he would be taking the same route a day later.

Mother and sons lived in Almere, a Dutch town not far from Amsterdam. Samira's sons were born in Indonesia, but their mother had migrated to the Netherlands four years ago. The boys loved their new home, but they still held on to their Indonesian roots and traditions. They were popular and their mother welcomed their new friends into her home. Those who came to visit quickly called Samira 'Aunty', as is the Indonesian tradition, and removed their shoes before entering the house. Friends unexpectedly turning up for dinner were never a problem for Samira—her house soon became a regular meeting place.

Shaka had just finished high school at the International School of Almere and was going to Enschede to study textile engineering and management at Saxion College when he returned from his holiday. He had a passion for the native fabrics of his birth country and wanted to discover and develop new fabrics inspired by his heritage. Miguel would join his brother Mika at the International School after the summer holidays, starting in first grade. Miguel was an enthusiastic football player and a gifted go-kart driver; the S-bend was his specialty and he had recently obtained his go-kart driver's diploma. When he came back from holidays, he was due to start a specialised training course.

Much to their dismay Samira had fussed over her boys' luggage. Shaka realised he'd forgotten to pack socks; Samira promised to buy him some and send them along with Mika the next day. Later, outside customs, Samira had hugged and kissed her boys goodbye. They were well-travelled kids so she wasn't worried—she would have them all back within a month.

To her surprise, young Miguel had suddenly turned as he stood in line for the passport control rushing back into his mother's arms. He would miss her, he said, and he was also afraid that something could happen to the plane. The disappearance of MH370 three months earlier had been all over the news and it had left even the most level-headed and experienced traveller slightly unnerved. A plane with almost 250 people on board just vanishing into thin air was as unsettling as it got.

Telling him that everything was going to be alright, Samira had hugged her youngest child one more time. In an effort to reassure them both, Shaka told his mother not to worry, promising her he would take very good care of her baby.

Samira remembered looking on as her two boys walked away. Miguel turned back to his mother with big brown sad eyes. Moments later her boys vanished from view, disappearing behind the customs booth. Samira was heading for the shopping centre to buy Shaka's socks. The plane would have taken off by now and her boys would probably be watching the inflight movies or playing videogames.

Nick Norris of Perth had three grandchildren under his arm, or maybe the children had their granddad under theirs. With Nick it was sometimes hard to tell. His own children had found his wise and slightly 'neglectful' parenting style during their early years had instilled a sense of independence among the four of them as adults.

Sixty-eight-year-old Nick loved sailing, and he liked a beer. Always with a story on the tip of his tongue, he adored his grandkids and was taking three of them home to Perth so they would be back in time for the first day of the new school term. Twelve-year-old Mo, ten-year-old Evie and eight-year-old Otis Maslin had left their parents behind in Amsterdam so Anthony and Marite (Rin) could enjoy an extra three days of holiday. After the three generations of the family had toured Europe for several weeks, Grandpa Nick was taking on the task of getting

Mo back to line up for the Scarborough Sea Eagles next Sunday morning.

Mo and his sister Evie were star pupils at school, but for little Otis the great outdoors was where he loved to be. Otis had a fascination for creatures great and small, and he could be the life of the party when he was on a roll.

Anthony Maslin and Rin Norris knew their kids were in capable hands with Nick, Rin's father. He was a leading educator who had had a distinguished career teaching French. He was now a consultant and director of the company Collaborative Systemic Change, and he was by far the wisest man they knew. He'd been a headmaster, a lieutenant colonel in the army reserve, and he'd done his bit to change his part of the world. Throughout his career, he had been a strong advocate for language education and worked closely with individual teachers to plan and strategically strengthen the position of languages within their schools. Listening to Nick's well-crafted stories of his family life, army experiences and sailing was sometimes like being piloted through new waters.

Waiting at the gate, Nick had been on the phone talking to another of his daughters, Natalia. Chatting for a while, he finally hung up when the ground crew had taken their positions behind the counters. The last thing Natalia had told her father was that she loved him.

They had been Newcastle United supporters for as long as they could remember, and it was the game that brought them together. For diehard fans like 28-year-old Liam Sweeney and 63-year-old John Alder, their age difference was trivial. What made them mates was their love for the club, nicknamed the Magpies, and for the players—cheering them on and crying real tears over the club's losses. That was what had welded their friendship, making it strong and profound. They belonged to the Toony Army ('toon' playing on the Geordie pronunciation of the word 'town') and were proud of it.

Liam and John had arrived in Amsterdam on different flights from England that morning. They'd explained to the lovely woman at the Schiphol transfer desk that they were mates and would very much like to be seated next to one another on their connecting flight to Kuala Lumpur, which was their stopover on their way to their final destination of New Zealand.

The Magpies were on a preseason tour in New Zealand, and John and Liam had saved enough money to watch them play football on the other side of the world. Just a few days ago the two of them had been present at Newcastle's first preseason friendly against Oldham, and now they were finally on their way to another hemisphere for a game of football.

Neighbours and some friends at home had been somewhat surprised that they were willing to follow their team so far, but for Liam and John, travelling to the other side of the world to watch the club play was just what you did if you were a true-blue Geordie. And they were not the only ones heading Down Under. The two were part of a big group of friends, with some of their mates travelling to New Zealand on later flights. Not many could afford such a trip though.

Within the Newcastle United club grounds, Liam was known as the 'big friendly giant'. A large guy with a soft streak, his love for his club went so far that he even turned down the possibility of a management position at the supermarket where he worked for fear that the new responsibilities might interfere with attending games. He only held the job at the supermarket anyway because it earned him enough to pay for all the Magpie matches at home and beyond; it wasn't as if he aspired to a make a career there.

His mate, John Alder, felt the exact same love and loyalty towards the club. Alder was from Gateshead and his mates at Newcastle nicknamed him 'The Undertaker' because of his habit of always wearing a black suit and a white shirt to each game. He prided himself on having never missed a Newcastle United match since 1973—well, actually only one, when his mother died—and he travelled to every away match. He was willing to go far and wide to watch his beloved Magpies play: to America, Thailand and now New Zealand. The club was his life and he was a permanent fixture at every match; he was also the owner of the biggest collection of Magpie memorabilia on the face of the earth.

The woman at the transfer desk had smiled at their excited and lengthy explanation of their love for their club. The two had thanked her effusively when she handed them their boarding passes. Now as the plane settled into cruising mode they sat back comfortably on their adjacent seats. They could not have been more pleased.

British-born Rob Ayley was on his way home to New Zealand. He had been only two and a half years old when his parents left Guildford in southern England for New Zealand. They moved to Wellington for an adventure and never returned.

Although he talked like a Kiwi, Rob was incredibly proud of his British heritage and travelled on a British passport; he nurtured a lifelong obsession with Britain. During a trip back there with his parents at age four, he had painted a picture of the Queen's horse and carriage and insisted on sending it to her. His parents were doubtful, but eventually agreed to send it in an envelope together with a letter addressed simply to 'The Queen, Buckingham Palace'. They were stunned when a response arrived several weeks later.

Rob had just spent a month in Europe, pursuing his ambition to become the best dog breeder in New Zealand. His specialty was rottweilers. For four weeks he had roamed around Europe with a mate who was a dog breeder and kennel owner. They'd rented a small Peugeot to get them about and had spent weeks talking to breeders and establishing contacts, all the while gathering as much information as they could.

At the end of their trip the two had parted ways to fly home separately. Rob was in a hurry to get back and had phoned his wife that morning after he missed the bus that would take him to the airport. His wife and two small children were waiting for his return in Otaki and he was anxious to get home; he told his wife that he had no idea if he could get to the airport on time to make his scheduled flight home. But the Netherlands' efficient transport system meant the next bus was only minutes away, so he had managed to make it and board his plane on time.

Rob Ayley had left high school at sixteen and life hadn't always been easy for him. Diagnosed with Asperger's syndrome as a teen, he had struggled to read other people's emotions. He'd skipped from job to job—fast food, horticulture, cheese-making—and flitted between obsessions, from cars to drumming and eventually to rottweilers, after his parents bought him a puppy. He had also had his flamboyantly extravagant moments: he'd once dyed his hair blue and he was now growing dreadlocks. He felt and acted young, and he was known as a generous guy who would give you the holes in his pockets if you wanted them. Rob toted a bag full of dreams for the future.

With his passion for rottweilers, it was his personal ambition to introduce the best of Europe's bloodlines into his breeding program in New Zealand so that the breed could become the noble and safe dogs they had the potential to be. To achieve this, he had left his family behind for a month. Rob was not well-travelled and often highly disorganised, so his family had had their doubts about this trip. But in Europe Rob had come face to face with the world's most beautiful rottweilers, and he'd also made new friends and valuable contacts.

To be separated from his family for so long was hard. His wife, Sharlene, was his soulmate, and they had changed each other's lives. While Rob sometimes struggled with everyday social communications, their two boys, Seth and Taylor, had become people he could understand, love and trust. His kids were like open books to him and he was now eagerly looking forward to returning to them and Sharlene. It had been a long and exciting journey, but he was content to finally be heading home.

Seated in the first row of business class were Australians Albert Rizk, a real estate agent, and his wife, Maree. Returning home to Victoria after a holiday, they had spent the last month travelling through different European countries. The couple loved to travel and had hopscotched the globe, from Thailand to Fiji to Europe. This time the Rizks had nearly skipped the trip due to family commitments, but a change of plans freed them up to join their friends Ross and Sue Campbell. The Rizks and the Campbells had become more like family than friends ever since Sue and Maree first met at a mothers' group when their now grown-up children were babies.

Albert worked for Raine & Horne in Sunbury, forty kilometres north-west of Melbourne, and he was a committee member at the Sunbury Lions Football Club, where his son played. He was known to serve an exceptional Sunday roast. Maree dabbled in everything from property management and writing to volunteering at the Royal Children's Hospital in Melbourne and was a member of a community book club.

The Rizks took pride in their two children. Their daughter, Vanessa, was a youth worker at a local secondary school, while their son, James, was carrying on in his father's footsteps as a property manager at the rival Raine & Horne agency in neighbouring Gisborne.

With the Campbells, Albert and Maree had had a ball travelling through Italy, Switzerland and Germany; it felt like they'd laughed for a solid month. All four of them had realised a lifelong goal: climbing to the top of the Klein Matterhorn in Switzerland. Unfortunately, Albert and Maree weren't able to snag a seat on the Campbells' return flight, so they'd bought tickets on the same route a day later with Malaysia Airlines. It was high season in Europe and all flights leaving Amsterdam had been jam-packed. They had been lucky to get a seat at all.

Some of their friends were surprised that the Rizks were willing to fly Malaysia Airlines after the disappearance of Flight MH370. Maree's stepmother, Kaylene Mann, had lost her brother and sister-in-law in that disaster. But Albert wasn't too worried: their house had been struck by lightning a year earlier and Albert didn't believe lightning ever struck twice. So their house was safe and so was their flight.

The night before Ross and Sue Campbell were due to fly out, the four of them had gathered at an Italian restaurant for a final meal and made plans for a reunion back in Australia. On Saturday next, when they were all back home again, they would get together to feast on the delicious Dutch cheese they'd bought, drink wine and pore over their holiday photos.

Mary and Gerry Menke were seated in the second row of business class. Born in Hilversum in the Netherlands in 1944, Gerry was one of six siblings who emigrated to Australia in 1953 when he was just nine years old. Although he had lived in Australia most of his life, he kept in touch with his family in the Netherlands and was now returning from a European holiday.

Gerry had met his New Zealander wife, Mary, from rural Bignell near Christchurch, while she was working in a pub in Mallacoota, Victoria during her working holiday around Australia. After they met, easy-going Mary cancelled her travel plans; even though she and Gerry were polar opposites, the couple were caught up in a whirlwind romance and soon married in New Zealand.

Curly-haired Mary was a colourful woman in every respect. She was quick to claim the centre of attention whenever there was a party, whereas Gerry could often be seen looking on quietly at the side. From the day they married, the couple had rarely spent a day apart.

As the years went by, they had four children—two boys and two girls—and ultimately their children had gifted them five grandchildren, all boys. Activities involving their grandsons took up most of their spare time on a near daily basis when they were home and left little time for anything else. But the Menkes were proud and affectionate grandparents and loved to help out.

Very much in the Dutch tradition, Gerry had a lifelong fascination with the sea, despite suffering from terrible seasickness. The lure of the ocean had first led him to a become a diver in the abalone industry, which he did successfully for thirty-five years until he one day contracted the bends, ending his diving career.

His focus then shifted to pearling and he became a pioneer in a new industry, culturing wild abalone pearls to be fashioned into jewellery. The business was unique to Australia and the family company, MAPA Pearls, had recently received a local business award and was going to be the focus of an upcoming episode of the TV series *Coast*.

The Menkes had a bit of a reputation as a couple of adventurous world travellers, often embarking on unusual trips. Their love of travel had taken them to the African wilderness, diving with whale sharks off Ningaloo and hiking the jungles of Borneo. Despite all their roaming around, their hearts always warmed when they returned to their home in Mallacoota, where their kids and grandkids were.

As always after long periods away, the couple were looking forward to returning home, where they would enjoy the simple things in life, like pottering in the veggie garden, having a hit of tennis and helping out at the kindergarten in Mallacoota where their grandchildren attended. They had missed their grandchildren greatly and were happy to be heading home.

Chapter 6
Ukraine, January–March 2014

The protest movement in Ukraine had been in large part a fight for the country's economic future, for better jobs and prosperity. Ukraine had all the necessities to build a prosperous economy: a large potential consumer market, an educated workforce, a significant industrial base and good natural resources and rich farmland. Yet its economy was in tatters. Corruption, bad government and short-sighted reliance on cheap gas from Russia had caused political unrest.

The people were very much aware of all this and were not going to back down; they had clearly had enough. On 12 January 2014, large crowds of protesters marched through Kiev, reviving the movement after a Christmas and New Year lull. Three days later, attempting to stem the tide and keep matters under control, the Ukrainian parliament passed restrictive anti-protest legislation.

MPs from President Viktor Yanukovych's Party of Regions, the country's largest political party, pushed new laws through the Ukrainian parliament that imposed harsh punishments on those who did not comply with the anti-protest legislation and continued protesting against the government. The unauthorised installation of tents, stages or amplifiers in public places in Ukraine would be punished by a fine or detention, and people and organisations who helped to facilitate such meetings in any way would also be liable to a fine or even jail time. Spreading propaganda and wearing a mask or any face covering became illegal.

The message the government was sending to its people was clear: Yanukovych was done with the protests. The streets of the capital must be cleared and if the people would not accept this, their president could now send in the police to ensure the law was obeyed.

Western countries were quick to disapprove of the measures taken by the government. In Washington, Secretary of State John Kerry said the move was disturbing and wrong, but Ukraine's foreign minister Leonid Kozhara rebuked the West over its criticism, stating that such comments from the US were 'considered in Kiev as meddling in the internal affairs of our state'.

Yanukovych's new measures only added tension to an already highly explosive situation. In response, a stand-off between protesters and police began on 19 January 2014 in Kiev. In defiance of the new 'dictatorship laws', some 200,000 people gathered for a Sunday mass in central Kiev in protest; they urged Yanukovych to step down to enable the formation of a new government by the opposition and the implementation of economic reforms.

Many protesters ignored the face concealment ban, defiantly wearing masks handed out by the opposition parties, while others wore hard hats and gasmasks. The 'Euromaidan activists', as they were now being described, appealed to the military to support the Ukrainian people, rather than what they called the 'criminal regime', and begged members of the military and police not to carry out 'criminal orders' when those orders involved the use of force against civilians. The activists' leaders promised the police that those who were fired by the government because they refused to incite violence would be reinstated once a new regime for Ukraine was installed.

As time passed, with both sides not yielding an inch, matters lurched even further out of control. The crowds supporting the Euromaidan protests grew. No one was going home before this matter had been resolved and the ultimate goal of the protesters—Viktor Yanukovych's removal from office—had been met. It might cost lives but many at Maidan were willing to become martyrs if that meant the start of a better future for their children. The world looked on and held its breath.

Clashes between protesters and police began on 20 January 2014 as thousands descended upon parliament via Hrushevskoho Street and were met by police cordons and a blockade of military cars, mini-vans and buses. A police loudspeaker warned, 'Dear citizens, your actions are illegal and are against the state.' Warnings that advancing within three metres of police would be considered a threat to police officers' rights and would inevitably prompt a response were also blurted out above the heads of the crowd.

With tensions running high, an outburst wasn't long in coming. Both sides exchanged projectiles as the day wore on. The stun and smoke grenades the Berkut fired at the advancing protesters fuelled the crowd's anger. Protesters—some of them hooligans who had joined the protests for the thrill—attacked the police barricade armed with sticks, pipes, helmets and gasmasks. Police shot at demonstrators with rubber bullets, and rumours swirled that a storming of the main protest encampment, the heavily barricaded Maidan, by police could begin at any time. An additional series of riots in central Kiev outside the Dynamo football stadium, adjacent to the ongoing Maidan protests, followed. It was the day the protests went into history as the Hrushevskoho Street riots, and it was also the day the riots turned fatal.

The first death occurred when a 22-year-old man plunged from the thirteen-metre-high wall of the football stadium, suffering multiple fractures and spinal damage, and dying as he was rushed to hospital. In the early morning of 22 January, while he was climbing the barricades in the conflict zone, twenty-year-old Serhiy Nigoyan was killed by police gunfire. Suffering four gunshot wounds, including one to the head, he died on the scene. Mikhail 'Loki' Zhyznewski was the next fatal casualty. He was also shot dead by police with a sniper rifle. Two additional shooting victims were announced as deceased by Euromaidan medical service coordinators by Wednesday evening, but their allegations were based on TV footage in which police were seen dragging motionless bodies to their side of the fighting, and these deaths could not be confirmed.

On 25 January another victim, Roman Senyk, died in a Kiev hospital after being wounded in the chest.

According to medical workers on the ground, 300 people were injured and treated on 20 January, 250 on 21 January, more than 400 on 22 January, and 70 on 23 January. The injured were counted on both sides of the barricades, but the extent of the violence on both sides was beginning to split the protesters, with cracks appearing in the opposition. On one occasion, opposition leader Vitali Klitschko had attempted to bring calm, but he was sprayed with a fire extinguisher by a protester from the crowd and shouted down as a traitor.

Realising that Yanukovych was not going to yield and with the situation becoming hopeless, Prime Minister Mykola Azarov handed in his resignation. It was just hours before a vote of confidence that probably would have removed Azarov from power anyway. President Yanukovych signed a decree dismissing the whole of the cabinet, but it was decided that Azarov and his government would remain in office until a new election could be held. It was now 28 January, and nine of the twelve recently enacted anti-protest laws were repealed and a bill offering amnesty to arrested and charged protesters was issued.

Two weeks later, in mid-February, events took an unexpected and peaceful turn when Yanukovych, shaken by the extent of the violence, agreed to meet with the opposition. The deal was made by three politicians, Arseniy Yatsenyuk, Vitali Klitschko and Oleh Tyahnybok, who had emerged as negotiators on behalf of the Maidan protesters. Following peace talks with President Yanukovych, two of these opposition leaders addressed the crowd on Hrushevskoho Street to announce a proposed truce with the government in exchange for the release of all arrested or detained protesters. The news was poorly received by a disappointed crowd, which greeted them with chants of 'Liar!' and 'Freedom or death!' and booed the leaders.

Nonetheless, in an effort to de-escalate the violence, the trio managed to strike an amnesty deal between the two parties. The 234 protesters who had been incarcerated between 29 December and February would receive amnesty if, in exchange, the opposition was willing to vacate the government buildings and unblock the streets in the city centre. But not everyone was on board, and reports suggested a possible rift between the Euromaidan camp and the more radical participants on Hrushevskoho Street.

On 14 February, in compliance with the amnesty, the protest leaders agreed to restore traffic on Hrushevskoho Street. On that Sunday morning anti-government demonstrators also vacated Kiev's city hall, which they had been occupying for almost three months. But this was the only building the protesters were willing to cede and many of them remained suspicious of the government's willingness to live up to its promises. 'This does not mean that we are surrendering the buildings, this does not mean that we are pulling down the barricades, this means that we will partially unblock Hrushevskoho Street to restore traffic,' one Maidan activist said, reiterating that protesters would remain on Hrushevskoho Street. Many protesters were appalled that a deal had been struck up with a person they deemed a 'murderer', and the temporary agreement didn't resolve the opposition's main demand that President Viktor Yanukovych leave office.

Yanukovych was considered a traitor by the protesters, not someone to be trusted and not someone who would keep his word, so not all the buildings were surrendered and not all barricades were taken down. And although protesters partially unblocked Hrushevskoho Street, the situation turned into another tense stand-off, with police controlling one side of the street and protesters controlling the other.

The EU, however, welcomed the end of the city hall occupation and called on Ukrainian authorities to close 'all pending court cases, including all house arrests'. To the West, the pro-European message coming from the protesters was promising and hopeful. But former US secretary of state Henry Kissinger offered Brussels the advice that Russia should be included in any talks to resolve the situation and Moscow should be assured that Ukraine would not join NATO. His advice was ignored.

On 17 February an activist was stabbed in the lung after he crossed onto the police-controlled side of the barricades. It was also the day that Russia boosted Yanukovych with a fresh US$2 billion cash injection. The next day, with protesters angered by yet another death and the sellout to Russia, clashes erupted with rekindled force. On 19 February, eighteen people were reported dead after scuffles with police and the military.

A day later Maidan was transformed once again from a protest site into a killing ground. From 20 February at least eighty-eight people, some say more than a hundred, were killed during forty-eight hours of conflict in Kiev. Eighteen police also lost their lives. Hundreds were badly wounded in clashes between protesters and police. It was the bloodiest two days in

Ukrainian history since the Second World War. Both police and protesters suffered significant casualties and the conflict was threatening to turn into a civil war.

American and European leaders called on Ukrainian president Viktor Yanukovych to de-escalate the situation and withdraw security forces immediately. They stated that they would not hesitate to sanction any individual officials responsible for the violence. Meanwhile, Russian president Vladimir Putin also stressed that Ukraine must take 'urgent measures to stabilise the situation and suppress extremist and terrorist attacks'. But there were fears that Russia would intervene once the world looked the other way.

For the moment, Russia was busy hosting the 2014 Winter Olympics in Sochi, which was held between 7 and 23 February 2014. It was the first Olympics to be held in any of the former Soviet Union states since its break-up in 1991. These were the most expensive Winter Games ever to be staged; for Putin they were intended as a showcase for Russia. But there was concern that once the all-important Olympics were over, Russia would intervene in the crisis because if Yanukovych was driven out, Putin would be left empty-handed. Just three months ago he had won in the game of chess between Europe and Russia; this had been an important victory for him because Ukraine represented the last stronghold in a region where NATO was advancing steadily towards the western borders of Russia.

The violence and bloodshed had prompted a mass defection by the president's shocked allies in the Ukrainian parliament. What had happened in Kiev had been filmed by professional and amateur journalists, and widely distributed on the internet. There was no denying the atrocities and Yanukovych, his back now against the wall, agreed to participate in negotiations.

On 21 February an agreement was signed by both Viktor Yanukovych and opposition leader Vitali Klitschko. The most important points were that the constitution would be restored and that new elections would be held as soon as this happened, but no later than December 2014. Restoring the constitution meant that Ukraine would revert to being a parliamentary republic, in which the prime minister and the parliament had more power than the president. All parties were to refrain from any violence.

However, although this agreement had been signed by the two main parties in the conflict, the protesters remained unwavering in their demand that Yanukovych had to go immediately; no other deal would persuade them to go home. They declared an ultimatum, giving Yanukovych until the next morning to officially resign from office.

So it was that just forty-eight hours after Ukraine suffered the deadliest day in its three-month uprising, President Viktor Yanukovych suddenly disappeared. A day earlier he had inked a deal with his parliamentary opposition's leaders to hold early elections and limit his powers. Now, in the space of a day, everything had changed once again.

Once it was discovered that Yanukovych had 'fled', parliament was called into session. By an overwhelming majority of votes, the interim parliament, now running the country, chose to remove the president from power. New elections were quickly set; they would be held on 25 May 2014. In Brussels, the European Commission acknowledged Oleksandr Turchynov, a Ukrainian politician, screenwriter and economist as the 'interim president' until elections could be held. The elite Berkut police unit, blamed for the deaths of protesters, was disbanded and Yulia Tymoshenko was immediately freed from prison. She arrived in Kiev soon after to talk to the people still crowding the capital's streets. Security forces stopped guarding administrative buildings, at last siding with the protesters.

A criminal case was filed against Ukraine's former leaders for the mass murder of civilians. Overnight Yanukovych and several other members of parliament became fugitives, wanted men. Russian president Dmitry Medvedev questioned the legitimacy of the new Ukrainian authorities, stating that the acting authorities had come to power by way of an 'armed mutiny' so their legitimacy was causing 'big doubts'.

No one knew where the actual president had gone. He seemed to have vanished into thin air. Rumours spread that Yanukovych had fled to an unknown location in the country's east or south, near the Russian border, where his support was still strong. In the days prior to his disappearance his government had crumbled all around him; now there were reports in the media that Yanukovych had departed Ukraine altogether and had possibly taken refuge in Russia. To most observers it was obvious that his reign had ended, but it soon became apparent that the former president held quite a different view of his status.

The goings on in Kiev were monitored warily by the inhabitants of the Ukrainian peninsula in Crimea. Tensions were mounting there as the fall of the old government became inevitable and a new interim government was installed.

The people of Crimea were mainly pro-Russian. In January 2014 the Sevastopol city council on the peninsula had called for the formation of a people's militia, to ensure the strong defence of the city from what they called 'extremism' emanating from Kiev. Now concern about what was going on in the country's capital began to manifest itself in demonstrations against the new interim Ukrainian government, but soon the pro-Russian protests in Crimea started to rapidly escalate.

Pro-Russian protesters gathered in front of Sevastopol's city hall chanting, 'Russia! Russia!' Anataly Mareta, head of a Cossack militia in Sevastopol, claimed that extremists had seized power in Kiev: 'We must defend Crimea. Russia must help us with that.' The head of the city administration in Sevastopol quit amid the turmoil, and protesters replaced a Ukrainian flag in front of the city hall building with a Russian one.

In the chaos and confusion, 82-year-old former Soviet leader Mikhail Gorbachev called for unity. 'The political turmoil in Ukraine looks like a real mess, but it is important that the country holds together in the battle for influence between Russia and the West,' he said.

Days later Viktor Yanukovych suddenly resurfaced, making his first public appearance since vanishing. Appearing not at all defeated, he surprised friend and foe with the words: 'If a president hasn't resigned, if he hasn't been impeached, and if he is alive—and you see that I am alive—then he remains the president. I intend to continue fighting for the future of Ukraine against those who use fear and terror to gain control of the country.' The press conference with Yanukovych was held in the Russian city of Rostov-on-Don.

Chapter 7
17 July 2014

AIDS researcher Joseph (Joep) Lange had boarded MH17 on 17 July 2014 together with his colleague and partner Jacqueline van Tongeren. The couple were heading for an AIDS conference in Melbourne being held that coming Sunday, an event organised by the International AIDS Society every two years and always held in a different country. The International AIDS Conference was the largest conference on any global health issue in the world and brought the leading AIDS and HIV scientists and doctors together, providing a unique forum on the subject. The single transfer and stopover for Joep and Jacqueline on their way to Melbourne would be in Kuala Lumpur, where a second plane would take them to their final destination.

Lange had spent quite a lot of time in the air lately, flying around the world. He was known as one of the world's leading AIDS researchers, a man who spoke at important meetings held on every continent. At the beginning of his career in the 1980s, in the early days of the AIDS epidemic, the young doctor had led international research on the clinical evolution of the HIV infection, and in the nineties he was instrumental in the development of anti-retroviral therapy. His ambitions, however, were not limited to furthering scientific knowledge. As ever more drugs came onto the market to lengthen the life expectancy of those infected by the disease, Joep made it his mission to widen access to the drugs in developing countries, fighting to improve HIV/AIDS care in the world's poorest communities. One of the first clinics he opened was in the Myanmar capital, Rangoon.

Back in the 1980s, AIDS had been considered an illness with little prospect or hope of being cured for those infected. The prognosis for a patient at that time was usually grim. Colleagues often warned Lange about tackling AIDS: it wouldn't boost his career and in the long run his efforts would get him nowhere, certainly not up any notable medical ladder anyway. If he valued his career as a medical specialist, he would be better off choosing a more promising field. Lange refused to listen to his colleagues' advice. He wasn't in any way interested in fame and fortune: he was interested in making people well again and easing their pain. But first and foremost he wanted to find a cure for this disease that was killing millions of people, not only in rich Western countries but also in the poorest countries in the world.

Over time Lange proved the sceptics wrong. Not many doctors were interested in AIDS during those first years of the discovery of the cause of the illness, the HIV virus, so if a lone doctor worked hard in the field he soon acquired a degree of standing. For many years Joep Lange worked in Africa for the World

Health Organization (WHO). HIV and AIDS were running rampant on that continent and it was there that his first ideas about finding a solution for the catastrophe surfaced. His work was often dismissed as unimportant and he could hardly contain his anger at times when journalists had the gall to criticise what he was doing. When one of them sneered at the relatively small number of people he was able to help, his annoyed answer was: 'If I can save a few thousand people in Africa, I wouldn't call that trivial, although I agree that it should be millions.'

Lange was not only a great virologist, he was also the driving force in the war against AIDS and a superb diplomat. Always good at talking about money, he was able to attract finance to his projects by approaching the rich and famous, who often donated generously to the cause. His charmingly informal manner got him what he wanted. Many were stupefied by the funding and public awareness he was often able to raise; he appeared to have the dual gifts of charm and persuasion.

There was however one great downside to his work: Lange missed out on a lot of his children's lives. With his former wife, Heleen Stok, he had fathered five children, and he had been absent for a large part of their lives. They were now pretty much grown up, the youngest being seventeen years old.

Lange had met his current partner, 64-year-old Jacqueline, in the course of his work. He had known her for years. Lange, the AIDS scientist, and Jacqueline, the AIDS nurse, shared a common goal. Since the early eighties they had both been highly involved in AIDS research. It had taken a while for the two of them to become involved romantically. The attractive and charming Jacqueline worked as head of communications for Joep Lange's Amsterdam Institute for Global Health and Development, a job that fitted her like a glove. As a team they envisioned a world where access to proper and affordable medical care for each and every person would be considered a right and not an exception.

Joep and Jacqueline were not the only ones heading for the AIDS conference. Lucie van Mens, director of support at the Female Health Company, and WHO media coordinator Glenn Thomas had boarded the plane with them.

For years Lucie had striven to educate prostitutes on the subject of sexual health. Creating websites where prostitutes, their pimps as well as medical professionals came together to exchange or gather information, Lucie and her team had found that approaching men, women and professionals through the internet was a very effective way of getting all the parties to talk due to its anonymity.

Lucie van Mens had been instrumental in finding new and effective ways of approaching this vulnerable target group. In 2005 she had become head of Stop AIDS Now!, a program that educated teenagers about AIDS. The enormous impact that AIDS was having on the lives of so many girls and women worldwide, and the small amount being done to turn the tide, infuriated her. Her priority became making sure that women themselves were able to organise protection for sexually transmitted diseases and were not dependent on others for their sexual safety. It was vital that women took responsibility for their own sexual health.

Forty-nine-year-old Glenneth Thomas was also going to the conference. Originally from Blackpool, Thomas lived and worked in Geneva as a press officer for WHO, which was based there. He'd been to a lot of places but never to Australia, so he was really looking forward to this trip. Luckily the football season was over because he hated to miss a match when the Tangerines, the Blackpool Football Club, played. Although he lived in Geneva, Glenn made time to attend the matches as often as he could, hopping on a plane to England.

Glenn was known as a sociable guy, always in for a party, organising barbecues and inviting everyone round. However, for his next birthday his twin sister, Tracy, would be the one making plans. They would be turning fifty and were set on celebrating the event together. The party was planned for September and was intended to be the highlight of what had turned into a sad year after the death of their father just a few months before.

Glenn wasn't medically trained; he had graduated with a degree in economics from Bangor University in 1987. His first job was in television, working as a journalist and producer for the BBC. Glenn's life as a gay man had made him especially aware of the dangers of AIDS and the need to prevent or to cure the disease. Frustrated by the world's slow response to tuberculosis and Ebola and the consequent proliferation of drug-resistant strains, the former BBC journalist had become involved in educating people on the subject of AIDS. He was also a communication officer for WHO's tuberculosis and

Ebola campaigns. Tuberculosis, considered one of the 'big three' diseases—the others being AIDS and malaria—had an especially terrible impact on people with HIV, with one in four dying of tuberculosis rather than AIDS. Glenn had become acquainted with Joep Lange in Geneva where Lange had worked for WHO at the beginning of the nineties. Joep was already an important researcher back then and his clinical research into preventing and treating tuberculosis and other diseases contracted by AIDS patients efficiently and cheaply was being taken very seriously even in those early days.

Martine de Schutter had played a significant role in AIDS Action Europe from its establishment in 2004. Under her leadership the organisation grew into a network of over four hundred non-government organisations from Europe and central Asia, becoming a major force in the European HIV policy field. Martine's work took her across the world and, like her other colleagues on the plane, she was looking forward to the Melbourne conference.

Like Joep, Martine was very involved in the struggle against inequality where health was concerned. It was difficult for her to accept that the level and the quality of medical treatment a person received depended on the country where they were born. The unfairness of it disgusted her. After working for WHO in South America, Martine returned to the Netherlands to work in the international fight against sexually transmitted diseases in Europe and central Asia. She worked passionately at keeping AIDS prominently on the European health agenda. She also worked hard at getting it onto Eastern European agendas, but that was a much more difficult proposition.

Martine was a single mother; raising her child alone had been a conscious choice. People around her told her she had a big heart, but Martine knew that although she loved people, the most prominent space she had in her heart belonged to her son. A proud mother, she frequently talked and boasted about her sixteen-year-old; although she was almost constantly on the road to somewhere, she never left her boy alone—he was always in safe hands with her younger sister, who was also his guardian.

This year Martine had stepped up another ladder and become the managing director of Bridging the Gaps, which aimed to provide vital drugs to those marginalised groups most vulnerable to HIV/AIDS across Africa, Asia and Latin America. She loved the work and she was good at it. She had a natural ability to connect people and she was making significant progress in identifying ways to break down the barriers for these groups to access crucial health services. Now the job she loved was taking her to Melbourne.

Pim de Kuijer worked as an HIV lobbyist, trying to convince the Dutch government to allocate more money to finance AIDS programs in regions where it would make the biggest difference. A political activist and parliamentary lobbyist for Stop AIDS Now!, he worked relentlessly to expand and build upon the quality of the AIDS effort from the Netherlands to developing countries. His experience in politics—he had previously interned for two former Dutch members of the European parliament and was a member of the liberal political party D66—and his incredibly detailed knowledge of the Dutch parliament were crucial in understanding who to approach in seeking support for his work for the Stop AIDS Now! group.

It was his aim to head back to his beloved Kuala Lumpur after the Melbourne conference, to meet up with old friends and colleagues. The 33-year-old Dutchman had always been a cosmopolitan who loved city life but some years ago, after working for the European Commission in Kuala Lumpur, he had returned to the Netherlands by train, journeying through the heart of China and Russia on the Trans-Siberian Railway. He'd loved the adventure of it, meeting and talking to people from all walks of life while travelling.

The AIDS movement had previously gone through a rough patch when, in 1998, Jonathan Mann, the former director of WHO's international AIDS program, had died when a Swissair flight from Geneva to New York came down over Nova Scotia. It had been a big blow for a movement that had become accustomed to losing its leaders, mostly struck down by the illness they worked so hard to combat. But new scientists and lobbyists had stepped up and taken hold of the baton. People like Joep Lange, Pim and the others on their way to the AIDS conference had the combined expertise to possibly one day find a cure to the disease that was mercilessly killing millions and then to promote that cure throughout the world.

Because he longed and hoped for a just world, where all people could live without being subjected to discrimination and could enjoy freedom, Pim was regarded by his colleagues as an idealist. Believing politics could change the course of history, he had arranged training workshops for politicians in Sarajevo and gone on several election missions. Pim had been in Ukraine working as an international observer during the elections in 2006 and 2007. He believed in democracy and had supported Yushchenko and Tymoshenko; he felt honoured that he had been able to contribute to a better future for all Ukrainians.

On his way to Australia for Stop AIDS Now!, he would be flying over the country he had tried to help find its way along the difficult path towards democracy. He was sadly aware that Ukraine had a long way to go and that to this day it was still subject to controversy, corruption and ethnic clashes. Ukraine was in turmoil and the country hadn't found democracy; instead it had tumbled into a war.

Chapter 8
Crimea, February–March 2014

The remarkably quick and mostly bloodless coup in Crimea may go down in history as one of the smoothest invasions in modern times. Days before, maybe weeks before, President Vladimir Putin had asked his parliament to approve his request to use force in Ukraine if it was needed to protect Russian interests there. By that time the Russian chess pieces were already in place. For much of February thousands of Russian soldiers had quietly taken up positions on Russian bases in the south.

Russia, like the US, had military bases on foreign soil, and existing agreements with Ukraine made it possible for their biggest base to be situated at the Crimean peninsula on the Black Sea. During the weeks of protest in Kiev, Russian forces had already begun moving around Ukraine, apparently legitimately and according to the terms of their military agreement. Crimea, with its many ethnic Russians, was suddenly full of Russian armoured trucks and aircraft.

This was an infiltration, not an invasion, and it was welcomed by a large portion of the local population. As tension in Ukraine mounted towards the end of February, with Russians and the EU accusing each other of interfering in the internal affairs of another country, the rest of the world looked on, expecting Russian ships and armed forces to arrive and capture Crimea when in fact this had already happened by stealth.

After Yanukovych fled his country in February, thousands of Crimeans flooded the streets of their capital, Sevastopol, in protest against the new authorities in Kiev. More than 71 per cent of the 379,000 inhabitants of the city were ethnic Russian. Sevastopol had never previously had a mayor because a governor for the city was always appointed by the president of Ukraine who also fulfilled the role of mayor. Now thousands of protesters chanted that they wanted a Russian mayor for a Russian city. Protesters waved Russian flags and chanted 'Putin is our president'. The next day more protesters rallied outside the Sevastopol administration offices. The pro-Russian rally chose Aleksei Chalyi, a Russian citizen, as their new mayor.

Rumours spread that the protesters in Crimea were in fact Russians who had been smuggled into the country during the weeks of protests in Kiev. On 26 February, media claimed that Russian troops or local volunteers had taken control of the main route of access to Sevastopol, creating a military checkpoint, with military vehicles under a Russian flag set up on the main highway. The next day the residents of Crimea woke up to find the Ukrainian flag over the regional parliament had been replaced by the Russian tricolour. Polite 'little green men' in military gear without insignia had in fact seized the Crimean parliament, raising the Russian flag. Apart from being well behaved, it was also claimed that they were professionals and heavily armed.

Although the parliament had been unlawfully seized, the Crimean prime minister, Anatoly Mogilev, said on a televised broadcast that the men who had taken over the building were not showing any signs of aggression, and he claimed that the situation was under control and that negotiations were underway to come to an agreement with the invaders.

Feeling compelled to become involved, the Crimean Tatars, an ethnic group that had originated in Turkey, now joined the protests against the Russian takeover. They, like the northern and western Ukrainians, were pro-Europe and had no affectionate memories of the Soviet Union. In May 1944, the entire Tatar population of Crimea was exiled to central Asia, mainly to Uzbekistan, on the orders of Joseph Stalin. They were deported as a form of collective punishment. The Tatars were not allowed to return to Crimea from exile until the beginning of Gorbachev's perestroika in the mid-1980s. They did not want to answer or belong to a country that had treated them so terribly in the past; the democratic forces in Ukraine had always been able to count on the support of these people.

Many Tatars feared that a Russian takeover would leave their relatively small population—roughly 12 per cent of Crimea—subject to ethnic backlash and repression. So on 26 February 2014 about five thousand of them rushed to the city council building in Sevastopol in a show of support for the Euromaidan protests. They were met there by supporters of the pro-Russian party. In an effort to avoid provocation, the Tatars mainly pleaded for unity, for respect and for protecting churches, mosques and synagogues. There were scuffles, but nobody was seriously injured.

For twenty years different nationalities, religions and denominations had lived side by side in Crimea without any major conflicts. It was probably the only territory in the post-Soviet space that had been able to avoid that so far. But even though the Kremlin and the new Crimean government immediately expressed their strong sympathy for the Tatars' concerns, the Tatars were in no way reassured; they had not forgotten their past and the atrocities they had suffered under Russian rule.

On the morning of 27 February, what were identified as Berkut units from Crimea and other regions of Ukraine seized checkpoints on the Isthmus of Perekop (the narrow strip of land linking the Crimean peninsula to mainland Ukraine) and on the Chonhar peninsula (another entry point to the region). It was reported that they were toting armoured personnel carriers, grenade launchers, assault rifles, machine guns and other weapons. From that moment on they controlled all traffic by land between Crimea and Ukraine.

Suddenly armed men were seen driving into the two airports in Crimea. In the early hours of 28 February, a group of armed men in military uniform without signs of identification seized Simferopol International Airport. Airport authorities later denied that it had been 'captured' and said that it was still operating normally, despite the continuing armed presence. Later in the day, Sevastopol International Airport was occupied in a similar manner as Simferopol's airport.

There was still uncertainty as to the precise identity of the gunmen holding the parliament and the airports. They claimed to be part of an informal self-defence group that had sprung up in response to the revolution in Kiev. When asked, they said they were just volunteers helping to maintain order at the airport. But others doubted this. 'This is not a ragtag force,' said Brigadier Ben Barry, a specialist on land warfare at the International Institute for Strategic Studies. 'When you see a new militia, they will have a jumble-sale look. This lot are uniformly dressed and equipped, and seem competent and efficient.'

There were no reports of looting and, although their behaviour seemed threatening, no civilian was attacked. In the days that followed, other groups appeared. These were genuine volunteers, who had come from Moscow to join what they saw as the liberation of Crimea.

After nine Russian-marked vehicles were spotted on the road between Sevastopol and Simferopol, Secretary of State Kerry said the US was watching to see if Russian activity 'might be crossing a line in any way' and had urged the Kremlin against action that might be misinterpreted as a violation of Ukrainian sovereignty. The Russian foreign ministry said movements of vehicles belonging to the Russian Black Sea Fleet were prompted by the need to ensure the security of its base in Sevastopol. Russia rebuffed calls from European leaders to withdraw troops from Crimea, saying the volunteer 'self-defence' forces were not under its command.

On 28 February, a missile boat of the Russian Federation blocked Balaklava harbour, where ships of the Ukrainian Sea Guard were stationed. For Russia these events ensured, for the time being, that Ukraine's new government would not join NATO, and also that Kiev would not evict Russia's Black Sea Fleet from its long-established base in Sevastopol.

Protests against the new authorities in Kiev and in support of the Russians in Crimea occurred throughout eastern and southern Ukraine on 1 March. The Crimean prime minister appealed directly to Putin in a signed statement officially calling for Russia to 'provide assistance in ensuring peace and tranquillity on the territory' of Crimea.

When Europe and the US protested against the 'violent' Russian land grab, Putin ridiculed the idea that events in Crimea amounted to Russian aggression. He said there had been no shots fired and no casualties listed during recent weeks: the outcome was what the vast majority of Russian-speakers in Crimea really wanted, and there was little need for Kalashnikovs in the streets. Within a week, Russian special operations troops had seized control of all strategic locations across Crimea, while the regional authorities moved to declare independence and schedule a referendum that would make it possible for the peninsula to become part of Russia again.

Russia vehemently denied any interest in expanding its hold within Ukraine. 'Don't believe those who say Russia will take other regions after Crimea. We don't need that,' Putin said. But Putin also said that Russia would always be ready to stand up for the rights of fellow Russians. He mentioned, seemingly in passing, that Russians in eastern Ukraine, in the cities of Kharkiv and Donetsk, had been subjected to the same sort of abuse at the hands of Ukrainian nationalists that he said had led him to act in Crimea. Putin said he was also reversing what he described as an 'historic injustice' inflicted by the Soviet Union sixty years ago. 'After a difficult, long and exhausting journey, Crimea and Sevastopol have returned to Russia—to their home harbour, their home shores, their home port,' he said.

Wasting no time, Crimea's pro-Russian leadership voted to join Russia and set a referendum for 16 March 2014. President Barack Obama warned that a referendum would violate international law and ordered sanctions on those responsible for Moscow's military intervention in Ukraine. The referendum was denounced by the new government in Ukraine, and by the US, the EU and Canada. However, after the votes had been counted, officials declared that 97 per cent of the voters were in favour of joining Russia. The referendum had only offered two options: join Russia or enhance Crimea's independence.

Following the referendum, Russia officially annexed Crimea two days later. According to Russia, this was based on the free and voluntary expression of the will by the people of Crimea at the referendum. While this action provoked renewed denunciations and threats of tougher sanctions and diplomatic isolation, it long remained unclear how far the West was willing to go to punish the Russians. The White House warned that Russia's actions would ultimately result in economic and political isolation. After weeks of warning about the consequences, the US and EU ordered sanctions, mostly limited to Putin's allies and people linked to events in Crimea. However, the economic sanctions did cause the rouble to plunge in value. In Crimea, celebrations were held to mark the Russian annexation; in Kiev, Ukrainian government officials said they would never recognise or accept the loss of the peninsula.

This was the first time the Kremlin had officially expanded the country's borders since the Second World War. After a Ukrainian soldier was shot and killed by gunmen who stormed a military base in Simferopol, the authorities in Kiev stated that the conflict had now reached a 'military stage'. Ukraine withdrew its forces from Crimea in order to protect their men.

With sanctions against Moscow now in place, on 24 March leaders of the Group of Seven nations came together in The Hague without Russia and agreed to hold their own summit later in the year and to suspend Russia's participation in the G8 until the country changed course. But in Russia the annexation of Crimea strengthened Putin's unchallenged political authority and enhanced his wild popularity. It unleashed a nationalistic fervour that drowned out the few voices of opposition or even the voices that cautioned about the potential costs to Russia. To many Russians the new leaders in Kiev were seen as fascists and the new government leading Ukraine was characterised as a junta.

Russia warned that it would protect its 'own people' not only in Crimea but, if need be, also in the rest of Ukraine. John Kerry warned that the US would take extreme measures if Moscow meddled in Ukraine's internal affairs. By the end of March Russia partly withdrew its troops along the Ukrainian border in the southern region of Rostov in Russia following talks between Russia's foreign minister and his US counterpart. Meanwhile, Russia's prime minister, Dmitry Medvedev, visited Crimea, promising funds and pay rises.

In this climate of animosity, realising they had the support of the citizens of Russia, the pro-Russian separatists' movement in southern and eastern Ukraine swelled. On 6 April as pro-Moscow demonstrations erupted in these regions, unidentified gunmen seized key buildings in several cities, including Donetsk, and replaced the Ukrainian flag in front of the regional government office with a Russian one.

Chapter 9
17 July 2014

They had met on a beach road many years ago. Liam Davidson and a couple of friends had been on a surfing trip at Victoria's Wilson's Promontory, surfboards strapped to the roof. Francesca was on the roadside with two girlfriends, thumbs out. Naturally the lads pulled over to pick up the three girls, insisting on giving them a ride. Liam instantly took a shine to the one in the wide-brimmed straw hat. Francesca White, whom friends called Frankie, and Liam Davidson had been together ever since.

Their passion for travel had taken them around the world, hiking in Spain, living in France and visiting their daughter, who was volunteering at an orphanage in Nepal. In 2011, Frankie and Liam visited the Annapurna Self-Sustaining Orphan Home in Pokhara, Nepal, where they were both touched by the incredible work being done. Berlin was their latest adventure—a visit to their son, Sam, who had made the German capital his home.

Liam and Frankie had been teachers at Toorak College, a private girls' high school south of Melbourne, for almost thirty years, but they were so much more than just teachers. Liam loved cycling, and almost every Saturday for fifteen years he clipped into his pedals and started the weekend with his mates. The group of fifty keen cyclists would greet the sunrise with a 35-kilometre loop across the Mornington Peninsula, and enjoy a coffee together afterwards.

But most of all Liam and Frankie were master wordsmiths. At Toorak College, 54-year-old Frankie taught English, history and humanities subjects and had supervised hundreds of students during twenty-eight years as a teacher. She had an enduring passion for arts and literature. But it was Liam, fifty-six, who had taken his love for words one step further. He began writing pieces for small publications as a prelude to his first novel, *The Velodrome*, which was published after being short-listed for the Vogel Award. His second novel, *Soundings*, won the National Book Council Banjo Award for Fiction in 1993. Some of his books were short-listed for the Victorian Premier's Awards. Liam Davidson became a critically acclaimed author in Australia.

The couple had travelled around Europe now for weeks and had met up with Sam during the last week and their daughter, Milly, had also joined them there in Berlin. The four of them had had a picnic in the forest and played Scrabble till late that evening. Having that time together had been wonderful. The whole trip had been especially wonderful.

Frankie and Liam, as well-seasoned travellers, knew that every trip contained at least one bad day. One of those days might be when the rain wouldn't stop, or you lost your luggage or missed a train or bus. Some incident would always turn up eventually during one leg of any trip, but their European vacation had been nothing but sunshine, happy moments, laughter and good times. It had been perfect, every single day of it.

In Berlin they took a connecting flight to Amsterdam, where they boarded MH17 for the next leg of their journey home. Although they had had great fun, boarding the plane and going home had been no punishment. For the two of them it was time to get back to Australia, time to share stories with friends over a bottle of wine or a pint of Liam's home-brewed beer.

If it had not been for the typhoon raging in the Philippines, the Gunawan family would never have boarded Flight MH17. The Gunawans were a close-knit musical family; Hadiono (Budy) Gunawan was born in Indonesia and his wife, Irene, was from the Philippines. Strangely enough they met in Japan. After high school, Irene moved from the Philippines to Japan to sing and become the drummer in a band, and it was there that she met Budy, a guitarist who joined the same band. The two later went on to tour Europe together, playing music and eventually falling in love. After their marriage they settled in Amstelveen in the Netherlands, where Irene gave birth to Darryl and Sherryl, who were now nineteen and fourteen.

The family visited Asia every year; they were always able to secure cheap fares because Budy now worked as a supervisor at Malaysia Airlines in Amsterdam. But this year they had had to postpone the flight they had planned for a day earlier because a typhoon was lashing the Philippines. They decided to wait it out and by chance they managed to nab business class seats on MH17 the next day.

Back in the Philippines, Irene was regarded as the light and laughter of her clan. The fifth of six children, she had always been outgoing and music-loving. At an early age she had decided that she wanted to see the world that existed beyond her sleepy rural village, so after finishing high school she spread her wings and took off. But during her long stays abroad, home tugged at her heart and Irene often flew back to 'Heaven', the name of her family's neighbourhood in the town of Pagbilao.

Irene had a great voice and at reunions she belted out her favourite Norah Jones and Diana Ross songs. This year, the couple and their two children were once more flying to Pagbilao, but now their son, Darryl, was bringing his DJ equipment along.

Irene and Budy had passed their musical genes on to their two children. Although Darryl Dwight Gunawan studied medicine, he was passionate about developing a career as a disc jockey and was already known as an up-and-coming artist; having won a Dutch DJ contest at the age of fifteen, Darryl now taught others slightly younger than himself the tricks of the trade. He had founded a company called Dwight Media, which produced the music of young emerging talent.

His little sister, Sherryl, a fourteen-year-old high school student, had one main passion, dancing, especially street dance. She was part of the hip-hop team Dance Tech at her dance school in Amstelveen. The team was good, very good—so much so that they had been chosen to compete in the world championships for street dance, to be held in Glasgow later in the year. The three-day event would host dancers from more than thirty countries, including the US, South Africa, China and Australia. For the students of Dance Tech it would mean competing at an elite level. Acts from *The X Factor* and *Britain's Got Talent* were due to appear, and Sherryl had been working hard at her moves, as well as working hard at the local supermarket to raise the money for the flight to Glasgow.

Back in economy class, two families had settled in their seats looking forward to the vacation they would spend together. They lived in the same street and the husbands played in the same amateur football team, their kids went to the same school, and now the Trugg family and the Wels family were heading for Bali together. Needless to say, the two families were close friends. Living across the road from each other in the town of Rosmalen in the south of the Netherlands, their homes faced one another across a grass square with swings and park benches.

Leon and Conny Wels, both thirty-nine, and Yvonne and Remco Trugg, both forty, had to contain the excitement of their children when they told them of the plans to visit Bali earlier that year. After Leon and Remco's football team won the season's competition, the men thought a combined trip would be a nice way of rewarding themselves and their families. Young Sem Wels was close mates with the Trugg girls, Tess and Liv. The kids had been over the moon at the prospect of spending time on a tropical island.

Remco had been a member of the OJC Rosmalen football club since he was eight years old, his father being the chairman there. Most of the men in the team had grown up in the same neighbourhood and known each other for years. After Leon came to live in the same street, he soon became friends with his new neighbour across the road. They shared a common profession, both of them working in finance: Remco Trugg ran his own financial service company and Leon worked as a personal banker. Remco soon introduced the newcomer to the local football club and Leon blended naturally with the tight-knit group of friends.

OJC Rosmalen's seventh team was a very close group: they held parties and birthdays together, and as many as five of the team's families would sometimes spend their summer holidays together. Everyone on the team was around forty years old, and they were all married and had young children. Whenever the team played, the wives and their children would come along to cheer them on.

Under her maiden name Stuiver, Conny had once been a well-known ice skater. In the early nineties she was one of the top Dutch figure-skaters and in 1992 she came second in solo skating at the Dutch championships. After her career as a skater ended, she became a choreographer and trainer for a Dutch figure-skating club. With her natural knack for coaching, some of her pupils went on to achieve medals and national titles. Although she still coached, she now also worked for an accountancy firm.

Their son Sem's passion had originally been gymnastics, until physical problems arose from the intensive training. To his dismay he was forced to stop, but he soon found another vocation. The ten-year-old joined an inline skate club and remarkably, after just six months of training, he came first in a contest. His mother's skating genes had undoubtedly contributed to his success.

Forty-five-year-old Hans van den Hende was a survivor. Although he never made a big deal of it, his colleagues at work knew it was a significant achievement that just before he left for Europe, he had been told that he was clean, no more cancer cells. He had battled leukaemia and won.

Moving to Australia seven years ago with his wife and three very small children, Hans and his family had fallen in love with the country. It had become their home. Hans was Dutch and had grown up in Veendam in the Netherlands. After high school he went to the far north city of Groningen to study chemistry, and from there he went to Brighton in England to get his PhD. In Brighton he met his Malaysian wife, Shaliza Dewa, who was also studying for her PhD. They had sealed their love with marriage in December 1995; in fact, a double marriage—one in Malaysia, in traditional Malay dress, and one in the Netherlands. For the next twelve years the couple had lived in Kuala Lumpur, where their three children were born.

The family had then moved to Australia, where Hans was offered a job at Securency, the banknote printing development company owned by the Reserve Bank. He'd been diagnosed with bone-marrow cancer very soon after starting the job and for many months he was absent from work while he underwent therapy. However, he ultimately returned to work and had now been in remission for five years, the statistical milestone which usually signifies a future free from the disease.

Hans was known for his very dry Dutch wit and his unassuming intelligence. With a PhD in chemistry, his colleagues knew he was probably the smartest guy in the room, but he wasn't one to take himself too seriously. This was underlined when he sometimes wore his clogs to work, just to get a rise from his colleagues.

The Van den Hende family loved Australian life and it was their intention to stay there. They lived in a neat weatherboard house in western Melbourne on a relatively new estate called Eynesbury. The three children attended Bacchus Marsh Grammar School, a twenty-minute bus ride away. Their eldest son, Piers, played football at Melton Phoenix Football Club and had had a hit of golf with a junior development squad at Eynesbury. Their middle son, Marnix, was a promising swimmer, a talented butterflyer who had made the Victorian state team. Hans often spent his pre-dawn hours driving his son to the pool in Melton and back home again before taking the long arc of Melbourne's Western Ring Road into work.

Their youngest, Margaux, was the one who lit up the room for the couple. She loved to dance and had joined a dancing school, and she often practised her routines in the middle of the kitchen for them to see. The children had forged deep bonds in the community during the short time they had lived there, and Hans and Shaliza often enjoyed sharing a glass of Australian wine, a cold beer or a cuppa with their neighbours.

A few months ago, Hans and Shaliza had decided it was time for the family to visit the Netherlands. Hans's mother and father, the kids' Dutch grandparents, had never seen the two youngest children in person. Hans had returned home every year or two, but not with his family; the cost of such a trip had been simply too high. But this time he set off, together with Shaliza and their three children—Margaux was now eight, Marnix twelve, and Piers fifteen—for a European adventure.

They had spent a week with Hans's parents and the elderly couple had been overjoyed to finally be able to hug and hold the youngest of their grandchildren, who had greeted them with two fluffy koalas. With Hans's sister and her family having come over from Denmark, it was the first time that the Van den Hende family had all been together.

Hans and Shaliza took their kids to Brighton during their European trip, going back to the university where they had met and fallen in love during their PhD studies. Then they had travelled to Denmark, visiting Hans's sister and her family, and of course the kids had made a visit to Legoland at Billund while they were there. The final week had been spent back in the Netherlands before their flight home to Australia on MH17, via Kuala Lumpur.

Helicopter rescue pilot Cameron Dalziel was also flying home to his family. Although born in Durban, Cameron, like Rob Ayley, also travelled on a British passport. The 43-year-old pilot had flown for the Canadian CHC Helicopter Corporation, working for them in Mozambique first of all. CHC Helicopter had its headquarters in Canada and operated in thirty countries around the world. In 2002 they had struck up a deal with Malaysia for offshore helicopter services and Cameron had recently applied for a transfer to Asia.

The application was granted and in October 2013 he had moved, together with his wife, Reine, and two sons, Sheldon and Cruz, to Miri, a coastal city in north-eastern Sarawak. Miri was an oil-mining town; he transported crews and personnel out to the rigs for Shell and Petronas and provided a 24-hour emergency backup.

Cameron Dalziel's colourful rescue career had started in South Africa, where he had been a lifeguard with Life-saving South Africa. Among the first helicopter pilots to be involved in swimmer rescues in South Africa, he flew all along the Durban coastline. Known as a very experienced and committed pilot, a veteran of countless missions, he was highly regarded by all in the field. He had been in Amsterdam for some time, completing a simulator training course there, but he had made a promise to his wife and kids that he would take them on a two-week holiday to South Africa once he got back home to Malaysia.

Chapter 10
Ukraine, March 2014

On 1 March 2014, separatist troops took over a government building in Donetsk city and raised the Russian flag. Just four days after this, the Ukrainian police charged the building and reclaimed it. A week later, 13 March was marked by violent clashes between pro-Ukraine and pro-Russian protesters in the city. A large group of pro-Russian protesters broke through a police cordon, attacking a smaller pro-Ukraine demonstration. A local pro-Ukraine activist was killed during these clashes while others, brutally beaten, were rushed to hospital. After this day of violence, pro-Ukraine residents of Donetsk decided not to organise any more peaceful demonstrations out of fear for their safety.

On 15 March, a crowd of pro-Russian protesters once again stormed government buildings in Donetsk and by mid-April thousands of activists had taken to the streets, demanding autonomy for the Donetsk and Luhansk regions, together known as the Donbas region (short for 'Donets Basin'). They wanted their region to become part of the Russian Federation, like Crimea. Some two thousand people came together at central Lenin Square in Donetsk chanting, 'Russia, Russia.'

In towns and cities across the Donbas, government buildings were suddenly occupied by armed pro-Russian separatist insurgents. Roadblocks were set up and violent scuffles were reported between pro-Ukraine police and soldiers and pro-Russian separatists. As the rebels expanded their territorial control, some government officers fled their police stations, leaving behind their weaponry. A number of Ukrainian soldiers joined the separatists and handed over their tanks, armoured cars and guns in the process. It was reported that eight Ukrainian tanks had been confiscated by separatists.

As a result, the Ukrainian government launched a counter-offensive against insurgents in some parts of the Donbas region. In the towns of Sloviansk and Kramatorsk a special operation against the rebels was carried out. Ukrainian special forces managed to recapture the airport of Kramatorsk and surround Sloviansk. But the situation was getting out of hand and rapidly turning into a civil war.

On 17 April, Russia, Ukraine, the US and the EU agreed at talks in Geneva on steps to de-escalate the crisis in eastern Ukraine. Ukraine's foreign minister agreed to suspend operations against pro-Russian militants in the east of the country over Easter. But the fragile truce was shattered when a gunfight broke out near the city of Sloviansk and three people were killed as Ukrainian security forces fended off a raid on a base in Mariupol and seized back control of the town hall in that port city. These were the first violent deaths in the east. Because of the hostilities, the Russian army resumed its exercises at the border with Ukraine.

Russian and Ukrainian sources differed greatly in the way they portrayed the pro-Russian demonstrators. The militants who had taken over government buildings in the Donetsk area were consistently labelled as 'rebels' and 'terrorists' by the Ukrainian authorities and the Western media, who typified them as a gruff and uncivilised lot who had seemingly come out of nowhere. They were said to be heavy drinkers, using coarse language; there was mounting suspicion that they had at some stage entered the country from Russia. When questioned by journalists, the soldiers often claimed to be 'volunteers', but authorities in Kiev believed some of them were in reality key figures in a proxy war tightly controlled by the Russian government.

Russian media and officials, however, referred to these men as 'supporters of federalisation', declaring that the Russian people merely sympathised with what they called 'modest demands' for adjustments to Ukraine's constitution. It was claimed that these demands were vital to protect the rights and interests of the Russian-speaking people in the east of Ukraine.

Disturbing photos of masked gunmen toting Kalashnikov assault rifles and RPG-26 rocket launchers taking over government buildings all over the east of Ukraine found their way into the media as the self-proclaimed rebel leaders started creating their individual nations. These 'leaders' were steadily taking over control in Donetsk and Luhansk in the Donbas region.

The separatists begged Putin to help them. They demanded protection from Russia and wanted their wish to become part of the Russian Federation recognised. But Putin was cautious and seemingly ignored their pleas; he insisted to the outside world that Russia had no hand in the violent seizure of government buildings across eastern Ukraine.

While the US and Russia blamed each other for the continuing unrest, the Ukrainian government was getting ready to launch further military operations. At the beginning of May, clashes in the Black Sea city of Odessa left forty-two people dead, most of them pro-Russian activists. Many of them perished while trapped in a burning building.

The separatists now decided to hold a referendum so that the people in the areas they currently controlled could have a say in the matter. After all, in Crimea the people's opinion had also been asked and the leaders among the rebels thought it only fair that the same should occur in the Donbas area. A date for the referendum was set for 11 May.

Hoping to establish a dialogue between the parties, Putin urged the activists to postpone the referendum date in view of an agreement that had been made in Geneva between the United States, European Union, Russia and Ukraine; it was intended to demilitarise and de-escalate the conflict. To meet the demands of the pro-Russian population, three pro-Russian activists were freed on 7 May in exchange for some officers from Ukraine's security force who had been captured by the rebel militia in Donetsk.

Initially both the separatists and the government in Kiev were cautiously positive in response to Putin's proposal, and both expressed their willingness to talk to one another. However, while the organisers of the referendum had initially considered a postponement, they in the end decided to maintain the original date. One of the separatist leaders claimed it wasn't his call to decide about the postponement—he was simply obeying the people's wishes.

On Sunday 11 May, large queues of people gathered in front of polling stations all over the region. The ballot papers in Ukrainian and Russian asked the voters to answer just one question: 'Do you support the Act of State Self-rule of the Donetsk People's Republic/Luhansk People's Republic?' The wording was vague, and it was somewhat unclear to voters what these words actually meant. Some of the electors who voted yes wanted more autonomy but not necessarily to split from Ukraine, whereas many people assumed their 'yes' would be a vote for the region to join Russia, much as Crimea had done in March. Some pro-Russian voters cast their votes to protect the region from 'fascists' in Kiev.

As the voting day approached, it had become evident that support for self-rule in the Donbas region threatened to deepen divisions in a country already heading perilously towards civil war. Ukraine's foreign ministry labelled the vote a 'criminal farce' arranged by a 'gang of Russian terrorists,' reflecting the government's view that Russian agents were behind the breakaway movement. The EU and US both announced that they would not recognise the outcome of the vote, which they deemed illegal. It was claimed that the polls were rigged, that voters were allowed to vote more than once and those who wanted to vote 'no' were often too afraid to head for a polling station. Nonetheless, the turnout in the region was massive, and the result of the poll left no doubt. It was a landslide victory, in which almost 90 per cent of the electorates in the eastern regions voted 'yes'.

After the official announcement of the results, state and military authorities quickly established control over the region. All Ukrainian military troops within the Donetsk and Luhansk regions were now considered illegal occupiers. Alexander Borodai, a Russian from Moscow, was appointed prime minister of the Donetsk People's Republic.

In Luhansk, Russian-born Marat Bashirov was installed as interim prime minister and his governor was Valeri Bolotov, also a Russian. The militia in the region were led by two Russians. It was a motley bunch: in the snapshots of these men and their associates that began to appear in the media, they disturbingly resembled a bunch of armed football hooligans or bandits. The West and Ukrainians alike were left wondering who these 'leaders' were. The conflict appeared to be throwing up self-proclaimed leaders, who preened themselves like dubious strongmen and had seemingly popped up out of nowhere.

The most notable figure was no doubt the self-proclaimed, and previously obscure, prime minister of the Donetsk People's Republic, Alexander Borodai, nicknamed 'The Fixer'. Borodai had been born in Moscow in 1972, where he obtained a degree in philosophy from the prestigious Moscow State University. In the 1990s he worked as a Moscow-based journalist for an ultra-nationalist newspaper, developing a reputation as an enthusiastic supporter of pro-Russian separatist movements across the former Soviet Union. In 1994 he worked as a military correspondent during the first Chechen war. After the Chechen war he worked as a political scientist specialising in elections, hence the nickname 'The Fixer'.

From 2001 Borodai headed a consulting business specialising in crisis management. It was rumoured that he was appointed deputy director of Russia's FSB (the successor of the KGB) security service after an article he wrote appeared in *Pravda*. But Borodai and the FSB swiftly denied any such thing. Borodai, however, never denied his involvement with the Crimean annexation, in which he had functioned as a political fixer and adviser to the new prime minister there. In the months to come he became the public face of the east Ukraine secessionist movement, always appearing comfortable with media attention and liking the spotlight.

An important military leader who had emerged in the region was Igor 'Strelkov' Girkin, who became the minister of defence of the Donbas. Born as Girkin, he was mainly known as Igor Strelkov, which loosely translates from Russian as 'shooter' or 'rifleman'. He had also been dubbed Igor Grozny ('Igor the Terrible'). He had previously worked closely with Borodai during the Crimean takeover; he had a long record of involvement in conflicts in which Russia was a participant, including service in Chechnya, Serbia and Trans-Dniester, a self-proclaimed republic in Moldova.

Born around 1970, Girkin was a shady character and little is known about his life. A Russian from Moscow, his record shows he worked for the Russian secret services. He took part in commanding Russian troops in their capture of the Crimea Simferopol airport. Clad in military camouflage outfit, he customarily travelled round in a black Mercedes with heavily tinted glass.

Ukrainian authorities claimed that he had been behind the 17 April kidnapping, torture and murder of local Ukrainian politician Volodymyr Rybak, as well as a nineteen-year-old student. When Rybak's corpse was found in a river, his head had been smashed and he had suffered multiple stab wounds to his body; the young student's mutilated body was found nearby. Ukraine authorities accused Girkin and one Igor Bezler of orchestrating these murders; Bezler, however, always denied his involvement. Although portrayed by his neighbours in Moscow as 'polite' and 'quiet', Girkin, after the discovery of the bodies, was described by Ukraine's interior minister as 'a monster and a killer'.

The actual commander of the pro-Russian separatist troops was Lieutenant Colonel Igor Bezler, nicknamed Bes ('demon'). Although Bezler's father was an ethnic German and his mother was an ethnic Ukrainian, Bezler considered himself Russian. Known for his walrus moustache and explosive fits of rage, he was feared by friend and foe alike. Because of his volatile nature, he was also considered somewhat of a liability by his superiors.

President Marat Bashirov and Governor Valeri Bolotov were the key players in the Luhansk area. Bashirov was a Muscovite who had previously worked as an employee of the Soviet Ministry of Internal Affairs and appeared to have no links to Ukraine; Bolotov had been born in Taganrog, Russia on 13 February 1970 and had participated in a number of conflicts including those in Tbilisi, Yerevan and Karabakh. The key players, however, came and went as their reputation deteriorated. As more and more 'volunteers' were called to take up arms, this also attracted criminal elements drawn in by the prospect of free access to weapons and the opportunity to steal and plunder. Girkin by now had reportedly shot two of his own commanders, claiming they were looters. He had also arrested the people's mayor in Sloviansk.

As ever more mercenary Uzbeks, Kazakhs, Ossetians and Chechen fighters joined the ranks, the armed and often drunk fighters were now frequently regarded as criminal gangs by the people of the region. Driving around in convoys, living in university buildings and hanging around on the streets, the gangs appeared to be much more interested in looting than actively fighting the Ukrainian army. Many citizens claimed these ragtag, aggressive 'invaders' were in no way helping the people's struggle for autonomy and were not even Ukrainian—or Russian for that matter. In Donetsk the question arose whether Borodai or even Girkin was really in charge of the disparate and often chaotic rebels, or were these gunmen actually running the self-proclaimed republic? To ease public opinion, Borodai publicly declared pride in his 'volunteers'.

Petro Poroshenko, the man who had climbed on the tank and tried to calm the protesters during the Maidan riots, was elected the fifth president of Ukraine on 25 May and inaugurated as Ukraine's president on 7 June 2014. He had captured more than 54 per cent of the vote in the first round, thereby winning outright and avoiding a run-off. Poroshenko was one of the richest men in the country and he also owned a television station; for some this made him a dubious leader. But he had also actively and financially supported the Euromaidan protests between November 2013 and February 2014, and this led to an upsurge in his popularity. For now, most Ukrainians were willing to give him the benefit of the doubt. When it became clear he had won the election he announced that his first presidential trip would be to Donbas, where armed pro-Russian rebels controlled a large part of the region. Poroshenko also vowed to continue the military operations by Ukrainian government forces to end the armed insurgency claiming, 'The anti-terrorist operation cannot and should not last two or three months. It should and will last hours.' Poroshenko and the rest of the world could not have fathomed then that five years later the Donbas would still be controlled by separatists and the fight for the region's autonomy would remain ongoing.

The second phase of the Ukrainian attacks on the separatist positions started around mid-May 2014 and, as the Ukrainian forces gained ground, it became evident that the pro-Russian fighters were actually only in control of the urban areas of the Donbas. During the clashes the rebels lost quite a number of men, but they were able to ruthlessly take revenge.

On 14 June 2014, a Ukrainian Air Force transport aircraft was shot down by forces of the self-proclaimed Luhansk People's

Republic during the Ukrainian anti-insurgent operation in the Donbas area. The incident came less than a week after pro-Russia rebels launched a series of attacks on Ukrainian forces at Luhansk International Airport. The airport had been under the control of government forces, but the rebels held most of the rest of the city. The aircraft was carrying troops and equipment; it was said that on its approach to land at Luhansk International Airport, it was shot down using an anti-aircraft rocket system.

A surveillance video that captured the plane's destruction showed a streak of light rising from the ground, then an explosion near the airport where the plane was making its final approach to Luhansk. Parts of the four-engine jet plane lay in a barley field and were reported to be scattered about and mangled beyond recognition, wholly unguarded by either side. All forty-nine people on board had died. It was the biggest loss of life suffered by government forces in a single incident since Kiev began its operation to defeat the insurgency in east Ukraine.

Chapter 11
17 July 2014

Willem Grootscholten was on his way to Bali to start a new life. It was there the 53-year-old had met the love of his life just a year ago. After selling his house, his motorbike and his car, he was now on a plane that would take him to the woman he loved.

Life had not been easy for this hugely muscled man, who weighed about 130 kilograms. He joined the army when he was twenty years old and was posted in Germany for years where he early on married and raised a family. Leading an outwardly settled life, he unexpectedly returned to the Netherlands poverty-stricken and alone. He never really told anyone what happened in Germany, but it was obvious that it had had a great impact on him. Never known as a man of many words but as someone who kept to himself, Willem did not appreciate the limelight.

After returning from Germany, the burly giant, who had once trained his muscles to the limit, was a shadow of the man he used to be; he started wandering aimlessly, even to the extent of becoming homeless for a short while. In an effort to get his life back together he applied for a security position; his military background and imposing figure helped him to get the job. Still, although he managed to find his feet again, there was always the feeling that something was lacking in his life.

When he went on a trip to visit a friend in Bali, all this changed. The friend had left his home in the Netherlands, burning all his bridges in order to settle himself in Indonesia. Willem fancied this idea and, when he fell passionately in love with a Balinese beauty, he decided to emigrate. Leaving his job as the bouncer at a local coffee shop, he was now on his way to his new life with his darling Christine, a guesthouse owner and mother of two.

The father of Christine's fourteen-year-old son and eight-year-old daughter had died six years before. The children soon bonded with the new 'father' and had already started calling Willem 'Daddy'. When he returned to Bali in May the previous year to celebrate Christine's birthday, he told her he wanted to spend the rest of his life with her.

Christine had never been happier. Willem had to sort out his life in the Netherlands first and sadly they had to say goodbye yet again. But this time it would not be for long, just a few months, and when he returned it would be forever.

The usually quiet and reserved Willem Grootscholten had enthusiastically spoken about the new turn his life had taken to the lovely woman at the Malaysia Airlines check-in counter at Schiphol. Smiling, she had wished him good luck and a wonderful life. As the plane he was on took him further towards his new life he knew exactly what he intended to do with the rest of his time on earth: lead a wonderful life.

Emma Bell was a school teacher in the remote Northern Territory town of Maningrida. Daughter of Peter and Barbara Bell and a sister to Sean, she was returning home after a four-week European trip. A homelands teacher for the last eighteen months, she loved her job. She had studied creative arts before discovering that teaching was her real vocation. The challenging area of Indigenous education suited her to a T: she travelled out from Maningrida College along bush tracks to service the smaller homelands education sites in Arnhem Land, teaching students aged one to eight. Emma adored the kids and was learning the local language.

The Aboriginal community had locked her into their hearts and one family had even adopted her and given her a 'skin name'. In most Indigenous languages, there is no word for 'stranger': everyone is related through the very complex kinship system of skin names. Now that Emma had been given one, it meant that she belonged to a family and that she would no longer be seen as an outsider in the communities.

Next to teaching, Emma's other great love was travel. In fact, she had searched online to see how she rated as an avid traveller and it turned out that she ranked within the 5000 most-travelled people in the world, coming in at 4283. According to this rating, she was the eighth most-travelled Australian female. She was curiously proud of this and was eager to have her place on the list go up a few notches in the near future. That would happen fairly soon because, after her latest visit to Europe, she was ready for bigger and more demanding journeys.

Her planned trip to Brazil during the next Christmas holidays peaked high on her list, but undoubtedly her greatest challenge was going to be her proposal to explore Africa during the coming year, travelling through most of the continent, visiting as many countries as possible. Her parents had been slightly horrified by the idea, but Emma, a young woman in the prime of her life, felt the need to live her life to the fullest.

Regis Crolla grew up in Amsterdam. After finishing high school, he had worked in a bar for a while. Then, not knowing if he wanted to go to university, much less what he would want to study there, he started to travel.

Taking to the road like a fish to water, Regis visited Thailand and stayed there for three weeks. After that he travelled around Asia with a friend and ended up in Cambodia doing voluntary work at a small orphanage. He loved travelling and meeting new people, but you needed money to do it, so he was soon forced to return to Amsterdam, picking up his old job as a barman and also working as a waiter in a restaurant.

Regis had always had a feeling for business. At the age of seven, having been refused a dog of his own, he started a dog-walking service; by the time he started high school he had bought a few boats and rented them out to tourists.

When he was a child, his big passion had been animals—rabbits and rats, but especially horses. He'd taken to horses after seeing horseriding contests on television, instinctively understanding what the riders were doing and what the horses were meant to do. After he took up riding he became very good at it, entering contests and winning a few medals. As with everything in his life, he became very passionate about horses and during those years he could be found at the riding school three times a week. But girls changed all that—when he was sixteen he discovered them, and they soon took over from the horses. He stopped riding almost overnight.

Now ready to start a course at university in Amsterdam, Regis decided to take one last trip before the term started. His mum had left with a friend for Bali the day before and his sister had left to spend her holidays in the south of France. His trips to Asia the year before had left a lasting impression, so he decided to follow his mother to Bali. He was able to get a business class seat on MH17 just a day after his mum left.

As he waited to board the plane, Regis sent a WhatsApp message to his mother: 'Boarding soon. See you at the beach.' After boarding he took photos of the aisle in the plane and posted them on his Facebook page. His mother sent him a message, telling him that she had made it safely to her hotel room, but she never got an answer back.

Benoit Chardome had just married and now he was heading back home to Bali. Chardome had been born in Belgium, but he lived in New Zealand for more than ten years before moving to Bali six years ago. He was a popular former Auckland

and Queenstown restaurateur: a maître d' at the well-known Parnell restaurant Iguacu for two years before acquiring two Queenstown eateries, the Pasta Pasta Cucina and Bathhouse restaurants.

Once known around town as 'Bathhouse Ben', Chardome had mentored a lot of staff now working in Queenstown, giving them their first jobs in the industry. He was sociable and good-natured, perfect assets in the hospitality industry. The enterprising 51-year-old had created his own holiday centre on Bali and was working on a community development program there for disadvantaged youths.

He was actually in the middle of his honeymoon when he boarded MH17. Because the two men could not officially marry in Malaysia, Chardome had taken his Malaysian partner, Puput, to his home country of Belgium to tie the knot in Antwerp. The couple had arrived in June and were supposed to spend their honeymoon right after the marriage travelling Europe, but Benoit had been summoned back to Bali to attend to some urgent business issues. Puput had wanted to visit friends in Switzerland and it was Benoit's aim to return to Europe to rejoin his husband after he had sorted things out in Bali.

The couple had brought their young friend, 24-year-old Wayan Sujana, with them to Belgium to be present at the wedding and he was now returning home, accompanying Benoit on MH17. Wayan was from a little village called Permuteran in the north of Bali. His family was poor; his father was a salt farmer and had barely been able to feed his children. Wayan was now earning sufficient money to be able to help his family financially, in fact the whole village was profiting from the young man's success.

A true self-made man coming from the humblest of economic circumstances, Wayan had become the backbone and future hope of his family. But they had known since he was very young that he would make something of himself; he had been a scholar and entrepreneur at an early age. At just ten years old, he had persuaded tourists to sleep in his parents' house so as to experience fully the authentic Balinese way of life. The tourists had paid just a few dollars a night, but for his family it represented a substantial income.

Wayan was talented and spoke excellent English. The young Balinese had visited Paris, Luxemburg and the Netherlands while he was in Europe and he could have stayed to pursue a career in any of those cities or countries, but he wanted to get back to Bali, to his family. He was paying for his brother and sister's studies and the people he loved and cared about were on Bali. 'It's all about family,' he told his friend Benoit.

On 1 June, Paul Guard had dropped his parents at Brisbane airport for the start of their seven-week European holiday. Roger, sixty-seven, was head of pathology at Toowoomba hospital, west of Brisbane. Jill, sixty-two, was a retired GP who volunteered for Meals on Wheels and helped Sudanese refugees settle into Toowoomba. They were devoted parents, had been married for forty-two years and had raised three children.

From the outset Jill knew that she would dearly miss their two grandchildren, two-year-old Kai and ten-month-old Ella. Thanks to the internet she had the possibility of keeping up to date with photos and videos. Ella would be walking soon and, if she did, Jill knew that she would not have to miss out—their proud daughter would send the video.

Roger had completed forty years of service as a Queensland Health pathologist. Away from work, he was an avid reader and interested in knowing how the world worked; fascinated by the endless complexity of nature, he was a scientist to the core. He was also a bit of a collector: he possessed a collection of *National Geographic* magazines that included every article printed since 1888, and he had stuck his fair share of stamps into albums and amassed an extensive butterfly collection. He even collected golf balls and was a keen bird watcher. Keeping lists of trucks he saw when driving across Australia was one of his strangest assemblages, a habit that some thought was a little eccentric. He was also passionate about running: as president of the Toowoomba Road Runners, he was involved in organising the Toowoomba marathon every year.

Jill had been a dedicated doctor who had worked in general practice for many years. She worked for most of her professional life at the Family Planning Clinic in Toowoomba, specialising in women's health. She had also committed herself to a wide range of worthy causes. As a piano and cello player in many local community music groups, she had encouraged her three children to take up an instrument.

The couple had experienced a wonderful holiday. First, they had visited relatives in Devon and then gone on a long trip travelling around Ireland and the UK. To top it all off, they had headed for Budapest, where they met up with Jill's sister, Liz, and her husband, Malcolm, who were fellow Australians on holiday. The four of them had booked a tour from Budapest to Amsterdam, where Jill and Roger boarded MH17. Liz and Malcolm planned to stay on in Europe and extend their holiday.

When the four of them had separated at Amsterdam on 17 July, Jill promised her sister that they would catch up after all of them had come home.

Stefan van Nielen loved everything about Asia—the people, the cultures, the weather—and Bali in particular had captured his heart. He'd visited the island a number of times. By telling enticing stories and showing off countless snapshots of enchanting Bali, Stefan had convinced his younger brother, Martijn, to go on a holiday there with him. The two brothers had not been on a trip together since they were kids and so, excited about the prospect of travelling to his beloved Bali with his brother, Stefan had searched the internet for flights.

It appeared that he could not get tickets. It was the height of summer and flights were booked to the max; they certainly wouldn't be able to book a flight together. He finally found one seat on MH17 for 17 July, and another for his brother on the same day but on a different flight.

Martijn could only get a ticket from Brussels to Paris to Kuala Lumpur, but he decided to take that route and meet up with Stefan in the Malaysian capital, from where they would travel on to Bali. They would have liked to have flown together, but this was a good alternative. Martijn's flight would arrive in Kuala Lumpur just a tad later than his older brother's.

Stefan and Martijn, although thirty and twenty-seven years old, still lived at home with their parents, but Stefan had been applying for a job on Bali. He desperately wanted to live there, and he had written letters to a number of businesses. An advertising company to which he had applied for a job looked promising, but he had not heard back from them yet. He was hoping to get a message from them in the next couple of days. His dad promised to phone him if a letter arrived while he was in Bali.

Chapter 12
Ukraine, June–July 2014

The downing of the transport plane led to a violent attack on the Russian embassy in Kiev. Positive that Moscow was largely responsible for what was happening in the eastern regions of their country, pro-Ukraine protesters tore down the Russian flag and threw Molotov cocktails and stones, smashing the windows of the embassy building. The furious horde overturned diplomats' cars, hacking into them with an axe while nearby police looked on and did little to stop them.

Moscow was outraged, and the US also strongly condemned the violent attack, calling on Ukraine to meet their obligations and provide adequate security. In retaliation for this attack, Russia turned off the gas supply. The message from Moscow was that poverty-stricken Ukraine would only receive gas if it paid for it in advance, which effectively meant the country would have to rely on their own supplies for the time being. It was June, summertime, but many Ukrainians knew their own

Naftogaz reserves would not stretch very far as soon as winter set in.

In an attempt to create an opening for peace talks, the newly installed president of Ukraine, Petro Poroshenko, on 18 June proposed a ceasefire in eastern Ukraine. He warned beforehand that he expected the proposed ceasefire to be very short-lived. The president promised that all rebels who surrendered peacefully, giving up their arms during the ceasefire, would receive amnesty, unless of course they had been accused of committing grave crimes during the hostilities. Government forces were ordered to withdraw from their positions to allow the rebels a chance to lay down their weapons. In the meantime, Russia resumed its build-up of forces along Ukraine's eastern borders.

It soon became evident that the pro-Russian separatists were ignoring the call for a ceasefire from the Ukrainian government. The violent clashes between government forces and separatists, which were now concentrated in the city of Krasny Liman, a town to the north of Donetsk and Luhansk, did not abate. Separatists reported that a hospital in the town had come under attack from Ukrainian forces, killing twenty-five people. Igor Girkin, commanding the pro-Russian troops in the town, said the Ukrainian military advance would completely cut rebel supplies to Sloviansk and he issued a desperate plea to Russia for military assistance. The separatists had suffered heavy losses and Girkin admitted that his troops were outgunned.

On 20 June Poroshenko officially announced a one-week ceasefire. He also proposed a peace plan that would increase autonomy to the regions as well as protecting the Russian language. The battle's pause gave the Ukrainian president the opportunity to visit his troops fighting in the east. During his visit he warned the separatists that the ceasefire did not mean that there would not be retaliation if the rebels showed any aggression against Ukrainian troops. Poroshenko stressed that the truce was meant only to give the rebels time to disarm. However, the pro-Russian insurgents showed no sign that they were willing to lay down their arms. The Kremlin initially dismissed the truce in a press release, saying it was 'not an invitation to peace and negotiations but an ultimatum'.

After talks with American president Barrack Obama, President Putin however later cautiously welcomed the Kiev ceasefire and on 23 June the pro-Russian separatists followed suit, agreeing to the truce. Alexander Borodai, the leader of the People's Republic of Donetsk, agreed to a four-day break in the hostilities, promising to start negotiations with the government.

But it soon became evident that the separatists were not united in their fight for independence. Many of them appeared to possess their own separate agendas and it became increasingly unclear who actually had the final say in the Dontesk and Luhansk regions. As the doubt about who was in charge in eastern Ukraine mounted, it slowly became obvious to the outside world that this depended on what area one was dealing with. Even the self-proclaimed leaders operating in the region appeared to only be in control of specific areas, villages, towns and cities in the eastern part of Ukraine. Several leaders had by now claimed their own autonomous states.

The truce was literally blown out of the skies just a few days after it had begun when a Ukrainian military helicopter was shot down near Sloviansk in the Donetsk region by separatists. The helicopter had arrived at Karachun (near Sloviansk) to unload and pick up a group of soldiers who were finishing their tour and going on leave. It was hit by a rocket just after take-off and nine servicemen and three crew members were killed as it crashed to the ground.

Donetsk leader Borodai claimed responsibility for the attack but blamed the Ukrainian military for inciting it, because of earlier provocations and violations of the ceasefire from their side. In response Poroshenko called the separatists 'terrorists' who were intent on maintaining a 'bandit state'. The helicopter incident was the most severe breach in the continuing violence, with both rebels and government forces accusing each other of breaking the ceasefire.

The EU, eager to pull Ukraine out of Moscow's clutches, offered Poroshenko a deal. So on 27 June, almost eight months after Viktor Yanukovych's refusal to sign an agreement with the EU, President Poroshenko signed an Association Agreement with the European Union. Using the same pen that the now overthrown President Yanukovych would have used many months ago if he had not backed out at the last moment, Poroshenko initialled the deal with the European countries.

Although the trade pact did not provide Ukraine with membership of the EU, it did mean that if the country was to successfully implement the Association Agreement, the EU would view favourably at a later stage their ambition to become full members of the union. For the pro-EU citizens in Ukraine it meant a renewed chance to become a modern European country after the missed opportunities of the past years. For Russia, the signing of the Association Agreement meant a grave setback, as it set Ukraine on a course towards Europe once again.

By the end of June, Poroshenko let the press know that he was considering an extension to the shaky ceasefire between Ukrainian and pro-Russian forces. But the next day he retreated from this and suddenly terminated the truce immediately. In explaining his about-face, he said that the talks with the rebels had not in any way been productive and they had failed to reach any permanent peace agreement. In light of this, further negotiations were considered useless. The Ukrainian Anti-Terrorist Operation (ATO) resumed their operations in eastern Ukraine with air strikes, artillery bombardment and infantry assaults.

The result of these renewed attacks on separatists' targets was a huge victory for Ukraine over the pro-Russian fighters. Just a few days after the termination of the ceasefire the Ukrainian military reported they had cleared as many as seventeen villages that had initially been held by separatists in the eastern regions. According to the Ukrainian claims, 150 pro-Russian militants lost their lives during aerial and artillery bombardments of the region, while only two Ukrainian soldiers were reported killed and four as wounded. A day later the Ukrainian troops freed the town of Sloviansk, once the symbol of the rebels' resistance. Igor Girkin ordered his separatist troops to pull back to Donetsk after he recorded an emotional appeal to President Putin, saying that he feared that 'Russia has abandoned us'.

A column of three tanks, three 'Grad' multiple rocket launchers and several armoured vehicles were spotted near the border with Russia in the region of Luhansk, in an area controlled by separatist troops. While there was no immediate indication that the Kremlin was enabling or supporting combatants coming from Russia into Ukraine, the pro-Russian separatists sometimes admitted that Russian citizens were present in their ranks (although others claimed these men were in fact Chechen mercenaries) and did not deny that they received military and financial support from Russian sources. It was hard, however, to assess how many Russians citizens or soldiers had actually joined the separatists, and the amount and type of military hardware they had received from across the border.

With Russia remaining reluctant to provide patronage publicly, the separatists became increasingly frustrated with Moscow and loudly complained that Russia was not providing enough men and materials, even after their leaders had repeatedly appealed to President Putin to intervene directly. But many leaders in Western Europe, the US and Ukraine believed that Moscow was highly involved in what was happening in Ukraine, and that the porous Ukraine border with Russia continually leaked men and weaponry, thus making the aid provided to the pro-Russian fighters less obvious to the outside world.

After being pushed out of Sloviansk and forced out of a string of eastern Ukrainian towns, Girkin and hundreds of separatists pulled back to Donetsk and fortified the city for a street war. Girkin believed that Donetsk would be much easier to defend than the smaller Sloviansk and, due to its importance to the Ukrainian economy, Ukraine's military might be reluctant to totally destroy the city in an attack.

The city up to now had been under the command of separatist military leader Aleksander Khodakovsky, who openly criticised Girkin for abandoning the people of Sloviansk. Khodakovsky promised the people of Donetsk that, if Girkin ordered his troops to flee from the city, he would not follow. He and his troops would never abandon the city and its people.

By coming to Donetsk, Girkin altered the shape of the conflict, because now all the firepower of the separatists was concentrated in just one place. Khodakovsky, who had had military control of the city, was now confronted by Girkin, who claimed command. Khodakovsky openly refused to subordinate to his superior, which made relations between the two edgy and tense. With neither party wanting to have on their hands an internal conflict as well as a war with Ukraine, both Girkin and Khodakovsky backed down for the time being, managing to avoid one another as much as possible.

As the separatists took up positions in Donetsk, three bridges were blown up on roads leading into the city. Although it was unclear who was behind the explosions, the Ukrainian media reported it had been done by the rebels in an attempt to cut off Ukraine's military advance. In the city many barricades were put up and even an old tank was snatched from a Donetsk museum to play its part in the coming conflict. Many residents, sensing the battle would be aggressive and fierce, fled. With armed troops roaming the city and the few remaining residents keeping indoors, the once lively Donetsk had now taken on the appearance of an eerie ghost town.

Clashes between Ukrainian troops and the separatists were reported as separatists tried to seize Donetsk airport on 10 July. A plume of smoke could be seen rising near the airport control tower and the loud sound of mortar was heard from within the city borders. A month earlier the separatists had taken the airport, but Ukrainian forces had managed to recapture it shortly afterwards. Throughout the months there had been a continually fierce fight to occupy the airport. Every fighter knew that it was a stronghold and that those who had control of the airport had a much better chance of gaining control of the city.

Positioned close to Donetsk with a good road transport network towards the city, and situated on high, flat ground, the airport offered a natural bastion that overlooked the city and afforded a platform for the deployment of armour and artillery that was within striking range of the city centre itself. This convenient vantage point allowed the Ukrainian forces to target separatist positions in Donetsk with artillery fire. The separatists, determined to capture the stronghold once more, fired endless rounds of mortar at the airfield. Their attack in the end failed and they were forced to pull back further within the city's borders.

As the fighting in the region intensified, economic sanctions against people and companies involved in the conflict were implemented by the EU and US. Those who were suspected of aiding the rebels were now no longer allowed to travel to Europe and their assets were frozen. Most separatist fighters shrugged at the measures: they weren't planning on travelling to Europe and they did not have bank accounts.

On 11 July a volley of rockets hit the village of Zelenopillya, killing thirty Ukrainian soldiers and injuring ninety-three of them. Poroshenko's answer came the next day when he sent war planes to bombard separatist positions along the front, causing huge losses to the rebels. The pro-Russian fighters were well aware that they would need better air-defence systems to defend themselves against the ongoing air strikes.

Now that the separatists were being pushed further back by the Ukrainian army, they became eager to display to the people who supported them that they were in no way defeated. Launching a rocket, the rebels managed to bring down yet another military transport aircraft, an Antonov An-26. It came down in an open field near the town of Izvaryne, close to the Russian border. Both pilots were fatally injured, but the six passengers managed to bail out just before the plane hit the ground. Jumping to safety, all but one escaped local separatist militia.

The Antonov had been flying at an altitude of some 21,000 feet. Its loss meant a crucial change in the way the war would need to be waged by the Ukrainian forces, because it was the first aircraft to be shot down while flying at an altitude out of reach of man-portable air-defence systems. Up to now, separatist militia were known to have portable surface-to-air missiles that worked up to about 3500 metres or some 10,000 feet.

Because Ukrainian officials did not believe that the separatists were in possession of the sophisticated military launcher needed to be able to shoot a plane out of the sky at an altitude of 21,000 feet, initially the theory was that either the missile had been launched from Russian territory or the plane had flown lower than the estimated 21,000 feet and was downed by a surface-to-air launcher. Officials also thought that the aircraft could have been attacked by a Russian fighter jet.

A defence analyst from London, Charles Heyman, doubted that the plane had been flying at 21,000 feet. Heyman thought it didn't make sense because the higher you fly, the more it costs, and the plane would have had to be pressurised. However, after a number of Ukrainian military planes had been targeted and brought down by separatist militias, crews were being advised to fly well above the suspected danger zone.

On the evening of 16 July, Ukraine authorities reported that a Ukrainian Sukhoi Su-25 jet had been shot down near Amvrosiivka, a village about fifteen kilometres from the border with Russia. After rockets hit its tail as the aircraft veered away from the border, the pilot was able to eject from the aircraft, and land safely. Ukraine authorities claimed the jet had been downed by a missile fired from a Russian aircraft. It was the first time that Ukraine openly accused Russia of using airpower in the conflict. Russia denied its involvement in the incident, calling the accusations 'absurd'.

By now there was a growing body of evidence that Russia had provided tanks, weapons and other support to the separatist rebels, and several separatist leaders had publicly identified themselves as Russian citizens. There was, however, still no proof of any active engagement in Ukraine by the regular Russian military, although the Ukrainian government had complained on several occasions that Russian aircraft had violated Ukraine airspace.

At the end of June 2014, a convoy of Russia's 53rd Anti-Aircraft Missile Brigade, a surface-to-air missile brigade of the Russian Ground Forces based near Kursk, travelled to the Ukrainian border, officially as part of a training exercise. Locals spoke to some of the soldiers in the convoy, who said that they were being sent to the border with Ukraine to strengthen border control. On 17 July locals reported seeing a convoy of military vehicles moving eastward towards Snizhne during the early afternoon. The convoy appeared to be transporting a missile launcher that was later reported travelling through Torez. The area was the hub of the fighting and it had been a noisy day in the eastern Ukrainian town, with plenty of military equipment moving through.

On 17 July, Associated Press reporters in the town of Snizhne saw a launcher aboard a flatbed truck with four SA-11 surface-to-air missiles parked on a street. The bulky missile system, also known as a Buk-M1, was a medium-range surface-to-air missile system developed by the Soviet Union and designed to counter cruise missiles, smart bombs, fixed- and rotary-wing aircraft, and unmanned aerial vehicles.

Three hours later, people living ten kilometres west of Snizhne heard loud noises. At first there was a weak boom, and then something that resembled explosions or multiple crashes. The blast came with so much force that windows shook and

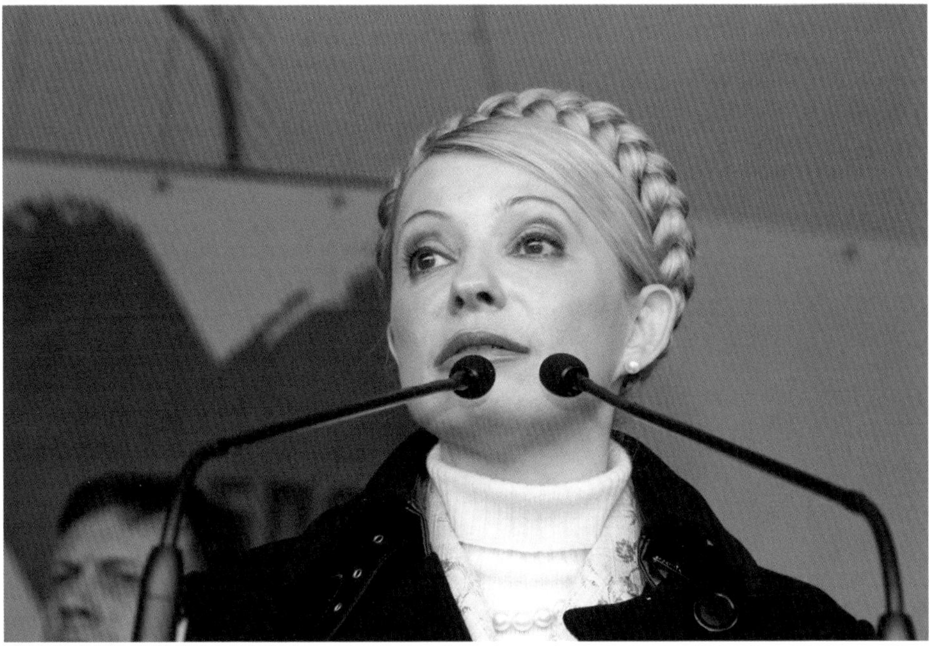

Yulia Tymoshenko campaigning on 18 February 2006 in Sevastopol, Ukraine. (Shutterstock/Alex Zabusik)

Kiev, Ukraine, 19 December 2013. The central street of the city lined with tents during the EuroMaidan protests. (Shutterstock/Zysko Sergii)

Thousands flock together on the Maidan Square, Kiev, 19 January 2014. (Shutterstock)

Viktor Yanukovych, President of Ukraine, at a press conference on 11 March 2014 at Rostov-on-Don, Russia. (Shutterstock/Oleg Pchelov)

Protests against President Yanukovych in Kiev turn violent, January 2014. (Shutterstock/Lena Osokina)

Russian soldiers marching in Perevalne, Crimea, on 5 March 2014. Russian military forces invaded the Crimean Peninsula on 28 February. (Shutterstock/photo.ua)

Proclamation of the Donetsk People's Republic, 7 April 2014. (Shutterstock/Govorov Evgeny)

Igor Strelkov (Girkin) and Alexander Borodai at a press conference on 10 July 2014. (Shutterstock/Denis Kornilov)

Smoke plumes from MH17 after it was shot down over Donetsk on 17 July 2014. (Shutterstock/gaponoffsound)

Wreckage near Rozsypne. (Shutterstock/Denis Kornilov)

Flowers outside the Netherlands embassy, Kiev, 18 July 2014. (Shutterstock/Dragunov)

Frans Timmermans, the Dutch foreign minister rushes to Kiev. (Dutch Ministry of Foreign Affairs)

Australian foreign minister, Julie Bishop, at a press conference shortly after MH17 was downed. (Shutterstock/ausnewde)

Wreckage from MH17. (Netherlands Ministry of Defence)

Australian prime minister Tony Abbott immediately after he accused Russia of being involved in the downing of MH17. (Shutterstock/Drop of Light)

One of the fighters guarding wreckage near Hrabove, 19 July 2014. (Shutterstock/Denis Kornilov)

Members of the repatriation mission hold a minute's silence before entering the crash site. (Netherlands Ministry of Defence)

Plane fragments in the Hrabove forest, 17 July 2014. (Shutterstock/Alexander Chizhenok)

Dutch and Australian forensic officers are finally allowed to search the crash site for remains. (Netherlands Ministry of Defence)

Wreckage at one of crash sites. (Netherlands Ministry of Defence)

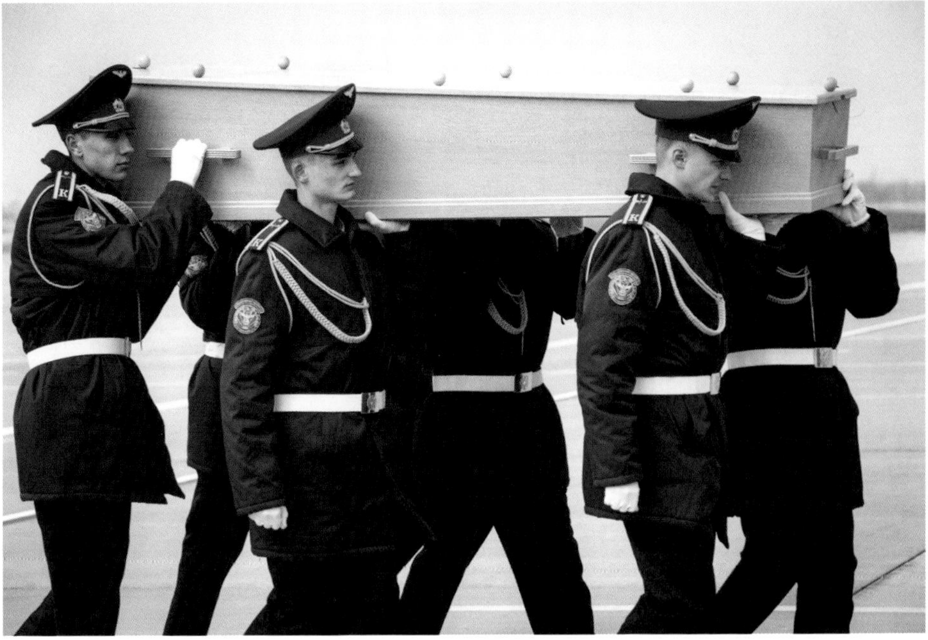

Ukrainian military carry coffins to a waiting plane at Kharkiv. (Netherlands Ministry of Defence)

A military salute as the coffins arrive at Eindhoven Airport. (Netherlands Ministry of Defence)

Coffins are carried to waiting hearses at Eindhoven Airport. (Netherlands Ministry of Defence)

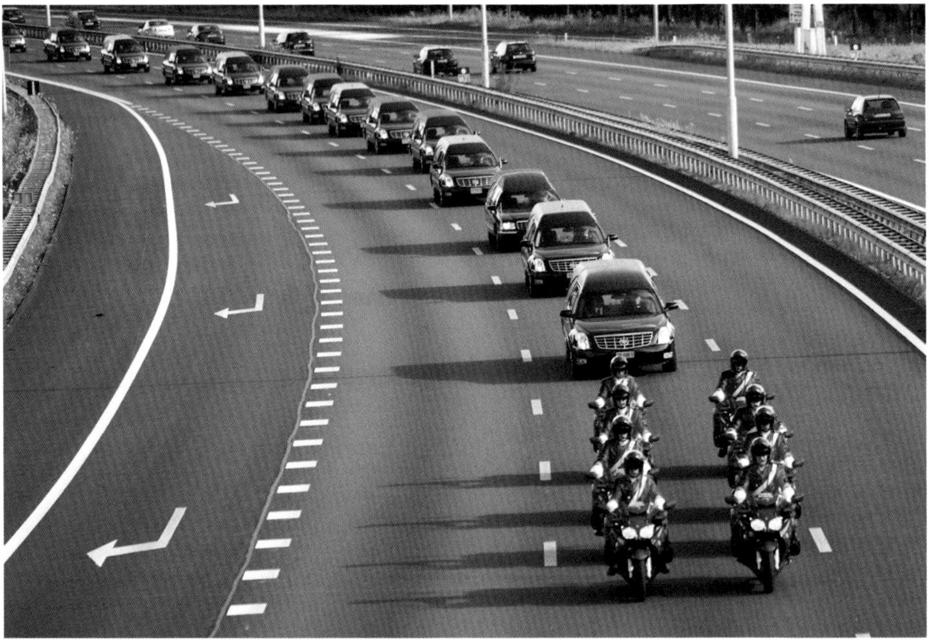

Members of the Royal Dutch Marechaussee escort the hearses carrying remains. (Netherlands Ministry of Defence)

Sunflowers in front of Schiphol Airport, Amsterdam. (Shutterstock/TW van Urk)

The forensic repatriation mission was aborted at the beginning of August 2014 due to dangerous conditions on the ground. The team returned to the Netherlands. (Netherlands Ministry of Defence)

Forensics at work at Korporaal van Oudheusden Barracks, Hilversum, the Netherlands. (Netherlands Ministry of Defence)

Rubble laid out ready to be transported to the Netherlands. (Netherlands Ministry of Defence)

The first convoy carrying parts of the wreckage arrives at Gilze Rijen Airbase. (Netherlands Ministry of Defence)

Wreckage in a hangar at Gilze-Rijen airbase. (Netherlands Ministry of Defence)

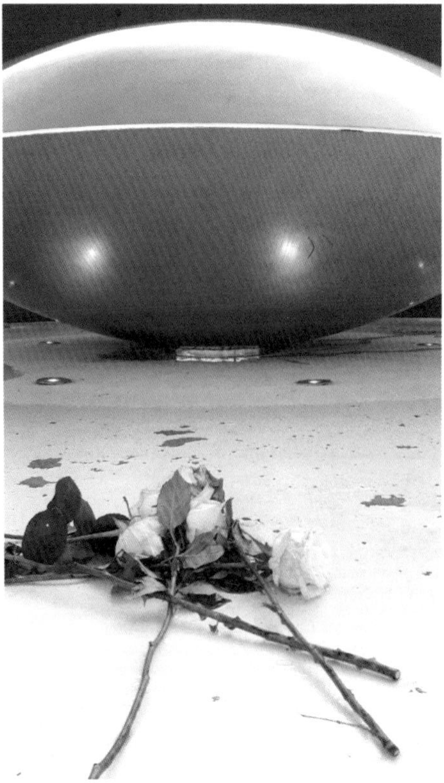

A monument to the victims of MH17 at Park Vijfhuizen, Schiphol Airport. (Marianne van Velzen)

The names of victims on the Park Vijfhuizen monument. (Marianne van Velzen)

The sunflower became a symbol for peace and remembrance of the victims of MH17. (Shutterstock/suncity)

shattered in houses. At 4.20pm local time in the town of Torez, Rostislav Grishin, a 21-year-old prison guard, raised his head to the sounds coming from above and saw a plane falling through the clouds.

Chapter 13
17 July 2014

Aerospace engineer Fatima Dyczynski was returning to Perth at the end of a five-year stint in the Netherlands, where she had been studying for a master's degree in the Faculty of Aerospace Engineering at the Delft University of Technology. In the course of her studies she had established her own space and nano-satellite company, Xoterra Space. The company website described her as a 'thought leader, scientist, creative space enthusiast, motivated entrepreneur, public speaker, all world traveller and absolute futurist'.

Although Fatima liked the Netherlands, her heart belonged to Australia and mainly to the city of Perth. Ten years ago, at the age of fifteen, Fatima had moved from Germany to Perth. It had been her dream to live in Australia and her parents—Jerzy Dyczynski and Angela Rudhart-Dyczynski—decided to share the dream with their only child, moving from their home in Germany to the Perth riverside suburb of Nedlands. In Perth

Fatima completed her secondary schooling at John XXIII College in Mount Claremont and after that the world became her oyster as she headed back overseas for further studies.

For the highly intelligent Fatima, however, the world alone wasn't big enough; her ultimate aim and dream was to become an astronaut. Her bucket list had always reached to the outermost regions of space. For the first twenty-five years of her life she had certainly not been idle: she had travelled through many countries and learned to speak four languages; she'd had a few gigs as a guitarist in a rock band; she liked glider flying and wasn't bad at kung-fu. She was known as outspoken, ambitious and incredibly motivated; those around her were confident that this young woman was going places.

As she waited to board her flight from Schiphol airport earlier that morning, she talked to her mother and father in Perth via Skype. They were excited at the prospect of having their daughter back soon and had prepared a surprise gift for her homecoming: a blue BMW Z roadster was secretly waiting in the family garage.

Karlijn Keijzer, twenty-five, was from Amsterdam but had been studying in the United States at Indiana University for her PhD in computational chemistry. She spent long days in the lab preparing a computer simulation for bryostatin, an anti-cancer drug and a promising candidate for treating Alzheimer's disease.

The blonde student had one great passion, rowing, and she was good at it. At Indiana U in Bloomington she had rowed with the fastest boat crew on the campus. After participating in the European Rowing Junior Championships in 2006 and the World Rowing Junior Championships in 2007, she had quickly developed into a leader on the team and was known for her fine technique. As the best athlete on the 2011 women's team at Bloomington, Karlijn rowed from the 'stroke seat' as the leader of the boat.

The Americans sometimes winced at her Dutch boldness and directness—her words tumbled out, saying everything she wanted to say without inhibition—but friends claimed she remained true to herself and never lost sight of who she really was. She was often the one to pat a back when someone was having a rough day and she could make people smile, like the time she showed up at a team party dressed as a gigantic ear of corn, a tongue-in-cheek dig at Indiana farmland culture.

Karlijn was now travelling to Indonesia with her boyfriend, 32-year-old Laurens van der Graaff. She had fallen head over heels for this sporty guy, and the couple appeared to be a perfect match. Laurens taught Dutch at a high school and they were both active members of the student rowing club, Skoll, where they had first met. But Laurens's real passion was writing: he wrote for the student magazine at university and he made no secret of the fact that his aim in life was to one day write a book. Meantime his mission was to fire up his teenage pupils with enthusiasm for literature and poetry. Whenever he could, Laurens visited Bloomington, where Karlijn would treat him to basketball games, wineries and restaurants.

Hoping to finish her studies in America in two years' time, Karlijn intended to return to the Netherlands for good and to move in with Laurens. It was school holidays now and, in between semesters, the couple had decided on a holiday to Indonesia to meet up with two friends: Boudewijn van Opstal, the rowing coach of the national rowing team of Indonesia, and Elizabeth Kleipol, a friend of Karlijn's from her high school days.

Gary Slok snapped a smiling selfie of his mum and himself just before the plane was due to take off. The sixteen-year-old did a lot of travelling with his 53-year-old single mother, Petra van Langeveld. On a previous trip they had been to Ecuador together.

When Petra announced their plan to travel to Borneo, Gary's father, who had remarried, had laughed and joked about it. As it happened, Jan Slok knew his son didn't much appreciate trees, or bugs for that matter, and the father was wondering how the boy would cope in the life-infested rainforests of Borneo, which were renowned for their wide variety of creepy-crawlies. But Gary and his mum were sure they would be able to overcome such trivial inconveniences and were confident that this trip would turn out to be their dream holiday.

The pair were joining a group tour designed for single parents and their children. Petra's sister-in-law worked for a travel agency and had suggested travelling via Vietnam, because it would be cheaper and a shorter haul, but that itinerary was fully booked so they decided to fly via Kuala Lumpur with Malaysia Airlines.

Petra, an energetic, outgoing person who was involved with elderly care groups, had just started her own business called

The Helping Hand. She had founded the venture because she noticed that more and more of the elderly were opting or forced to stay in their own houses rather than move to a retirement home. To be able to survive at home this age group needed a little help with a variety of matters, varying from a friendly chat in order to combat loneliness to assistance with filling in their tax returns. Petra was also the driving force behind a group of friends who called themselves the Golden Girls. Every Wednesday night they would come together for a fun evening, a drink of wine and a meal. The four of them had been friends for eons.

After his parents' divorce, Gary had moved from Rotterdam to Maassluis with Petra, about twenty kilometres away. Gary visited his dad every weekend and the two of them would talk incessantly about football; they were both loyal supporters of the Rotterdam football club Feyenoord. They would go to matches together as much as possible.

Gary himself played football and was goalie for his local club in Maassluis. He was really looking forward to this holiday and, when the plane prepared to taxi onto the runway, he sent the selfie and a message to his father: 'Here I go.' Now he and his mother were well underway.

Cor Schilder and Neeltje Tol were born and bred in Volendam, a small and attractive Dutch fishing village popular with tourists. They had gone to school there, grown up and fallen in love there. Young and dynamic, the couple ran a flower shop, simply called Neeltje's Flowers, in a shopping mall in the village. They worked hard, taking only two weeks off every year to go on a well-earned holiday. This year they had booked for Bali. Cor loved Malaysia and Indonesia and had spent many a holiday in Asia.

The couple had just bought a new house in the village; life was good and their futures looked bright. It was the peak of the holiday season and they had put up a sign in the shop window that morning that they would be back in two weeks, wishing all their customers a wonderful holiday. Then they had taken off for Schiphol.

Apart from fishing, nearly everyone in Volendam was involved in music, either as a singer, musician, producer or as simply a vendor of records and CDs. Through some strange quirk of genetics, just about everyone in the village could sing and most were gifted with wonderful voices. Musical talent had run for centuries through these families and almost every Volendammer could play some instrument or other. There were many local bands.

Cor was drummer in a band called Vast Countenance and sang the backing vocals under the stage name Cor Pan. Neeltje was the band's most devoted fan, always up the front and cheering them on at every performance. The group were about to celebrate their fifteenth anniversary and were working hard to produce a new CD, practising whenever they could for a special concert to be held in October.

Cor loved life, but his favourite pastime was lazing in a hammock with a beer and a cigarette. He was also a practical joker, known for his corny humour and silly gags. Always up for a laugh, he had taken a snapshot of Malaysia Airlines MH17 as he and Neeltje waited at the gate. His friends had teased him about the disappearance of Flight MH370; Cor decided to go along with their tease and posted the snapshot to his friends just before boarding.

The caption that accompanied his photo read: 'In case it goes missing, this is what it looks like.'

Chapter 14
Ukraine, 17 July 2014

Malaysia Airlines flight MH17 had left Amsterdam Schiphol almost three and a half hours ago and the crew were busy serving lunch. The plane was well into Ukraine territory, taking the shortest flight path over Eastern Europe before flying on to central Asia and over the Bay of Bengal and Thailand before reaching its final destination, Kuala Lumpur in Malaysia. Outside the oval windows, above the clouds, the sky over Ukraine was a perfect blue. From that height the situation on the ground below looked incredibly peaceful, and no one would suspect that blood was being shed and a war was raging on the ground. Some thousand feet above them Singapore Airlines was cruising leisurely a minute behind them, and Air India was also just minutes away. Together with Malaysia Airlines, some 150 other aircraft were using this same air corridor every day.

It had been smooth sailing from Amsterdam, but now Captain Eugene Choo, glancing at his radar, noticed a small patch of bad weather ahead. In the cockpit with Choo was First Officer Rahim.

The forecast had been for thunderstorms in eastern Ukraine, so when it became evident that MH17 was on course to fly into the storm, Choo intended to ask the air traffic controller if he could divert from his flight route. It was standard practice to deviate from a route if there was good cause, but a plane needed permission from the air control centre to do so.

However, before Choo could call in to ask for permission to bypass the storm, a communication came in from one of the air controllers at the flight control and information centre at Dnipropetrovsk (commonly known simply as Dnipro), asking if he could perhaps take his aircraft to a higher altitude.

Flight MH17 up to now had been flying at flight level (FL) 330, equivalent to 33,000 feet. The controller asked him to take his plane to flight level (FL) 350—35,000 feet—but Choo declined. His reason is not clear, but it may have had to do with the detour that Choo was planning. The air traffic controller did not ask for an explanation.

It was a busy day in the skies above Ukraine and there were several other aircraft in the area at the time. The Singapore Airlines flight was still trailing behind MH17 so, to give both planes some leeway, the controller felt the need to direct one of the two to fly higher. Singapore Flight 350 let Dnipro control centre know that taking the plane to a higher altitude did not present a problem.

The airspace below 26,000 feet had been closed for civilian aircraft as a result of the Notices to Airmen that had been issued on 1 July and later, on 14 July, the Ukrainian Air Traffic Service (UkSATSE) applied restrictions to airspace in eastern Ukraine, banning flights below 32,000 feet. Any aircraft flying at or above the assigned airspace was considered to be safe from insurgent air attacks.

Captain Choo at this stage put in his request to divert around the storm: 'Dnipro, Malaysian one seven, okay, start to two zero miles to the left of track due to weather?'

The answer came immediately: 'Malaysian one seven, roger.'

It was almost 1300 hours UTC (Universal Time Coordinated). At Ukrainian ground level it was around four o'clock in the afternoon.

Five minutes later MH17, having made its way around the bad patch, was back on its original flight path. But now Choo, feeling the need to make up for lost time, asked the air controller if the altitude at FL340 was free. This would take the plane up another thousand feet.

'Malaysian one seven, is flight level three four zero available?'

With Singapore Airlines 350 flying at almost the same altitude, the controller refused the request. He had just been able to give the two planes some room and allowing MH17 to fly higher would cramp both planes' airspace.

'Malaysian one seven, maintain flight level three three zero for a while, three four zero is not available for now.'

It was no great setback for the pilots of the MH17; they could deal with a loss of five minutes and they might be able to win back the lost time at a later stage. The MH17 crew now settled into the flight as they prepared to be handed over from Ukraine to Russian airspace. There was a war on the ground but, when it came to commercial aviation, the two countries fully cooperated with each other. The Ukrainian controller directed them to proceed to Romeo November Delta (RND, the flight centre at Rostov-on-Don in southern Russia). The last call from MH17 to Dnipro control centre was clocked at 13.19.56 hours. 'Romeo November Delta, one seven.'

Hrabove (also known as Grabove or Grabovo) is a small village in the Donetsk region of eastern Ukraine. Its population is estimated at about 740, although no one would have known that if strolling its streets. The sleepy village appeared quite deserted as the only 'busy' time of the day approached, when the village school would empty its pupils onto Hrabove's streets.

Two-thirds of the population were known to speak mainly Ukrainian and identified with Ukraine. Located on the Mius River, some ten kilometres from Tirez, Hrabove in July 2014 was also located in the very heart of the conflict zone. The area was under the control of pro-Russian separatist groups although, so far, the actual fighting had bypassed the small village. Villagers could frequently hear rumbles just thirty-five kilometres away, coming from the Ukrainian military and the separatists who were fighting a bitter battle over who would take control of the border area between Russia and Ukraine.

But 17 July 2014 was the day the people of Hrabove realised the war had finally come to their village. Hearing loud crashing and booming sounds at a very close range, villagers assumed they were being bombed with rockets and artillery. The population, mostly farmers and miners, scrambled from the fields, calling for their wives and children to rush to their basements and take cover. As things quietened, some of them dared to cautiously emerge from their hiding places.

From a nearby field ashen black smoke arose, smudging the sky where it slowly spiralled upward. The smell of burnt aviation fuel, burning grass and death hung heavy in the air. The fields where farmers grew wheat and sunflowers had gone eerily silent. Even the birds appeared to have been silenced by what had just happened. As if the heavens themselves could not contain their emotions, it started to rain.

The residents' first thoughts were that yet another Ukraine military transport plane had been downed by separatists. But, even from a distance, they could see there was so much debris that they doubted if it had been just one plane that had crashed. The only sound coming from the field was the crackling of fire and an occasional hiss as the rain managed to extinguish small flames. The surviving sunflowers appeared to turn their heads in shame.

One man wondered out loud where the pilot was, but the destruction of the plane left no doubt that nobody could have escaped from this. The aircraft parts had fallen so close to their houses that it was a miracle no villagers had been injured.

The thick black smoke and fire rising from the field made it hard for the villagers to assess what exactly had happened. Nothing prepared them for the horror they were about to encounter as they approached to take a closer look. Edging nearer, they at first saw nothing but black and smouldering earth where just earlier that day wheat and sunflowers had swayed in the gentle breeze. Parts of the aircraft—the motor, the fuel tanks, landing gear and a large section of the hull—had landed just thirty metres from a couple of houses.

Standing at the edge of the disaster area, bringing the scene into focus, people now began to notice items that would never have been on board a military aircraft. Stuffed animal toys, travel guides and family photos emerged from the blackened wreckage, and then bodies and body parts also became visible.

Curious children were hastily pulled away from the scene, ushered back to the village by their horrified parents. The town's mayor began piecing together the letters on the different parts of the plane's hull. As the words 'Malaysia Airlines' emerged, it suddenly brought home to him the reality that this had been no military plane. The shock and horror of what he and his villagers had stumbled onto became clear.

This wasn't an Antonov; this plane had carried civilians. People and families going on a holiday, going home to their relatives or on business trips. These men, women and children were playing no part in the war in Ukraine. The people in Hrabove were shocked and appalled. How could this have happened?

Four seconds after the air controller received confirmation from the MH17 captain that the plane would proceed to Rostov in Russia, he contacted MH17 again with extra information on how to proceed on that flight path.

'Malaysian one seven, after Romeo November Delta, expect direct to TIKNA.' (The TIKNA waypoint is located east of Rostov in Russia.)

But now no answer came back and, as he checked his radar, the controller noticed the plane had suddenly disappeared from his screen. A green dotted line, what controllers called a synthetic track, had appeared where the plane had disappeared. The synthetic track displayed on the air controller radar is also known as 'coasting'. After an interruption on the radar screen, the position and altitude are predicted and displayed by the green dotted line; the dotted line's course is based on the previously received radar data and flight plan information. It is a kind of 'ghost' track.

It was 13.20.10 UTC, about 4.20pm in Ukraine. Wondering why the plane had suddenly vanished from his radar, the controller, with growing concern, tried to make contact.

'Malaysian one seven, how do you read me?'

Nothing.

'Malaysian one seven, Dnipro Radar.'

After he had repeated his call three times, the controller was at a loss as to what could have happened. There had been no distress call. Nothing. Just a blip where the plane had gone off the radar, leaving only the ghost line.

Two minutes after the plane had vanished, the Ukrainian controller decided to call his Russian colleague in Rostov.

'Rostov, do you observe the Malaysian seventeen by the transponder?'

The answer from Rostov wasn't what the controller wanted to hear: 'No. It seems that its mark has started to break.'

The Dnipro radar told the same story: just the synthetic line where the plane should have been, and nothing to indicate where it had gone. Both controllers checked their devices, but the MH17 did not appear on any of them and appeared to have just vanished.

Dnipro control, running out of options, decided to contact the nearest aircraft flying close to the spot where MH17 had disappeared. It was the Singapore Airlines 350 flight. The controller asked the captain if he had detected something or could see the aircraft from his position.

But Singapore Airlines could only give Dnipro a negative. The captain said they could see no plane in the vicinity, not on the radar and not from the windows.

For minutes after that the Dnipro controller frantically tried again to make contact with MH17; he was still at a loss as to what could have happened, but he was slowly beginning to fear the worst. Rostov control contacted his Ukrainian counterpart to let Dnipro know that he had reported the incident.

To check the possibility that there was perhaps something wrong with MH17's instruments, Dnipro suggested that his Rostov colleague search for another Malaysia Airlines plane flying in the neighbourhood. It might help if Malaysia called the plane using its own radio. But there was no other Malaysia Airlines plane flying in the area.

After trying to locate MH17 for almost thirty minutes, RND control centre informed Dnipro that everyone at Rostov was by now rushing around on high alert, desperately trying to figure out what had happened.

Igor Girkin was one of the first to mention on social media that the separatists had managed to down yet another Ukrainian plane: 'In the vicinity of Torez, we just downed a plane, an An-26. It is lying somewhere in the Progress Mine. We have issued warnings not to fly in our airspace. We have video confirming. Residential areas were not hit. Civilians were not injured.' The post came just thirty minutes after MH17 went missing.

It was almost dinnertime in the Netherlands. People were lighting the barbecue or returning home from work. It had been a beautiful day and everyone appeared to be looking forward to a warm and relaxing evening ahead.

Many missed the extra news bulletin at 5.35pm with its special report, but not the mother of Hans van den Hende. She and her husband, Ko, watched the TV news with mounting shock and disbelief. A passenger plane that had left Schiphol airport earlier that day had likely crashed near the Ukraine–Russian border; there were reports that it may even have been shot down. When they saw it was Malaysia Airlines MH17, they knew. If this were true, their son Hans, his Malaysian wife, Shaliza Dewa, and their three beautiful children—Margaux, Marnix and Piers—had apparently crashed. The two elderly people sat in front of the television, stunned as the news was relayed again and again.

All around the Netherlands phones began to ring. Confusion erupted, and hearts broke.

Anthony Maslin and Rin Norris, still holidaying in Amsterdam, landed in a hell beyond hell as realisation settled in that they had not only lost Rin's father but also their three precious children.

In Amsterdam, Samira Calehr had just finished buying the socks she had promised her son Shaka when her phone rang. It was her friend Aan. 'Where are you?' he screamed. 'The plane crashed!'

Jan Slok, Gary Slok's father, was driving home when he heard the news that a plane had crashed en route to Kuala Lumpur. He knew in an instant it was the flight his son and his ex-wife, Petra, were on.

In Bali, Christine, fiancée of the friendly giant Willem Grootscholten, received a phone call at her guesthouse. She dropped the phone, collapsing in grief to the floor.

Robert Crolla was home alone. His wife had left for Bali the previous day, his daughter, Fleur, was holidaying in France and his son, Regis, had left for Bali that afternoon to join his mother for a holiday before he began university. Robert was looking forward to a peaceful evening when a telephone call came in from a sister-in-law. The plane Regis had boarded late that morning had crashed.

The news hit especially hard in the Netherlands. Two-thirds of the passengers on Flight MH17 were of Dutch or of dual-Dutch nationality. When the national news broadcaster NOS announced what had happened, night had already fallen in Australia and New Zealand. The relatives of those returning home on MH17 were asleep and unaware of the heart-rending news that would change their lives forever. In the morning they would awake to a world that had turned alien in a blink.

Word of the disaster spread quickly across the internet. It was too early to point the finger, and no one knew yet what exactly had happened. The Dutch as a nation aren't very prone to speculation; the people of the Netherlands, digesting the news in a state of horror and disbelief, waited for the facts to be revealed. As news agencies scrambled to collect data about the downed plane and the circumstances under which it had so tragically crashed, everyone involved held their breath, in anticipation of what would happen next.

The Dutch news broadcast lasted for more than two hours. Bit by bit the information trickled in. The first footage came from CNN and the images of the dismal smoke plumes rising from the Ukrainian countryside left little hope that anyone could have survived.

In Kuala Lumpur, family members and friends of the passengers of flight MH17 started arriving at the airport expecting to pick up their relatives. The plane had been due to touch down at 6.10am. But the plane didn't land, and over the next hours, as they waited, it became apparent that something was dreadfully wrong.

That morning Martijn van Nielen had been driven to Brussels airport by his father to board his flight to Paris. But after landing at Charles de Gaulle, his plane had been delayed for hours. It appeared something was wrong.

He was told there were many delays on the route to Kuala Lumpur: a plane had apparently vanished while flying over Ukraine. There wasn't much additional information. Ultimately his plane took off hours later for Kuala Lumpur, where he expected to be met by his brother, Stefan. At Kuala Lumpur he discovered that Stefan's plane had not yet landed. Thinking his brother had encountered the same delay that he had, Martijn waited in vain for Stefan to arrive.

As the news spread in Malaysia, anxious relatives tried to find out what had happened to their loved ones and family members. Initially Malaysia Airlines used its Twitter account to announce the news to the public: 'Malaysia Airlines has lost contact of flight MH17 operating from Amsterdam to Kuala Lumpur on 17 July 2014. The last known position was over Ukrainian airspace. For latest update, please follow our Twitter account @MAS.'

Heartbreaking scenes of sobbing relatives arriving at the airport—reminiscent of the aftermath of the MH370 disaster just four months before—dominated the news. Some people had not heard about the tragedy and arrived at the airport expecting to pick up their loved ones. Instead they were told that their family members would never arrive at Kuala Lumpur airport.

Tirso Pabellon waited at the airport. He was confused because his younger sister, 54-year-old Irene Gunawan, was supposed to be arriving along with her Indonesian husband, Budy, and her two children, Darryl and Sherryl. They were on their way to attend the annual family reunion in her hometown of Pagbilao. Tirso saw the plane had disappeared from the arrivals board, but it had not landed. There were disturbing but persistent rumours that it had crashed.

Ad van Nielen frantically tried to call his youngest son, Martijn. He did not want the boy to be alone when he heard the news, but Martijn wasn't answering his phone.

Not everyone was certain that their families were actually on the missing aircraft, and families and friends could be seen roaming Kuala Lumpur airport, frantically seeking information and confirmation. But the desks at the airport were mainly empty. Grieving families soon started to demand to see the passenger list, but no employees from Malaysia Airlines were to be found anywhere.

Furious relatives waited for hours at the arrivals hall, unable to speak to officials from Malaysia Airlines. Some grieving relatives tried to push their way into the operational areas but were met by security guards. Police guarding the area then had to call for calm as the now hysterical families began demanding that the flight manifest be shown to them. Everybody appeared struck not just with horror but with sheer disbelief that Malaysia had lost yet another aircraft. 'I am shocked by reports that an MH plane crashed. We are launching an immediate investigation,' Malaysia's prime minister, Najib Razak, said on Twitter.

Robert Crolla managed to get a phone call through to his wife on Bali. A plane has crashed and Regis is on it, he told her. She didn't understand until she turned on the TV in the hotel room. He kept trying to phone his daughter but her phone was busy.

Sixty-eight-year-old Yasmine Calehr had travelled from her home in Texas to Malaysia. She had once lived on Bali for years with her Indonesian husband and still owned a villa there that looked out over the rice fields and palm trees. Because she lived in the US and her grandsons lived in the Netherlands, they would travel to the villa every year to spend a vacation together. Yasmine had left Houston hours ahead of her grandsons, Shaka and Miguel who travelled from Amsterdam. The plan was for her to be there well ahead of them to meet them when they landed at Kuala Lumpur. Their brother Mika would arrive a day later.

Yasmine's flight was slightly late and she was afraid that she would miss her connection and also the boys when they landed. When her own plane landed, she grabbed her bag and turned on her Blackberry, because she knew the boys would ring her if she was late. But the phone rang immediately. It was her daughter, Samira. She was crying.

Chapter 15
17 July 2014

Around 6pm Dutch time, the GHOR, a Dutch governmental organisation responsible for leading and coordinating help during disasters and crises, was called to Schiphol to assist relatives and friends of the victims who were expected to arrive at the airport. As the sun began to set at the end of that warm summer day in July, distraught relatives drove their cars to Schiphol airport. Wondering where to go, they approached airport staff in the departure hall, but no one appeared to have any idea where to direct them.

Robert Crolla was one of the first people to arrive. Not knowing where to go or which way to turn, he headed for the bar area, where more relatives soon joined him. For the time being, bewildered and in shock, they sought each other's company, grouping together and waiting at a bar inside the hall.

The European managing director of Malaysia Airlines, Huib Gorter, a Dutchman who grew up in New Zealand, was sitting in his garden in the Netherlands enjoying his day off when he received a telephone call from the Malaysia Airlines area manager: radio contact with Flight MH17 had been lost. It was a Code Red. For everyone in the aviation business, this was their worst nightmare.

His phone did not stop ringing after that. Huib Gorter had quit smoking months ago, kicking the habit after years of addiction. But when he left the house he stopped at a local store and bought a packet, his first in ages. He thought he would need it.

Rushing to his office at Schiphol, he saw rows of TV network vehicles and realised that he must prepare to talk to the press. But first he had to meet the relatives. Minutes later, Gorter left Schiphol in a police car with its lights flashing, leaving no doubt that disaster had struck. The flashing police car took its passenger to the Steigenberger Hotel; the plan was that relatives were to be brought there and informed about what had happened.

The distraught groups that had flocked to the bar area at Schiphol airport were now gently ushered away by police and guided to waiting shuttle buses. They were told they were being taken to a private location. As they moved off, the faces peering out through the bus windows appeared stunned, as mothers, fathers, brothers, sisters and friends tried to process the pending reality that their family members and friends might never come home. Baffled by the growing realisation that their loved ones had most likely died far from their homes, in a tragedy caused by a conflict none of them had any part in, all they could do was wonder why. There was no sense to it, no logic.

A pastoral counsellor met the relatives at the hotel, but most of those first arrivals had to wait for hours while many more distraught next of kin and friends were collected at the airport and brought to the hotel. In the meantime, these frightened and distressed people continued to demand answers but were forced to wait as scant details trickled out of a remote area in Ukraine where a separatist insurgency was raging. The Malaysia Airlines and Schiphol officials in the room appeared to know as little as they did, but what little news there was could be found mainly on social media and it soon became evident that it wasn't good. There were no reports of people being found alive from the crash site. By now everyone was fearing the worst.

When Huib Gorter finally addressed them, he understood that he was facing the hardest challenge he had ever had to tackle in his life. It was something he knew that everyone in the business feared, a situation his colleagues hoped they would never experience. The room was unusually quiet and you could almost hear a pin drop. As he tried to form words to console the waiting next of kin, the mood changed and he was suddenly faced with their anger, their despair, their denial. There was no shouting or displays of heated emotions as at the airport in Malaysia, but people did demand answers. It was all directed at him because, for the time being, there was no one else.

Gorter knew very little about what exactly had happened to flight MH17 at that point, and the one thing he could not give the waiting crowd was answers. Copies of the passenger list were distributed by assistants to the relatives; people's lives were shattered as their family members were crossed off that list when they were confirmed as having boarded the ill-fated plane.

Unable to contain himself, Huib Gorter cried along with the people who had been so shockingly betrayed by this dark twist of fate. He knew he would not see his bed that night, but that was the least of his problems. Slowly but surely, as the evening progressed and more details emerged, it became evident that no one on the plane could have survived the crash.

After being informed about the disaster by Ukraine president Petro Poroshenko, Dutch prime minister Mark Rutte hastily returned to the Netherlands. Rutte had left for a holiday at the Bodensee in Germany earlier that week after having just ended a somewhat difficult EU summit. Arriving at Schiphol airport, a visibly emotional and drawn Rutte addressed the media: 'I am devastated. The whole Netherlands is mourning its loss. This beautiful summer day has ended in the blackest possible way.'

At 10.30pm Dutch time, Huib Gorter finally conducted a press conference at Schiphol airport. Press from all over the world had been waiting for hours and now heard a lot of heartfelt sympathy and words of comfort for the relatives, but little information about the cause of the crash and why the plane had been flying deep into a conflict zone above Ukraine.

'For those relatives who wish to travel closer to the site of the tragedy, a flight will be provided to Kiev, possibly departing tomorrow,' Gorter said. But he also warned about the difficulty in reaching the crash site, which was about a seven- or eight-hour drive by car from the Ukrainian capital. Probed repeatedly by the press, who wanted answers as to why the plane had been flying over a war zone, his answer was: 'It is classified as a safe area to fly over, otherwise in our industry we would not be able to file a flight plan over an area that is dangerous.'

Sunrise came to Australia and New Zealand, and with it the devastating news of a plane shot from the skies. In New Zealand, the frantic family of rottweiler-fancier Rob Ayley began sending him messages; they hoped his email about missing the bus meant he'd also missed the flight.

In Melbourne, Ross and Sue Campbell had just arrived home to Greenvale when they heard that a Malaysia Airlines plane had been shot down over Ukraine. Fearing the worst, they rushed over to the house of their friends, the real estate agent Albert Rizk and his wife, Maree, to check on their children. And for the second time in five months, Maree's stepmother learned she'd probably lost another loved one to a Malaysia Airlines disaster.

Australia's prime minister Tony Abbott phoned his Dutch counterpart Mark Rutte that same evening and held a televised press conference in Australia a few hours later. Where Rutte had refrained from publicly accusing any nation or person until more was known about the circumstances surrounding the crash, Tony Abbott was quick to lay the blame.

'These were innocent people going about their lives and they have been wantonly killed by Russian-backed rebels, quite possibly, maybe probably using Russian-supplied equipment,' Abbott said. 'The idea that Russia can somehow say that none of this has anything to do with them because it happened in Ukrainian airspace frankly does not stand up to any serious scrutiny.'

Russia reacted as if stung by a bee: 'Without bothering himself about evidence and operating only on speculation, Mr Abbott assigned guilt,' the foreign ministry said in a statement. 'Abbott's statements are unacceptable.'

President of the United States Barack Obama called the deaths 'an outrage of unspeakable proportions'. He went on to say: 'From the days of our founding, the Dutch have been close friends and stalwart allies of the United States of America. And today, I want the Dutch people to know that we stand with you, shoulder to shoulder, in our grief and in our absolute determination to get to the bottom of what happened.' He described the downing of the plane as a global tragedy—'an Asian airliner was destroyed over European skies, filled with citizens from many countries'—and called for an international investigation into what had happened. Later that night he called Rutte personally to offer his condolences.

In the course of the evening the nationalities of those who had perished became known. The Dutch had suffered the most casualties. One hundred and ninety-six Dutch men, women and children had died. Malaysia suffered forty-two casualties, Australia twenty-seven (although a total of 38 victims called Australia home), Indonesia eleven, the United Kingdom ten, Belgium four, Germany three, the Philippines three, Canada one and New Zealand one. Because some victims had dual citizenships, the numbers and nationalities varied.

Before the tragedy, many people had never heard of the conflict in Ukraine; they did not know about Ukrainian pro-Russian separatists or the annexation of Crimea. Articles about the country's troubles had hit the news and over the past months more articles appeared, but for most people Ukraine was a country they were not able to point at on a map, a country that did not concern them, a country that was tucked away in a far corner somewhere in between Europe and Russia. Not nestled in the collective conscience, never known as a hot tourist destination, it had now suddenly emerged from its obscurity, albeit for all the wrong reasons.

Slowly, as the realisation of what had happened and its likely implications for the parties involved began to dawn on everyone, the separatists and Ukrainian government forces started to accuse one another of being responsible for shooting the plane down. And disturbing reports were trickling in that insurgents were hindering access to the crash site.

Outraged at the attack itself but also horrified by the footage coming out of Ukraine, the deep grief and distress of families, friends and world leaders slowly evolved into a general feeling of anger and incredulity. Disturbing images—of charred metal, of luggage and documents, of broken and burned human bodies left unattended and uncared for—were flooding social media and broadcast on television news over and over again.

Robert Crolla, the father of Regis, saw those terrible scenes on his television, but he soon turned it off and refused to watch anything connected with the disaster for weeks. Stefan van Nielen's friends were furious when it became evident that the plane had been blown from the skies: someone wanted this to happen, they said, someone targeted Stefan and all those other people, all those children, and that person consciously pulled the trigger.

The worst outrage was the prevalence of looting. Cameron Dalziel's widow reported that her husband's credit cards had been stolen and used. After hearing about the crash, desperate relatives tried calling the mobile phones of their loved ones, only to find them being answered by strangers with 'eastern European-sounding voices'.

By now relatives of the deceased around the world were becoming increasingly angry at how the disaster was being handled at what people were now calling the 'crime scene.' The plane had come down in a foreign place far from where the passengers had boarded and there was no easy access to the site, so the relatives could only guess at what state the bodies were in. Human remains had been lying out in the open in the summer heat.

News coverage of the crash site gave the impression that security was very lax: villagers and separatists strolled through the mangled remains of the aircraft, poking at personal belongings with sticks. In North Tyneside, Barry Sweeney, the father of dedicated Newcastle United fan Liam Sweeney, said: 'I am sickened at reports of what has been happening over there and I just want Liam home.'

The bereaved demanded to know why it had taken an unbearably long time for the relatives to receive confirmation from Malaysia Airlines that their family members had even been on the plane. But, although the passenger list from Malaysia Airlines was available almost immediately after the crash, this wasn't sufficient to establish who had actually boarded.

Passenger lists of most airlines are often unreliable and incomplete. The nationality, date, country and place of birth are often not mentioned on aviation lists and it took Malaysia Airlines a couple of days to retrieve all the reliable information from their databases. Most families had thought this information could be retrieved at the press of a button. The entire process of collecting, distributing and verifying the information necessary to inform the relatives about the fate of their loved ones took a while to process.

But there were other questions families and friends wanted answered. One that quickly arose was why Malaysia Airlines MH17 was even flying above a war zone. In the last week alone two Ukrainian military aircraft had been shot down and a third had been damaged by a missile. How could it be possible that an aircraft was cruising around in the Ukrainian skies as if nothing was wrong?

The answer was simple enough. The aircraft was there because the airspace had not been shut down. Malaysia Airlines crew filed a flight plan, and Russia and Ukraine both accepted the aeroplane into their airspace. Although Malaysia Airlines was aware of the conflict on the ground in east Ukraine, they did not consider this a reason for monitoring the area more closely because they had no destinations in Ukraine and they would be flying at a high altitude.

A day before the tragedy, an Antonov An-26 flying at 21,000 feet had been downed with a weapon system that could reach planes flying at cruising altitude, but few airlines or aviation authorities knew that there were medium- or long-range surface-to-air missiles in the area. Military jets typically fly at lower altitudes. It was thought that it would be hard for insurgents to misinterpret an aircraft cruising at great height as a threat and most ground-based weapons couldn't reach such an altitude anyway.

But some families suspected that operators had continued to fly across the zone until 17 July because it was the quickest and therefore cheapest route for some flights. And this was in part probably true. Ukraine is huge: in area it is the second-largest country in Europe; only Russia is larger. The flight path was known as the 'highway to Asia'. Avoiding it would have meant a long detour and this would have been quite expensive in terms of extra fuel, as well as being disruptive for the carriers that took this option. Not a single state or international organisation, with the exception of the USA's Federal Aviation Administration, had publicly warned of any risks to civil aviation, and not a single state prohibited its airlines from using the airspace.

Of course, Ukraine itself had not closed its airspace. To do that, Ukraine would have had to admit that their sovereignty above eastern Ukraine could not be guaranteed. Moreover, every plane flying over Ukraine paid a fee and closing the airspace would have meant losing a significant amount of income for the country.

In the whole of Ukraine, 1300 flights were registered on 17 July. It was a grim version of Russian roulette that blew the MH17 from the skies that day. Most passengers on board, as they drank their beverages and watched their movies, were likely totally unaware that their flight path would take them over a country engaged in a war. And if they had been aware, they would probably not have realised that the airspace was in any way dangerous.

There were huge concerns among family and friends about how the passengers had died. The one very important question the relatives and friends were asking themselves was had their loved ones suffered? That this might have been the case was probably the hardest knowledge to accept.

It was widely assumed that death, or at least unconsciousness, had come quickly for the 298 people aboard the Boeing 777 when it came apart in the oxygen-thin, icy cold air at 33,000 feet. At this altitude, the lack of oxygen would lead to unconsciousness within thirty seconds to a minute. Still, thirty seconds, or double that, was a long time.

It was also suggested that the sudden loss of cabin pressure could have led to serious internal injuries. Those not strapped into their seats would have suffered a higher chance of injury than those who were, as they could have been hit by flying luggage and parts of the plane. Passengers' bodies very likely went into shock with the sudden extreme changes in temperature when the aircraft broke up. It's possible that some passengers and crew were immediately sucked out of the crippled fuselage into the minus-57 degrees Celsius oxygen-deprived air. A number of those killed were found in their seats, their seatbelts buckled.

Based on past plane explosions, it probably would have taken one or two minutes for MH17 to descend from its cruising altitude of 33,000 feet to the earth. But most passengers died due to decompression, reduced oxygen levels, extreme cold, powerful airflow and flying objects. It cannot be ruled out that some occupants remained conscious during the sixty to ninety seconds before the plane crashed. None of those falling to the ground could have survived. It was almost certain that the victims would barely have been able to comprehend the situation in which they found themselves. No indications of any conscious actions, such as sending text messages, were later reported.

Chapter 16
Chaos

Much of the scene at the disaster area was still in chaos twenty-four hours after the plane was brought down. The aircraft had broken to pieces as if it had exploded in mid-air. Parts of the wreckage were scattered over an area of about fifty square kilometres, in close proximity to the villages of Hrabove, Rozsypne and Petropavlivka.

The cockpit of the plane had crashed in a field of sunflowers near Rozsypne. It appeared to have broken off from the rest of the plane. The luggage racks, cargo area and the cockpit roof had come down in the fields surrounding Petropavlivka, and the villagers soon realised that it was short of a miracle that none of them had been hurt or killed because much of the debris had also landed in the village itself. The hull of the plane, the tail, landing gear and motor all came down in Hrabove. Bodies of the victims rained down over different areas. Parts of the aircraft, including at least one engine, exploded near Hrabove when it hit the ground, leaving an area of blackened rubble once the fires were put out.

Abandoned shoes dotted the fields; boxes of tablets spilled out of a medical cabinet and lay in a patch of grass; empty suitcases and articles of clothing were strewn around. Some villagers started to collect items, putting them in plastic bags and storing them in their sheds for safekeeping, ignorant of the fact that they were contaminating a crime scene and that their actions would later be regarded as looting. During those first hours after the crash the quiet fields were suddenly transformed into a busy centre of interest; journalists, local residents and separatists wandered largely unimpeded through the ashes and charred wreckage.

Although the disaster had taken place on Ukrainian territory, the authorities in Kiev could not start a rescue mission. The separatists were not likely to give Ukrainian officials permission to enter the area and any Ukrainian representative entering the Donbas would most likely be arrested if he or she was not shot first. A handful of local emergency workers arrived on Thursday evening, rushing to the scene of the disaster a few hours after the news was announced.

Darkness was setting in and, with no victims alive at the scene, at first they seemed uncertain about what to do. But eventually they put up their tents and set up floodlights in the field; they decided they would search for bodies in the morning. Just being there was a tricky business, they soon realised, as the constant sound of mortar fire and shooting in the distance served as a reminder of the conflict raging.

The next day rebel fighters in combat fatigues arrived, 'guarding' the scene and patrolling the area with Kalashnikovs. As a few more local emergency workers arrived, the armed rebels watched the proceedings nervously. They were now aware that Kiev had accused the separatists of shooting down the plane, but they vehemently denied playing any part in the downing of the civilian aircraft.

When the rescue workers started combing the fields, they called for the separatists and villagers to help them search for the bodies that were strewn over a very large area. Separatists clearly controlled the site, but the belief was that they could help out while doing so. Asked to help search and to mark with a white cotton ribbon attached to a stick any spot where remains were found, the tough men entered the fields.

They came across burned rubble, travel guidebooks, twisted metal, brightly coloured suitcases and headphones. They also found many human remains, some of them small children. It left the battle-hardened fighters shocked. Fighting had scarred and torn the region apart, but this was the most unlikely and heartbreaking battlefield they had ever witnessed.

As more and more white-ribboned beacons fluttered in the fields, another problem presented itself. The rescue workers soon realised that the local morgue would never be able to hold all the bodies the men were finding. Weeks before, some fifty people had died during the battle of Donetsk airport and the morgue at that time had been unable to hold that number. Now the morgue would have to deal with hundreds of bodies.

Most of the remains in the fields, once they were found, were covered by plastic sheeting weighed down by stones. The thunderstorms that had struck the area the day before had now disappeared; the rain had stopped and the sun had come out again. It was the height of summer and, with temperatures likely to rise to thirty degrees Celsius, everyone knew that soon these remains would start to decompose.

As it became more obvious that the plane had not just crashed but had most certainly been shot out of the sky, world leaders and the media scrambled to identify the perpetrators. Ukrainian president Poroshenko appeared positively convinced that the pro-Russian rebels had targeted the plane, calling it an act of terrorism. People on the ground and on social media claimed that a Russian-made Buk missile launcher had been seen and also photographed in the area. The next morning the same Buk launcher was videotaped travelling through the town of Luhansk. In the footage the launcher was loaded onto the low-loader truck and now appeared to be missing one of its four missile rockets.

Russia insisted none of its military's weapons had entered Ukraine. The Donetsk People's Republic prime minister, Alexander Borodai, said the allegation that the separatists had been responsible for the crash had come from the Ukrainian military, but his men had no such sophisticated weaponry. He claimed he was concerned about the imminent decomposition of the bodies of the passengers and crew, but he highly distrusted Ukraine and did not want Ukrainian officials coming to the area and possibly tampering with the remains.

'Bodies of innocent people are lying out in the heat,' Borodai said. 'We reserve the right . . . to begin the process of taking away the bodies. We ask the Russian Federation to help us with this problem and send their experts.'

From the outset, Russia denied any involvement. Its defence ministry spokesman claimed that none of its armed forces' weapons, including its Buk surface-to-air missile systems, had crossed its borders into neighbouring Ukraine. The Kremlin website let the world know that Putin's thoughts were with the friends and families of the victims and he sent his condolences to the Malaysian prime minister, Najib Razak.

According to a statement from the Kremlin, President Vladimir Putin in a phone call on 18 July with Dutch prime minister, Mark Rutte, offered his condolences and called for a 'thorough and unbiased' investigation into the crash of Malaysia Airlines Flight MH17. Later, English prime minister David Cameron and his Dutch counterpart called for the European Union to 'reconsider its approach to Russia' in the light of evidence that pro-Moscow separatists had most likely brought down MH17.

Russian state television released what it said was a satellite photograph showing that a Ukrainian fighter jet had shot down MH17; it later said that if a missile was responsible for the downing of the plane, it must have been launched from Ukraine-controlled territory. The satellite photo, released on Friday 18 July by Russia's Channel One and Rossiya TV stations, supposedly showed a Ukrainian fighter plane firing an air-to-air missile in the direction of Flight MH17. The channels had received the photo from a Moscow-based organisation, which had obtained it via email from a man who had identified himself as an aviation expert.

But in an interview just after the disaster, a highly placed separatist officer said that the plane was shot down by a mixed team of separatist fighters and Russian military personnel, who believed they had been targeting a Ukrainian military plane. No one was really sure about what had happened, but if the separatists had shot MH17 out of the sky, then it had certainly been a mistake on their part.

In Australia, the Netherlands, Malaysia and Ukraine, flags were flying at half-mast as the victims were mourned. Prime Minister Tony Abbott instructed all government establishments in Australia and overseas to fly Australia's flag at half-mast as a symbol of respect.

Malaysia Airlines informed close relatives of those who died on Flight MH17 that they would be offered the opportunity to visit the crash site in eastern Ukraine. A number of relatives expressed their emotional need to visit the site where their loved ones had died, but most of them had no idea how remote and dangerous the crash site was. By car it was more than seven hundred kilometres from Kiev. It would take seven to eight hours to get there, travelling through extremely difficult terrain; upon arrival they would most likely find themselves in the middle of a war. The area was off-limits even for the authorities and investigators who had flocked to Ukraine. It was much too dangerous, so the prospect of large groups of civilians travelling to the area anytime soon seemed unlikely.

Jerzy and Angela, the parents of Perth's promising aerospace engineer Fatima Dyczynski, refused to believe that their daughter was dead. They were determined to go to the crash site despite government officials in Australia, Germany and the Netherlands advising victims' families against immediately travelling to the crisis-torn country. Hoping that, through some miracle, they might find their daughter alive, they became the first relatives to arrive at the crash site. Unable and unwilling to believe that no one had survived the crash, they walked through the rebel-controlled fields with mounting horror at what they witnessed. The disaster area revealed a different story to the one they wanted to believe. Nevertheless, they vowed that they would not give up the search until they had found Fatima alive.

Emma Bell's father said while he wanted his daughter's body to be brought home, he did not want to visit the crash site. 'Ukraine is not Emma and that crash site is not Emma,' he said.

At the end of Friday 18 July, Dutch minister of foreign affairs Frans Timmermans arrived in Kiev. With him were the Dutch National Forensic Investigation Team (LTFO) as well as the Dutch Safety Board (the DSB, or OVV in Dutch). The DSB had already established an incident team in The Hague; now they would set up another in Kiev.

In view of the fact that a number of countries had let Ukraine know that they would be sending investigation crews to repatriate their dead and help with forensic work, the Ukrainian government asked the Netherlands, who had lost the most civilians in the disaster and had remained neutral and refrained from pointing an accusing finger during those first days, to lead and coordinate the investigation. Forensic teams from different countries would take on the task of identifying the victims and the DSB was to investigate what had actually caused the crash. It would be a difficult task, as there were by this time three major crash locations. This disaster had destroyed so many lives—not only of the dead, but also of their relatives and friends—and the DSB realised they would be under enormous pressure to find answers to questions that probably could not be answered either quickly or easily.

Earlier that day members of the OSCE, the Organization for Security and Co-operation in Europe, had visited the site and demanded access, but they had been held at bay by separatists, who fired gunshots into the air to let them know they meant business. They left in a hurry. The OSCE had already experienced the drama of eight of their international observers being taken hostage in east Ukraine in May that year, four abducted in the region of Donetsk and four others in the region of Luhansk. After being held prisoner for almost a month, they had suddenly and unexpectedly been released on 27 June. The separatists appeared to be answerable to no one and their actions were highly unpredictable. The OSCE was not going to put its people's lives on the line.

Timmermans, who had previously rushed to Kiev during the Maidan riots, was hoping that his presence would secure access to the crash site. He wanted his teams to be allowed to do their work without interference, but they were soon denied access to any of the sites. According to the rebels, the area was much too dangerous to enter at this time and no one could guarantee the safety of the teams. They would have to wait; it was anyone's guess how long the delay would be.

Dismayed at the prospect that the site would continue to be contaminated, the teams could do nothing other than obey the rebels' orders. Being unarmed civilians, they weren't in a position to argue with people bearing heavy arms.

Rod Anderson, a forensic police officer from Canberra, was heading towards Ukraine. Rod's usual job was station sergeant at Gungahlin police station in the Australian Capital Territory. His working days were normally focused on investigating traffic crashes, but on the morning of 18 July he awoke to the news that a Malaysia Airlines plane flying through Ukrainian airspace had crashed. Lots dead, although reports were not sure about any Australians. Anderson had barely finished his coffee that morning before his phone rang; the caller was the Australian Federal Police's chief forensic scientist and national disaster victim identification (DVI) commander, Dr Simon Walsh. Anderson was Walsh's ACT counterpart in essential DVI business. The two took turns heading to the frontline when Australians were in trouble.

The Dutch had asked Australia to help form a multinational search party that was assembling at Donetsk. The flight to Kiev fell to Anderson.

As valuable minutes turned into hours, the forensic teams waited. International concern about the contamination of the crash site mounted as images of armed separatists delving through the rubble were broadcast. Some thought the stalling and rummaging through the rubble was a deliberate effort to make evidence disappear. Australian prime minister Tony Abbott described what was happening at the scene as a cover-up: 'After the crime comes the cover-up,' he told reporters. 'What we have seen is evidence of tampering on an industrial scale and obviously that must stop.'

Australian minister for foreign affairs Julie Bishop sat in the Commonwealth Parliamentary Offices in Sydney on the morning of 18 July watching TV images of pro-Russian separatists picking through belongings of victims of Flight MH17. She realised immediately that access to the crash site was imperative. The Abbott government's National Security Committee of Cabinet had decided within hours of the tragedy that international backing in the form of a United Nations resolution was needed to safeguard access to the crash site so that victims' remains could be retrieved and a proper investigation could begin.

Rushing to New York, Bishop met up with her Dutch counterpart, Frans Timmermans. A UN resolution that the two had thrown together in just a few days, backing access to the site, would be presented to the United Nations Security Council. Before the meeting Bishop had strategically laid out copies of Australian newspapers with the horror headlines about the tragedy. There was a heated discussion with Moscow, whose representative refused to support the resolution.

In an emotional and powerful speech to the UN Security Council, Frans Timmermans, the Dutch minister of foreign affairs, called upon Russia to take action, urging them to back the resolution tabled by Australia, demanding that armed groups immediately surrender control of the crash site of Flight MH17 to allow for the repatriation of victims. It proposed an international investigation into the attack.

Pausing at times to contain his emotions, Frans Timmermans spoke to the United Nations of his shock at the treatment of the bodies, the indignity of the news coverage, and the obfuscation of the details of the crash. In his speech he recalled how men, women and a staggering number of children had lost their lives on their way to holiday destinations, their homes and loved ones. He pondered as to what had happened during those final moments of their lives: 'Did they lock hands with their loved ones? Did they hold their children close to their hearts? Did they look each other in the eyes, one final time, in a wordless goodbye? We will never know,' he said.

Timmermans stressed that the Netherlands, like Australia, had one priority that clearly stood out above all others: 'to bring the victims' remains home.' He expressed gratitude for Australia's role in drafting and negotiating the resolution, especially thanking Australia's minister for foreign affairs, Julie Bishop; he thanked the countries that had expressed support for it. He demanded respectful treatment of the crash site and dignity for the victims and the multitudes who mourned their loss. 'My country will not rest until all the facts are known and justice is served.'

The United Nations unanimously adopted Resolution 2166. The resolution expressed support for the 'efforts to establish a full, thorough and independent international investigation into the incident in accordance with international civil aviation guidelines' and called on all United Nations member states 'to provide any requested assistance to civil and criminal investigations'.

With the resolution in place it was now a question of making sure it was implemented, so Julie Bishop flew to Kiev with Timmermans. Thinking they had a deal, she travelled to Kharkiv, where bodies of victims were due to arrive by train. There was no Australian embassy to back her in Ukraine so not all relevant information was passed on to her. When the news came through that the parliament in Kiev had broken for the summer recess, she was stunned. The signature needed from the Ukrainian government to implement the resolution could not be obtained. Bishop found herself flying back to Kiev together with Timmermans that same evening where the two 'made complete nuisances of themselves' in an effort to have the Ukrainian parliament recalled. Four days after MH17 was downed, the resolution was signed by all parties including Ukraine.

Despite Bishop's and Timmermans' efforts, access to the site remained uncertain. On 21 July 2014, Angus Houston, a retired senior officer of the Royal Australian Air Force, was appointed the prime minister's special envoy to Ukraine, with the objective to 'lead Australia's efforts on the ground in Ukraine to help recover, identify and repatriate Australians killed in the MH17 crash'. He was starting to put together a recovery team in Kiev. Thinking there was an agreement with the separatists, Houston and his men made their way to a checkpoint only to find they were not allowed through. Ukraine's parliament had approved access by armed Australian police, but the separatists then insisted they be unarmed. Australia and the Netherlands consented despite their initial reluctance, but access to the site remained very uncertain. The days were hectic for everyone involved and National Security Council meetings were often called for during the early morning hours in Kiev. It was on one of those early mornings that Bishop, normally fashionably dressed, was called to discuss matters with Australia's prime minister. Sleepy-eyed, she stumbled downstairs to the conference room in the hotel where officials had installed a secure phone line for her to talk to the prime minister and senior colleagues back home. Barefoot, clad in a set of Qantas-issued pyjamas, she did not realise she would be beamed in back to Canberra from Ukraine via a video link instead of by phone. It was too late to do anything, and as the video link between Canberra and Kiev connected, silence fell in Canberra. Cabinet colleagues and senior officials stared at the foreign minister in her nightwear until one of them broke the silence with the inquiry: 'Going casual today, Julie?' Keeping a straight face, Bishop got right down to business.

As precious hours passed after the crash there were pleas for ceasefires, but none of them were acknowledged. Putin said in a televised public appearance that the downing of the airliner must not be used for political ends and urged separatists to allow international experts to access the crash site. Borodai and Putin both called on the militants to lay down their arms so that the remains of the victims could be removed from the site, but many separatists did not feel accountable to either Putin or Borodai. So the fighting went on.

It became apparent that neither Borodai nor Putin had full control over the different rebel groups; small pockets of militants seemed to be engaged in their own private fights. The Ukrainian government appeared to be dealing with the same problem. When they were asked why Ukrainian troops were still fighting thirty kilometres away, the government in Kiev denied sending the regular army into the Donetsk region; they claimed small 'self-organised' pro-Ukrainian groups, over which they had no control, were fighting the rebels in the city. More than twenty civilians were reported to have died in scuffles in Luhansk on 18 July. Journalists travelling to the crash site reported that the road from Donetsk to the site was punctuated by five different rebel checkpoints, all running their own separate document checks.

There was fear that the victims' belongings would become a magnet for looters who, according to Ukrainian politicians, had descended on the site of the crash in the hope of salvaging valuables. People in the Netherlands and Australia were beside themselves with rage. A furious Mark Rutte, no longer able to maintain a neutral stand, said that Putin had 'one last chance to show he means to help'. But some journalists visiting the scene said they had not witnessed any looting and that the only people tampering with belongings or bodies were the rescue workers. The local Ukrainians were not uncaring people. It was as much a tragedy for them as for the victims, and they were all working under very difficult circumstances. But the televised footage of rough, armed and seemingly drunken rebels holding stuffed animals and victims' passports up to the camera had set the mood.

Initially the 298 victims of the attack had been left to lie where they fell, but finally over the first weekend, beginning on Saturday 19 July, a chaotic clean-up operation began. Young men and emergency workers, armed with body bags and green plastic gloves, were sent into the fields to retrieve bodies. On Sunday 20 July, local rescue workers claimed that they had found most of the corpses—some of them largely intact, others mangled—and that they were now in the process of transporting them.

By early afternoon, the line of body bags had expanded from very few to very many. From a logbook kept by a Torez firefighter, Sergei Michenco, it became clear that most bodies had been found in the area of Hrabove. According to Sergei's logbook, 282 more or less intact bodies were found at the three crash sites, plus an additional eighty-seven body parts. The remains of the victims were now lined along the roads at Hrabove, Rozsypne and Petropavlivka. The Dutch and Australians were frantically negotiating with the authorities to have the bodies transferred from the crash site to Ukraine-controlled territory so they could finally be brought home.

Later that day these bodies, wrapped in black plastic, were piled high onto the back of trucks in the sweltering heat before being carted off to a refrigerated train waiting at Torez, twelve kilometres away but still well within rebel territory. For the families, those scenes of the bodies heaped onto the trucks was the most undignified and painful sight imaginable. By now the news coverage of the disaster had become so upsetting that most families and friends had simply stopped watching it.

In Melbourne on Sunday 20 July, the International AIDS Conference was held. Some 12,000 delegates were expected to attend the three-day conference, but it soon became known that six delegates, among them the most brilliant minds in the HIV field, would be absent. On the Saturday night the names of those killed when their plane was shot down over eastern Ukraine were revealed: the former society president and professor of medicine Joep Lange, his partner and Amsterdam Institute for Global Health and Development public health official Jacqueline van Tongeren, AIDS lobbyists Pim de Kuijer and Martine de Schutter, director of support at the Female Health Company Lucie van Mens, and World Health Organization media coordinator Glenn Thomas.

Red HIV ribbons adorned the doors of buildings throughout the precinct and people wore them on their shirts; these symbols of the conference taking place had now also become a sign of remembrance for the six researchers. Distraught and teary-eyed delegates pushed past the cameras as they headed into the building.

During the minute's silence that was held in memory of those who had died, the devastation and anger in the room became palpable, more so because what had happened appeared to be not just an accident. If it were established that the plane had been shot from the skies, that would turn the death of nearly three hundred people, including their six colleagues, into an act of murder.

Chapter 17
Outrage

Shortly after the crash, rumours started circulating in the news that the separatists controlling the area where MH17 was brought down had recovered its black boxes and were now considering what to do with them. For the investigators of the Dutch Safety Board, the black boxes were a crucial find. After any plane crash investigators always turn for answers to the plane's flight data recorder (FDR) and cockpit voice recorder (CVR), known as the black boxes.

Because they did not trust the Ukrainian authorities, the separatists' first instinct was to send the boxes to Moscow for further examination, but the Ukrainians protested that they in turn did not trust Russia. The parties finally agreed to hand over the flight data recorder and the voice cockpit recorder to the owners of the plane, the Malaysians.

In a bizarre late-night press conference on 21 July, Alexander Borodai handed the black boxes over to a Malaysian delegation at the headquarters of his self-proclaimed Donetsk People's Republic in Donetsk. 'Here they are, the black boxes,' said Borodai, guarded by a group of Kalashnikov-wielding rebels, as an armed rebel soldier placed the bright orange boxes on a desk. 'Today is a quite important day in the history of the Donetsk People's Republic,' he added.

The visibly uneasy and probably terrified Malaysians thanked 'His Excellency Mr Borodai' for agreeing to the transfer and Colonel Mohamed Sakri of the Malaysian National Security Council said the two black boxes appeared 'in good condition'.

The voice recording could hold crucial information: the audio from the cockpit, in particular, might show if the plane had crashed due to other circumstances or, if it was indeed struck by a missile, whether the pilots knew their plane had been hit. The black boxes weren't going to solve the mystery of who downed the Malaysian airliner, but the flight data recorder would give investigators information about engine settings, pressurisation and electronic communications, among other details. Handing over the black boxes was a significant step forward in an investigation that had been stalled for days.

After the handover the Malaysian delegation negotiated with Borodai into the early hours of the next morning. The result appeared to be a deal that secured the safe passage of the MH17 victims' bodies out of the rebel-held territory and unfettered access to the crash site for international investigators. But in return the Malaysians had offered the rebels a semblance of legitimacy with their thanks to 'His Excellency Mr Borodai'.

In spite of the progress made by the Malaysians, widespread international outrage continued to mount in Western capitals. The rebels and their suspected allies in Moscow were being accused of tampering with evidence and insulting victims' families.

In the hours after the bodies arrived at Torez, it became evident that yet another delay had arisen. The separatists were refusing to allow the bodies in the refrigerated carriages to go any further. In the days to come this makeshift morgue—four windowless wagons housing hundreds of bodies and body parts—would become the scene of a tug of war in what evolved into an international squabbling match.

The pro-Russian separatists distrusted Ukraine's authorities and wanted the train to head for a city under separatist control. The Dutch, Australians and Malaysians wanted the train to go to Kharkiv, which was under Ukrainian government control. The separatists, in turn, said they would hand over the bodies only to international representatives, not to Ukrainians. But the separatists also explained that letting the train head for Kharkiv meant that the bodies as well as the forensic team would be subject to dangers on the 128-kilometre route. There was still heavy fighting going on, one of them told the team, and the twenty-eight kilometres to the Russian border was a much safer and quicker option. From there the bodies could be transported to any destination, whatever the wishes of the forensic teams or their superiors.

Pierre Chardome, brother of the dead Belgian entrepreneur Benoit Chardome, accused the rebels of using the bodies as a means of blackmail: 'How can you even consider such a thing?' Jijar Singh Sandhu, the 71-year-old father of Malaysia Airlines flight attendant Sanjid Singh Sandhu, appealed to the rebels ('I believe that they are all human beings with feelings') and pleaded with them to 'please let us have our loved ones'. Tracey Withers, the twin sister of WHO media coordinator Glenn Thomas, commented that: 'We just want them to show some compassion and let people in to try and get the bodies back.'

The Ukrainian government accused the rebels of deliberately holding up the train at the station. A statement from a government official said that the return of the victims has been delayed because 'terrorists are blocking its exit'.

As they waited for the separatists to make up their minds, the grief of the families turned to anger. In news broadcasts some of them called on President Putin 'to please send our children home.' In a statement on Russian television Putin said that it was essential to give international experts security to conduct an investigation. In his reaction Tony Abbott let his countrymen know that his government was doing all it could under the circumstances: 'It's absolutely imperative that we bring them home, but in order to bring them home we've got to first get them out. So that is what all of our energies and efforts are directed to. We want to retrieve the bodies, we want to investigate the site, and we want to punish the guilty. That's what we want to do.'

The Dutch National Forensic Investigation Team (LTFO) led by Peter van Vliet finally gained access to the crash site on Monday 21 July as part of the deal the Malaysians had succeeded in negotiating. The team, made up of two Dutch forensic investigators, a guard and Alexander Hug of the OSCE, stumbled across remains that had not yet been removed, and they also inspected the luggage of the perished passengers. The forensics team realised that the site had been contaminated as soon as the villagers and separatists started rummaging through the area, but these experienced professionals also knew that this by no means meant it would be impossible for the Dutch Safety Board to piece together what happened at a later stage.

They did not have sufficient time for any kind of methodical examination of the area before they were hurried away by separatists after the sounds of exploding shells were heard close by. When the rebels told them to leave, van Vliet certainly didn't even contemplate disobeying their orders: 'When a separatist, smelling of alcohol and waving an AK-47 from his clapped-out Hyundai, tells me not to go somewhere, I'm not going there.'

The members of the OSCE and the Dutch forensic team were then taken to Torez. The team had been given clearance by the separatists to inspect the storage of the bodies in the refrigerated railcars and to confirm that the remains could be transported adequately to Kharkiv. Before boarding the train, van Vliet and the other forensic experts stood for a moment, their heads bowed and their hands clasped in a show of respect to the dead, then they donned masks and latex gloves and climbed onto the train cars to inspect the bodies.

The victims' luggage, as much of it as had so far been salvaged at the crash site, was piled in a heap on the railway platform. Against the decrepit grey locomotive, this colourful pile was a grim and very sad reminder of forever lost lives, hopes and dreams.

After the separatists refused to let the train depart, van Vliet could do nothing but wait at Torez. Until now he had not been asked to sign any clearance forms and he was thankful for that. He had been given specific orders by the Dutch government not to sign anything that came to him from the separatists. Putting his signature on a separatist statement might be seen as an acknowledgement of the Donetsk People's Republic and the Dutch certainly did not want to give any such impression. So he waited, contemplating how he would handle the situation if the men guarding the remains insisted on a signature.

The bodies had now been exposed to hot summer conditions for four days and were steadily deteriorating; the smell of decay around the makeshift morgue train was becoming almost unbearable. There were reports that the refrigeration in the carriages had not been working consistently. Finally, on 22 July, the separatists let the train go.

But before they were willing to part with the train and its precious cargo, Peter van Vliet, to his great dismay, was asked to sign a number of documents in different languages. It was the Donetsk People's Republic's self-appointed minister of transport himself who entered the carriage waving a pile of documents.

As van Vliet contemplated what to do, he suddenly found himself looking down the barrel of a Kalashnikov.

Tired from the long and strenuous days, van Vliet still hesitated as the Uzi-waving separatists became visibly ever more frustrated. Impatient and angered at being kept waiting, the smell of death overwhelming in the muggy heat, the minister of transport waved the papers in his face. On the spur of the moment van Vliet decided to sign them. But under each signature he carefully wrote in Dutch: 'With this signature the Dutch in no way acknowledge the Donetsk People's Republic.'

Hoping the separatists would not be able to read his native tongue, van Vliet felt he had done the only thing he could, considering the circumstances. He told journalists that he was impressed by the work the recovery crews had done, given the heat and the scale of the crash site. 'I think they did a hell of a job in a hell of a place,' he said.

Silene Fredriksz-Hoogzand and Rob Fredriksz had lost their only son, Bryce (twenty-three), and his girlfriend, Daisy Oehlers (twenty), in the crash. The young couple had been on their way to a holiday in Malaysia, the trip being a present from Bryce's parents after a difficult year for the pair: Daisy's mother had died and as a result Daisy had failed her exams. A friend phoned Rob Fredriksz in the late afternoon of 17 July asking if he had dropped his son and girlfriend off at the airport. Silene and Rob had not slept since. In a Sky News broadcast the grieving parents addressed Putin personally: 'Please send my children home. Let them go to the Netherlands. I want my children back. We want to be able to bury or cremate them. We are sitting here waiting for them to return.' The images of the grief-stricken couple and their heart-rending plea were aired worldwide.

Urged by the Dutch forensics team and the leader of the OSCE team, Alexander Hug, who insisted that 'this train must move today', the separatists, after accepting Peter van Vliet's signature, finally gave the all clear. The long, slow and sad journey home had started at last, four days after the victims had plunged to earth.

As the stench got worse by the minute, the separatists who had been guarding the train for almost three days appeared visibly relieved to finally see it go. Walking alongside the makeshift morgue, clutching their automatic rifles as the train rattled into motion and chugged away, the separatists escorted the train out of the station. It would take twelve hours to reach Kharkiv, but the train was due to stop overnight in Donetsk, fifty kilometres west of the crash site.

Dutch prime minister Mark Rutte held a news conference to announce that the locomotive with its body bags on board was on its way to rebel-held Donetsk and would then travel to Kharkiv, which was in Ukrainian government hands. From there the bodies would be taken back to the Netherlands to be identified.

But fighting had flared again earlier that day in the separatist-held city of Donetsk. City authorities reported battles were taking place near the town's airport and warned residents to stay inside. Dutch forensic investigators feared that they would be held up again and would not be able to pass through the rebel stronghold. Much to everyone's relief the train stopped overnight in a relatively calm Donetsk before leaving for the government-held city of Kharkiv at about 3am.

All the efforts of the countries that had lost citizens in the disaster were now aimed at transporting the victims out of the war-torn badlands. On 22 July the train carrying the remains of the MH17 victims finally arrived in Ukraine-controlled territory.

It was early afternoon when the locomotive emerged from a gap in dense greenery hauling four decrepit refrigerated wagons, their door edges oozing globs of foam insulation that served as a makeshift seal. The clanking Soviet-built windowless locomotive with its grey refrigerated wagons came to a halt in the grounds of a dismal weapons factory, where the bodies were to be unloaded. The remains of the victims of the crash of Malaysia Airways Flight MH17 were being delivered to a disaster response team in Kharkiv.

Flying out of Canberra on 18 July, Australian forensic investigator Rod Anderson had first gone to Kiev. When news of the train of the dead came through, Anderson travelled on to Kharkiv and was assigned the job of taking control of the refrigerated train when it arrived and helping unload the bodies. Under Anderson's supervision, a team entered the wagons and carried the bags to the platform, where their formal documentation began.

In the absence of names, each bag was given a number and an evidence tag, which Anderson had fashioned from lengths of a specialist tape that police customarily use to ensure parcels of evidence are tamper-proof. It was the start of a huge assignment, and Anderson knew that this was the easy part. The hard part of the job was yet to come: identifying the bodies and body parts would take place in the Netherlands.

Days later Anderson was one of a small group of investigators who actually got to walk around the MH17 crash site, sent to search for remains that had been overlooked. He wasn't a foreigner at the gates of hell and he had previously been a witness to many a disturbing scene, but it was when he wandered through the crash site and came across the dead dogs that he was stopped in his tracks. They had been travelling in the live-cargo section of the plane and, although Anderson was there for the dead humans, the animals among the pile of suitcases and clothes suddenly brought home to him that 'it was not just people. It was everything about life; the victims lived lives, they had pets.'

In Kharkiv, international forensic investigators supervised the transfer to a Dutch transport aircraft for a flight to Eindhoven the following day. A Dutch military plane, a C-130 Hercules, was standing at Kharkiv airport ready to take the remains back to the Netherlands. There they would not just be identified but finally returned to their families. The heart-wrenching odyssey of these passengers, whose lives had begun in dozens of different countries and had tragically ended in an eastern Ukrainian sunflower field, would soon be ending.

Speaking before the UN Security Council in New York, Dutch foreign minister Frans Timmermans told members that bringing the victims' remains home was his country's top priority. 'To my dying day, I will not understand why it took so much time for the rescue workers to be allowed to do their difficult jobs, and that human remains should be used in a political game.'

Confusion remained as to the number of dead actually recovered from the crash site. It was impossible for the forensic team to determine how many remains had been loaded onto the train. The only limited access that investigators continued to be allowed to the crash site made it quite possible and probable that many body parts were still out there in the open.

On Sunday 20 July, the US claimed there was 'powerful' evidence that the rebels had shot down the plane with a Russian surface-to-air missile. They accompanied this accusation with video of a rocket launcher being driven away from the likely launch site with one surface-to-air missile missing. Phone calls from the separatists claiming credit for the missile strike had also been intercepted, but the only problem was that no one on the ground had reported seeing a Buk being fired. There were no photos, no videos of the actual flight path of the rocket, nothing. The launch of a Buk would leave an unmistakable long-lasting trail in its wake. No farmer, no miner, no peasant wife had reported seeing that trail; no one had presented any visual proof of a Buk being launched that day.

In an effort to have the US prove this accusation, Moscow asked the US to share any satellite images they had of the Buk launch. Russian officials denied that separatists had launched a Buk. They claimed they had evidence a Ukrainian Su-25 fighter jet had flown 'between 3 to 5 kilometres' from the Malaysia Airlines jet. It was this Ukrainian plane that had targeted the MH17 and shot it down, they declared. As early as May 2014 separatist fighters had accused Ukrainian Air Force jets of 'hiding' behind commercial airliners to avoid becoming a target.

The investigation into the cause of the crash was being led by the Dutch Safety Board. It had now ruled out most of the other possible causes of the crash and was becoming ever more convinced that the plane had been downed by some kind of surface-to-air missile. The plane had an excellent maintenance record. The feedback they were getting from the black boxes indicated that whatever had happened to the aircraft had been an extremely sudden event. The plane had flown around a thunderstorm and was flying in calm weather when it was hit, so it wasn't likely that it had been struck by any form of lightning. There was no meteor activity recorded that day, so that option had also been dismissed.

But the Dutch Safety Board had still not been able to inspect the actual crash site and were still stuck in Kiev, waiting for clearance to visit the area. Although a number of international forensic experts had been allowed access to the site for a short period of time to look for remains, the DSB team, which was to determine the cause of the crash, was almost losing hope that it would ever be granted access. The main objective of these team members was to locate and salvage the wreckage so they would need to gain access for lengthy and consecutive periods. They could only hope that by the time they set foot on the crash site there would still be vital pieces of wreckage left to salvage.

Chapter 18
Bringing them home

After days of international disgust at the callous and casual treatment of the bodies by balaclava-wearing militia, the victims were given the dignity they deserved the following afternoon when they were transferred into simple but proper coffins for their flights to the Netherlands. 'Operation Bring Them Home' had begun.

This was the name the Australian government had given to the mission to repatriate the bodies of those killed in the tragedy, and other countries mourning their own MH17 victims had adopted the name. Australian government personnel had been deployed to Ukraine and the Netherlands as part of the operation and it would also help in repatriating the remains to the Netherlands for further identification.

In the early morning hours of 23 July at Eindhoven Air Base, the Globemaster crew prepared their aircraft for the solemn and significant task of bringing the first coffins home. The Royal

Australian Air Force had flown its C-17A Globemaster aircraft to the Netherlands. From there it would fly to Kharkiv to pick up a number of coffins and bring them back to Eindhoven.

It was an unusually bright and sunny morning as the Globemaster's wheels skidded along the runway before it took to the air at 7.50am. A Dutch C-130 Hercules had flown to Kharkiv a day after the crash to be on standby, ready to transport the bodies home when they arrived. But this crew and aircraft had been waiting for days on the hot tarmac as hold-up followed hold-up.

The moment the Globemaster lifted its wheels from the tarmac in Eindhoven, forty hearses turned onto the military airport's runway. Parking in an impressive row, they would later that day carry a coffin each.

Eindhoven is a combined civil and military airport with a lot of general aviation as well, the second largest airport in the Netherlands. Eindhoven Air Base is the home base of all the Royal Netherlands Air Force's transport aircraft. Their most important task is the provision of air transport for worldwide military operations, humanitarian missions and special assignments. In addition, air force personnel are tasked with airport duties at Eindhoven airport day and night.

That morning, on the civilian side of the airport, the departure and arrival halls were thronged with vacationers arriving from and departing to their different destinations. Flight schedules for later that day had been changed: all scheduled take-offs and departures from 3.45pm to 6pm were now cancelled. Out of respect for the victims, from the moment the bodies arrived until they had left the air base, no planes would take off or land at Eindhoven airport. But for now, at the height of the summer holidays, the hustle and bustle of everyday life in the terminals was in stark contrast to the solemn preparations taking place on the military side of the complex.

That side of the air base was uncannily quiet as uniformed men received muted orders from their superiors. As the victims' mourning families and friends started to enter the airport grounds, their grief and incredulity was almost tangible. For most of them the arrival of the coffins would change everything. They had been forced to wait an almost unbearably long time for the bodies to finally come home, so for some it was a relief of sorts. But for others, bringing them home would also bring home the hard and undeniable reality of those deaths.

In the early afternoon in Ukraine, forty simple wooden caskets were being unloaded from a truck. Earlier that morning the truck had picked up the coffins containing the victims remains from the factory grounds in Kharkiv. Each casket was carefully laid out on the tarmac in preparation for its journey home. Ukrainian military personnel plus forensic experts and representatives from the Netherlands, Malaysia and Australia together formed an honour guard around the coffins.

'Today you start your journey home.' It was 10.15am when a Dutch representative began his ceremonial speech. 'It's a long journey but we want to do it properly, with dignity.' Moments later, white-gloved Ukrainian soldiers respectfully carried the coffins onto the aircraft one at a time.

At Eindhoven airport, national and international press had gathered. Some five hundred journalists, present to cover the arrival of the first victims, were met by a representative of the Dutch forensic team; he let them know that forty coffins would arrive later that day, but that the bereaved would be screened off to protect their privacy. The Dutch Hercules would arrive first with its transport of sixteen coffins and the Australian Globemaster was to follow with the other twenty-four coffins. The estimated time of arrival was around 4pm. The forty coffins were to be followed by more coffins during the week; it was expected that all the remains now still in Kharkiv would land on Dutch soil within the next four days.

In the meantime, the search for remains went on. Forensic experts hoped to examine the site in Ukraine for any overlooked remains or bone fragments in the following days. It was estimated that some sixteen victims were still unaccounted for. Finding them remained high on the list of priorities of anyone involved with the victims. However, the realistic expectation was that some were never going to have any closure because their loved ones would remain 'lost' forever: their bodies had probably disintegrated in the fire that broke out after the plane crashed to the ground. The impossible heat when the fuel tanks exploded left little hope of anything remaining of those caught in the fire. The forensic experts had also faced enormous difficulties in retrieving what was left from the crash site because of the limited and dangerous access.

Around midday, twenty members of the Royal Netherlands Marechaussee, a Dutch gendarmerie force performing military police and civil police duties, arrived at Eindhoven airport on gleaming motorcycles. The honorary escort would accompany the convoy of hearses to the Korporaal Van Oudheusden Barracks in Hilversum. There the Dutch forensic authorities, assisted by a large number of Australians, from forensic scientists to fingerprint and DNA experts, would start their disaster victim identification procedures. The Dutch experts included police officers, military personnel, forensic dentists and other medics, all tasked with collecting samples from close relatives around the country to help identify the 196 Dutch victims. The Dutch National Forensic Investigation Team, known as the LTFO, had already been collecting DNA samples, hair, fingerprints, and information about scars or tattoos or moles from family members.

As soon as a victim was identified by the LTFO they would first and foremost inform no one else but the family, to whom, after identification, the remains would be released and transferred. The identification process, even for experienced investigators, was expected to be so distressing that the team was assessed by a psychologist on a daily basis. The process for a single identification could take weeks, although it was more likely to take months. Every bone fragment found at the site would have to be identified; for some of the dead all that was left were fragments.

Large numbers of people who had been invited to attend the coming home ceremony were starting to pour into the military airport. Among them was Thomas Schansman, Quinn Schansman's father. His son had been eighteen years old when he boarded the MH17 for a holiday to Malaysia. Although born in the USA, Quinn had spent most of his life in the Netherlands and his parents were Dutch. His dual citizenship held promises for his future and he had been very proud of his American passport, envisioning a future as a CEO for himself in that country. Quinn had been the only person on the plane with an American passport.

A few days after the crash, being the only American casualty, Quinn's name was mentioned by Barack Obama during a press conference about the MH17. His father thought Quinn would have been proud of this, but for Thomas this wasn't the way he wanted to have his son commemorated. Quinn was supposed to have gone on to become a CEO in America—that was the plan, not this. As he waited for the planes that carried the coffins, Thomas assumed his son would either arrive in the first coffin or the last one. Either one would have been characteristic for Quinn. But it was anyone's guess who was in the caskets and it did not really matter. They were coming home, at last.

It was estimated that some 1200 people would be present, among them the bereaved, politicians and officials. Dutch King Willem-Alexander and his wife Queen Maxima, as well as Dutch prime minister Mark Rutte, headed the guests of honour. Australia had sent their minister for foreign affairs, Julie Bishop, and their Governor-General, Sir Peter Cosgrove. No representatives from Malaysia Airlines had been invited to attend the ceremony; this was later explained as an oversight.

Malaysia, however, had sent their foreign affairs minister, Sri Anifah Aman, and their minister of transport, Liow Tiong Lai, to represent the country. Belgium's Prince Laurent sat alongside David Lidington, the minister for Europe. The British ambassador to the Netherlands, Sir Geoffrey Adams, was among the attendees, and the entire Dutch cabinet sat in muted and solemn silence. Many world leaders had sent their condolences.

As the morning wore on, people from all over the Netherlands came to lay flowers at the entrance of the air base. The memorial spot was the old Dutch-built Fokker F-27 aeroplane that proudly stood guard at the entrance of the base.

The Globemaster touched down on Ukrainian soil at 10.50am. Just ten minutes later at 11am, the first plane, the Dutch Hercules, prepared for take-off from Kharkiv with its sad but precious load. As rehearsals for the ceremony in Eindhoven started, the second plane, the Australian Globemaster, took off at 12.30pm with its twenty-four coffins on board. The Globemaster, a much faster plane than the Dutch Hercules, would make up for lost time in the air. Both planes were now on their way, bringing a small number of the victims home at last to a waiting Dutch King and Queen and a nation in mourning.

Less than an hour after the Globemaster took to the skies, hostilities flared up once again when separatists shot down two government jetfighters in eastern Ukraine near Savur-Mogila; this was only forty kilometres from the spot where MH17 was shot down six days before. Ukrainian officials said that separatists had downed two of their four Su-25 planes flying near the border with Russia, where they were assisting military forces on the ground. After trying unsuccessfully to manoeuvre away from the surface-to-air missiles, the pilots managed to get out of their aircraft moments before impact, floating down to pro-Russian territory and into the hands of the enemy. The downing of the military aircraft signalled renewed hostilities in the area.

Meanwhile at Eindhoven airport, flags flying at half-mast flapped in the breeze. There was one flag to commemorate every nation that had lost citizens, as well as the Ukrainian flag. Although there were no Ukrainian nationals among the victims, it was thought that Ukraine too had suffered. At Schiphol the impromptu shrine outside terminal three, which had been little more than a pile of flowers just after the news of the downing of the MH17 broke, had now grown into an ocean of bouquets, teddy bears and candles.

Fifteen minutes before four o'clock a murmur rose from the crowd gathered at the airport. A small dot appeared in the cloudless blue sky, gradually getting larger as it approached its destination. At 3.47pm the first plane, the Hercules, landed, and just three minutes later the Globemaster followed.

Churches around the Netherlands started tolling their bells at five minutes to four. This lasted for five minutes. Just before 4pm a lone bugler sounded the traditional military farewell of the 'last post', marking the arrival of the two aircraft. It was a profoundly moving lament which echoed across the silent airfield, the last tones drifting away on the wind as the silence returned. At 4pm local time, at precisely the time the rear cargo doors of the planes were opened, a nationwide one minute of silence followed. From Amsterdam to Maastricht, the country fell silent. Trains and traffic ground to a standstill, and planes did not take off or land. The cranes in Rotterdam, Europe's largest port, ceased to swivel and haul. In supermarkets across the country, shoppers paused to remember the dead. The nation's iconic windmills were placed in 'mourning position', their wings tilted to the right. Courts suspended all trials, and even commercials were pulled from Dutch television and radio.

To coincide with the arrival of the two planes at Eindhoven, there was a small ceremony at Kiev. In front of the Dutch embassy there, the Ukrainian people had paid tribute to the dead by lighting candles or laying flowers. Among the carnations, sunflowers and roses were more than a dozen teddy bears for the eighty children and infants who had died in the crash. Some thirty members of the Dutch embassy staff walked in a line to stand in front of the endless rows of flowers, candles, soft toys and messages of condolence that the locals had left during the past five days. For five minutes they stayed motionless, until at a signal they wordlessly walked back inside in the knowledge that the victims had arrived home.

Back at the Dutch air base the eerie silence was broken only by the soft clinking of flagpoles whipping in the wind at half-mast. Then, on cue, members of the Royal Netherlands Air Force began to move. The men marched in formation, two lines, four pallbearers on each side, disappearing into the bellies of the massive planes and returning just moments later carrying a single coffin. Faced with that first coffin, some family members were unable to contain themselves. Confronted for the first time with the undeniable truth of death, a few screams cut through the dense silence.

It took ninety minutes for all forty caskets to be carried out and placed in individual hearses. The short rhythmic steps of the eight pallbearers were precisely accurate, never advancing more than one foot at a time. The solemn, dignified and painstakingly precise ceremony moved nearly all those attending to tears. Queen Maxima clutched her husband's hand, unable to contain her tears as the coffins were carried before the attendees.

The stark wooden coffins, bereft of any flag, hit home how anonymous the bodies still were. None of the families knew if their loved ones were among those now being carried to the hearses, no one had yet been identified, but it did not matter. Sir Peter Cosgrove later told the media: 'We were thinking to ourselves, "Is this person in this casket an Australian?" But today they were all Australians. They were all Dutch. And they were all of the other nations.'

Protected from the media glare and seated behind large shields, the bereaved watched and wept as the coffins were carried into the black automobiles. The Dutch King would later comment that 'the families' grief had ripped through his soul'. On the baking tarmac at the military airport, King Willem-Alexander and Queen Maxima stood and bowed their heads in remembrance as the last coffin was placed in a hearse.

Six days after they had perished in the wheat and sunflower fields of eastern Ukraine's countryside, forty of the victims had finally made it home. No words were spoken, and no speeches made that day. Out of the carnage, chaos and unspeakable horror finally came a moment of calm.

At 4.46pm the first twenty hearses moved off, slowly driving past the area where the families were seated before leaving the airport. Gone was the horror of the train of the dead, with its appalling odour and lethal gases, the remains were now on their way to a state-of-the-art laboratory at the Korporaal van Oudheusden army barracks.

As the cars started off on their ninety-minute journey to Hilversum, the convoy passed along roads and overpasses lined with thousands of members of the public, who applauded, threw flowers or stood in silence to pay respect to the dead as the cars drove by. White roses were dropped from a motorway bridge as the cortege of hearses drove past. When the cars finally arrived at the army barracks, a large crowd applauded the victims as the hearses passed. Some held their hands across their mouths in shock while others mourned and wept.

Everyone was aware that this was only the first group of victims, and that another 258 were to follow; some were still to be located and the remains of another 150 were waiting at Kharkiv for transportation to the Netherlands. As they arrived over the next few days, every coffin would be greeted with the same show of respect and the same painstakingly precise procedure, but without the assembled international dignitaries. Men in uniform carried the caskets from the aircraft into the waiting hearses and along the motorways people lined up day after day, throwing flowers and crying for the lost lives that passed them by.

On that first day and the days that followed, the images of chaos in a far corner of Europe were replaced with images of a country at peace but deeply affected by the senseless loss of lives.

For the 38 Australian citizens and residents who were killed on 17 July, it would take some weeks before they could be returned to the country they called home. First, they would need to be identified. The Victorian couple Mary and Gerry Menke, who ran their abalone pearling business at Mallacoota, were officially identified in August 2014; they were the first Australians to achieve this finality.

On 11 September, nearly two months after the tragedy, the bodies of several Australian passengers were returned home and met by a convoy of hearses at the Qantas hangar at Melbourne airport, where a repatriation ceremony was held for those killed in the crash. There was no confirmation of how many were repatriated that day or their identity, but at the beginning of December 2014 forensics in the Netherlands confirmed that all Australians had been identified and that their remains would now soon be returned to their families.

On 7 August, weeks before the first remains arrived, a national memorial service had been held in St Patrick's Cathedral in Melbourne. Melbourne was chosen to host the service because sixteen of the Australians killed were from Victoria. Victoria Police had been tasked with leading the Australian teams on the MH17 operation, with state and federal governments also involved. The cathedral was packed with mourners as hundreds of people filled the building. Governor-General Sir Peter Cosgrove, Prime Minister Tony Abbott, the ambassador to the Netherlands, the high commissioner for Malaysia, community and religious leaders joined relatives at the Melbourne service.

Where the Dutch had refrained from making speeches, keeping their ceremony sober and impressive, in Australia there was a need to express verbally the grief and heartfelt sorrow for the victims and their families. As flags flew at half-mast on 7 August, Australia's national day of mourning, Prime Minister Tony Abbott let the grief-stricken families know that the MH17 victims would never be abandoned or forgotten. 'There will be a time to judge the guilty, but today we honour the dead and we grieve with the living,' he said. 'We cannot bring them back, but we will bring them home as far as we humanly can.'

The memorial at St Patrick's was a multi-faith service; there were readings from the Torah, the Koran and the Bible as religious leaders of the Christian, Jewish, Hindu, Islamic and Buddhist faiths offered their prayers at the cathedral. Around 160 immediate family members placed sprigs of wattle on a memorial wreath, shedding tears for those they had lost.

Tony Abbott went on to express solidarity for the loved ones of the passengers. 'When those we love are snatched away, nothing can ease the pain,' he said. 'We who have not been bereaved must reach out to those who have and show by our love that love has not abandoned them.'

Federal opposition leader Bill Shorten told mourners that the memorial was not about why, or how, the disaster happened, but about those left behind. 'Some will call it closure, some will call it acceptance, some will call it letting go. Whatever it is, it will take a while,' he said.

Friday 22 August was declared the national day of mourning for the 42 Malaysians on board Flight MH17. Its government had been heavily criticised for its initial response to the missing jet, but Prime Minister Najib Razak had also won praise for brokering a deal with the pro-Russian separatists to ensure international access to the black box flight recorders and to allow for the return of all the bodies on MH17.

A plane carrying the remains of twenty of the people who had died in the tragedy touched down from Amsterdam just before 10am on Friday at Kuala Lumpur International Airport, as flags across the country flew at half-mast. Such a national day of mourning was the first ever to be held by Malaysia for ordinary citizens and had previously only been granted when a king or other important leader had died.

Much like the Dutch ceremony, the Malaysian one was muted, except for the roar of the plane's engines. Eight men dressed in traditional Malay attire carried each flag-draped coffin out of the belly of the plane while Malaysia's King Abdul Halim Mu'adzam Shah, Prime Minister Razak and other top officials looked on. Hearses and helicopters lined up to transport the victims on to their home towns for burial. In a slow march a team of eight pallbearers carried each casket to the hearses.

Dozens of Malaysia Airlines cabin crew and pilots gathered near the welcoming ceremony dressed in blue uniforms, holding Malaysian flags and flowers in honour of their deceased colleagues. The awareness that the incident had occurred only four months after Malaysia Airlines MH370 disappeared without a trace made it all the more difficult to come to terms with. Everyone was well aware that the families of the victims of MH370 might never witness a similar homecoming.

On the tarmac, relatives gathered together with political dignitaries for the solemn reception of the caskets. The motorcade carrying the twenty coffins moved slowly past the families and on towards two transport aircraft and three military helicopters that would fly seven of them to their respective home towns. The remaining coffins would be transported over land to their families.

Relatives waited at domestic airports across the country for the remains of their loved ones to arrive. A little over a month ago they had also awaited the arrival of their families and friends. They then still believed their loved ones to be alive and had expected to be reunited with them.

Malaysians all over the country had dressed themselves in black and the country, much the same as in the Netherlands, came to a standstill as people paused for a minute's silence. In this multi-ethnic country, where tension between different groups and religions can run high, mourners were united in their grief, with ethnic Malays and ethnic Chinese standing side by side as they recited prayers for the dead. Kuala Lumpur City Hall ordered all entertainment outlets to cease operations for twenty-four hours while Penang ordered toll operators at the bridge to the island to stop collection during the scheduled minute's silence.

Commuters who had streamed into the bustling streets of the capital earlier that morning were nearly all clad in black, including many Muslim women wearing black Islamic headscarves. State television continuously broadcast recitations from the Koran and photos of the Malaysian victims while newspapers bordered their front pages in black.

It had been a long and emotional journey for not only Malaysia but for all countries that had lost citizens.

Chapter 19
The Buk

Now that the bodies had come home, the important question remained: what had brought the airliner down? Was it an advanced surface-to-air missile, as most parties appeared to believe? If it was, who had fired it and why?

The most probable cause of the disaster was a missile attack, because the plane had been found in bits and pieces on the ground, spread over a large area. This must surely have been caused by an explosion of some kind: airliners simply don't fall apart, as this one had definitely done, once they have reached a comfortable cruising altitude.

Journalists were now allowed unfettered access to photograph and film what was being called the crime scene. As masked men holding guns stood watch, journalists photographed plane parts, personal items and whatever else they came across. Photos of the aeroplane parts, quickly loaded onto the internet, made it apparent that the damage and markings to parts of the body of the plane were consistent with something external hitting it. The holes in the aluminium parts of the plane were dented inward and that meant the plane had been hit by an external force and not, for example, by a bomb blowing outward.

The Dutch Safety Board's goal was to answer what, and not who, caused the crash. The DSB were not responsible for assigning the blame—that would become the Joint Investigation Team's (JIT) job. Although the DSB had not been able to visit the site, they too believed that some kind of explosion from outside the plane was the cause, most probably a missile. Although they did not yet rule out something like a freak meteor or meteor rain, they couldn't be sure until they were able to examine the shattered parts of the plane.

The general assumption in the Western countries was that the separatists or Russia had something to do with the plane crash, and this theory had been further boosted after rebels delayed and hindered the investigators' access to the debris field. 'A cover-up' the Australian government said in a statement and, although the Dutch were more careful in venting their suspicions, the overall feeling in the Netherlands was one of distrust towards the role Russia had played.

The DSB were waiting ever more impatiently in Kiev for permission to gain access to the site. Their safety had to be guaranteed before they could set foot in the disaster area. The OSCE had been allowed to inspect the crash site for a short period, but the DSB would need to remain on site for a much longer period to do their work. In order to conduct an effective investigation, the investigators must have the opportunity to move around the entire investigation site freely, examine materials and traces from up close, and secure them for further study where necessary.

The separatists, whose comrades were fighting just a few miles further down the track, could not warrant that DSB inspectors would be safe for any amount of time if they entered the site. Separatists had said they were happy for any investigators to arrive and work at the site, but they could not give them guarantees. Journalists, on the other hand, did not request any assurances for their safety and roamed the location at their own risk and were the first to deliver images to the DSB and to the public.

In the United Kingdom the flight recorders were being examined by the Air Accidents Investigation Branch (AAIB) at their headquarters in Farnborough, Hampshire. They had the responsibility for retrieving and downloading the crucial data, and then this would be sent to an international team of experts to be further analysed. The AAIB had been handed this task by authorities in the Netherlands because they were considered the best in their field.

The two recorders—the so-called 'black boxes', which are actually orange in colour to make them more visible and easier to find—were the flight data recorder and the cockpit voice recorder. If the information on them could be accessed, it would be possible to learn if the pilots had received any prior warning that something was wrong. In England the team of specialists were also tasked with the job of finding out if the boxes had been in any way tampered with.

Back in Ukraine, although they did not have access to the site, the DSB was not remaining idle. Their teams in Kiev, as well as in the Netherlands, were working around the clock analysing data from different sources—photos, videos and intercepted phone calls. In the Netherlands, forensic analysts had already received the first victims' remains from the crash site. Their findings would be sent on to the DSB to help in their quest for the truth.

Western officials and experts were united in their belief that separatist forces, aided by the Russian military, were the perpetrators and that the plane had been targeted by a surface-to-air missile, most likely coming from a Buk. Russia responded to these accusations by pointing its finger at the West, claiming that Ukraine's army may well have shot down the plane and that a Ukrainian military plane had been flying in close range of the downed aircraft just before it vanished from the radar screens. Moscow accused Ukraine's government of being complicit in the passengers' deaths, no matter how the disaster had occurred, because it had allowed civilian jetliners to fly through a war zone.

It was no secret that both the Russian and Ukrainian armies owned Buk missile systems and there was no disagreement that both countries' professional military departments possessed Buk surface-to-air missiles (SAMs). The contested question was whether separatist militia units also had access to these sophisticated weapons.

Although most Buk-M1 and Buk-M2 SAMs were thought to be under Ukrainian and Russian military control, reports from 29 June, coming from both sides of the conflict, indicated that Donetsk separatist paramilitaries had managed to capture a Buk-M2 unit from the Ukrainians when they tried to take over the airport at Donetsk. This capture had been immediately reported by sources on both sides of the conflict. The separatists had boasted about the steal, but Ukraine at the time did not appear impressed. It was an old Buk, they said, and, even if the separatists had actually gained access to a Buk, it wouldn't be much use to them, because they would not know how to use it.

Ukraine later denied that separatists had seized a Buk from its forces; instead it alleged the separatists had received Buks from the Russian military. Of course, this narrative was denied by Moscow.

Military experts outside the war were unanimous that even if the insurgents possessed a missile launcher, this didn't mean they were able to use it. At least not without help from a trained accomplice.

The Buk surface-to-air missile system was first developed in the early 1970s by the Soviet Union and then became part of the regular Russian defence arsenal. The Buk is a complicated air defence weapon designed to locate and engage targets by radar. While older versions were now no longer used by the Russians, having been replaced by a more sophisticated version, various types of the older Buk systems were still used by Ukraine as well as other former Soviet republics. The manufacturer of the Buk, Almaz-Antey, was quick to claim that the missile launcher that was thought to have brought down MH17 was a dated version of the Buk that was not used by Russia anymore and that this particular Buk launcher had been sold to the Ukrainian army some time ago.

Despite its age, the Buk is a highly effective battlefield weapon. It's able to engage several targets at once and strike at a distance of up to twenty-five kilometres, putting the MH17, flying at an altitude of 33,000 feet, well within its reach. It's also a highly complicated piece of equipment. A person off the street could no more step in and operate it than he could suddenly become an airline pilot. Trained officers needed at least six months' training to learn the basics and it could take a couple of years to become an experienced professional. It needs a whole team, well prepared, to operate it and make it work effectively.

The Ukrainian prime minister, Arseniy Yatsenyuk, told journalists that the missile required 'very professional staff' and 'could not be operated by drunken gorillas', suggesting that, if the Buk had been fired by the separatists, they must have had help from Russia.

A Buk system normally consists of six launch pads with four rockets each and a loading station with eight additional missiles. There is a command vehicle and a targeting radar post all mounted on their own tracked vehicles; this allows the system to move with other military forces and relocate quickly. Each missile on a Buk is 5.55 metres long, weighs 690 kilograms and carries a relatively large 70-kilogram warhead, which is triggered by a fuse. The warhead contains a cluster bomb that bursts into tiny metal fragments when it hits its target. Buk missiles are self-propelled warheads that can reach speeds of up to 850 metres per second. The chances of a missile hitting its target are 99 per cent.

The radar post is by far the most crucial element of the system. It provides information on how fast the target plane is travelling and, more importantly, what kind of plane it is. Without the radar serving as his eyes, the launching pad operator is virtually 'blind' and would have to guess what he is shooting at. The missile launcher pad does have its own radar, but it is inferior to that of the radar post and only allows the operator to see a moving dot on his screen; under those circumstances, he will know that it is an aircraft of some kind, but he will not be able to see what kind of aircraft he is targeting. If one shoots a Buk missile without the use of a radar post, it is totally random who dies and who doesn't. The Buk system operator's training is always based on a war situation and so, for the trainee, there are no civilian planes to take into account because, in a war, civilian airliners would normally be prohibited from flying over the area.

The separatists and Ukraine, however, were at war, fighting a bloody battle along the southern border with Russia. The separatists had conquered the eastern Donbas area up to the border with Russia. Along the country's southern border the Ukrainian forces held a small strip of land that ran from separatist-held territory to Ukraine's border with Russia. As the fighting intensified, the separatists tried to force a breach in the Ukrainian corridor from the town of Marinivka in separatist territory to the Russian border. This would leave part of Ukraine's forces trapped behind enemy lines.

To be able to keep their troops supplied with food and weapons, Ukrainian transport planes made daily flights over the conflict area. The Ukrainian forces commander, Sergei Mandalina, complained of food shortages and also a diminishing supply of ammunition. On 17 July the Ukrainian troops near Marinivka were facing heavy artillery from the pro-Russian separatists, but Commander Mandalina did not request air backup because too many Ukrainian planes had been downed by enemy missiles during the past week. The separatists had been targeting the Ukrainian air support for days; using their anti-aircraft weapons, they had managed to down a number of Ukrainian military planes, including two large transport planes with soldiers and supplies on board.

In the early morning of 17 July 2014, journalists saw a single launcher on a low-loader truck trundling through the gritty mining town of Snizhne; it was similar to a Buk system but without its usual accompaniments. Someone took a picture of the missile launcher as it made its way through pro-Russia controlled territory and posted it on the internet. A Twitter post on 17 July reported the sighting of a Buk at the intersection of Shakhtostroiteley Boulevard and Ilych Avenue in Snizhne, heading east in the direction of Marinivka. It suddenly became clear that not only did the rebels have man-portable air-defence systems, known as MANPADS, but they also had at least one Buk missile system, marked with the identification number 3X2 (where the X stands for a number that could not easily be deciphered).

A phone call between two rebel fighters, intercepted by Ukraine's intelligence services, suggested that the Buk had arrived in Donetsk with a crew. Less than half an hour after the plane crashed, the commander-in-chief of the pro-Russian separatists in Donbas, Igor Girkin, had celebrated the downing of a Ukrainian military jet with a post on his profile on the Russian version of Facebook, VKontakte. The post received over two thousand likes in a short space of time, but it was then quickly deleted. Later, Girkin claimed the post had been a fake.

On 18 July a video was posted online by the Ukrainian ministry of the interior. In this video, a Buk missile launcher, travelling through Luhansk, was now missing at least one of its missiles. On the side of the truck was a telephone number. It belonged to a truck rental company in Donetsk. The owner later said the vehicle had been stolen from him in June by pro-Russian separatists. The Russian Ministry of Defence claimed in a press conference on 21 July that the video had been in fact filmed in Ukrainian government-controlled territory—in the town of Krasnoarmeysk now known as Pokrovsk, which had been controlled by the Ukrainian military since 11 May—and not in the separatist-held part of the country.

Amid the disputes over who was responsible for this horrendous crime and the political fallout it caused, the bereaved families of 298 people were trying to come to terms with the loss of their loved ones. The general feeling was that, if it had been an accidental downing of a civilian aircraft, someone should have at least apologised. But over time the families of the victims no longer thought of the disaster as an accident—to them, killing their loved ones had been no accident; it was a crime. And now they wanted to know who had given the order and how a Buk rocket could have been launched without anyone seeing it happen.

The DSB, the one party who would be able to bring clarity to the bereaved and everyone else involved, was still waiting for clearance in Kiev in September 2014. Jordan Withers, who had lost his uncle, the WHO media coordinator Glenn Thomas, in the crash said he was shocked it could take so long to obtain justice: 'I find it unbelievable hundreds of people can be murdered and everyone can be so slow to react.'

Chapter 20
The wreckage

Normally when a civil aviation accident occurs, the investigators try to visit the crash site as soon as possible. Responsibility for the investigation of the disaster lies with the country in which the crash has occurred, together with the owner of the aircraft—in this case, Ukraine and Malaysia Airlines.

But the MH17 catastrophe followed a different procedure. At the request of the Ukrainian government and after consultation with the International Civil Aviation Organization (ICAO), the Dutch Safety Board was entrusted to take the lead in the investigation.

The DSB created a basis of cooperation between the states involved in the investigation of the downing of flight MH17—Netherlands, Ukraine, Malaysia, United States, United Kingdom, Australia and the Russian Federation. Representatives of these states were members of the international investigation team and had access to the investigation information as it became available, making it possible for them to study and verify it firsthand.

Although considerable effort was made to enable Dutch investigators to visit the crash site, because of the unstable situation there was no guarantee of their safety or that they would be able to conduct a long-term investigation. There were two small teams of investigators based close to the crash site at Kharkiv and Soledar, ready to travel to visit the wreckage area as soon as the situation allowed it. But in the end, it took almost four months before a proper investigation of the wreckage site could be made.

For the relatives, it had all taken much too long and they criticised the Safety Board. Although Ukrainians and Malaysians and observers from the OSCE had briefly visited the area and were able to take photographs during those first days, it had been impossible to stay at the site for long periods of time. Alexander Hug, the acting head of the OSCE mission in Ukraine, had left with his team to visit the disaster area just after he heard about the crash. After reaching the area, the team were confronted by separatists. 'A rebel leader stood in front of me,' Hug told journalists. 'A big, intimidating man armed with a machine gun. I could smell alcohol. He said: "This is as far as you go."'

The teams, however, were by no means sitting passively as they waited for permission to enter the area. A great deal of investigation data had already been collected and was being processed and analysed. Malaysians had handed over small parts of wreckage material salvaged from the crash site and there were photos and other data. A constant concern for the investigators was that the wreckage, spread over six sites, was mostly left unguarded and, by the time they could access it, it would undoubtedly have been seriously contaminated.

Mid-August it became known that rebel commander Igor Girkin had resigned his position as defence minister of the insurgent's Donetsk People's Republic. Rumours spread that the decision was made due to Girkin being severely wounded in combat, but there was no evidence that this was true. The leadership of the Donetsk People's Republic announced that Girkin was dismissed from his position of defence minister 'on his own request' and he was being assigned 'some other tasks'. Many people believed that the main reason for the removal of Girkin from the position of defence minister was because of the amount of attention created by the downing of MH17 and the negative impact on Russia's actions in Ukraine this had caused.

Alexander Borodai had also resigned as prime minister of the Donetsk People's Republic. In a press conference in Donetsk on 7 August 2014, Borodai announced his resignation and he stated, 'I came here as a crisis manager, a start-upper, if you want. I've managed to achieve a lot in the past several months, the DPR has been established as a state.' He further stated at this press conference that he believed a 'native Muscovite' like himself should not lead the Donetsk People's Republic. The fact that nearly all top figures in the rebel movement at the time were from Russia was awkward for the Kremlin, which maintained that pro-Moscow sentiment was indigenous in eastern Ukraine. Borodai stepped aside in favour of Alexander Zakharchenko, a former electrician from the area. Igor Girkin and Borodai both slipped back into Russia in 2015, deeming their job finished as 'patriots' in east Ukraine.

On 26 August 2014 at Nieuwegein near Utrecht in the Netherlands, Tjibbe Joustra, the chairman of the DSB, informed relatives of the victims of what progress the investigation had made. The Dutch Safety Board released a preliminary report based on information gathered from various sources in September; this showed that the aircraft had been in full operating condition and that no technical malfunctions had been reported. The salvaged fight recorders had not been tampered with and their data revealed that there had been no engine or aircraft system warnings prior to the crash. At the time of the event the plane was flying in unrestricted airspace at a height that was deemed safe from ground attacks. Absolutely no distress messages whatsoever were made by the MH17 crew and, in view of this, the DSB concluded that the moment of impact must have been very sudden. Photographs taken of the damage to the fuselage and cockpit suggested multiple impact points from 'high-energy objects outside the aircraft'. Damage to the aircraft wasn't consistent with any known failure of the aircraft's engines or its systems. Flight MH17 had evidently broken up in the air with different parts of the plane ending up in multiple locations.

Numerous experts claimed that the damage described by the safety board was consistent with the impact of a Buk missile that exploded as it crashed into the plane or just before, its shrapnel destroying the target. The DSB refrained from specifically referring to a Buk missile impact in its preliminary report; for the time being that was just a theory and they would not support it until they could prove it beyond any reasonable doubt.

All through the summer months the separatists and Ukrainian forces battled with each other while the DSB investigators were forced to wait endlessly for the situation to stabilise to such an extent that they could carry out their work in an acceptable manner. Former Australian defence force chief Angus Houston was coordinating the Australian response to the disaster. Multinational police teams, including unarmed Australian Federal Police, at different times sent out a team in advance; but often they could only make it halfway down the road, and sometimes three-quarters of the way, before the shelling started again and they were forced to return.

No one could point the finger at who was responsible for the shelling, although the Ukrainian government assured everyone that it wasn't them. If this was true then that left the question of who the separatists were targeting and why. No one provided an answer. There were reports that the remains of many MH17 victims might still be lying in the war-torn area.

It was October and the Australian government was by now getting increasingly frustrated by the situation. A G20 summit planned for November and to be held in Brisbane was fast approaching, and Putin had let Australia know that he would be attending. The countries forming the G20 had decided by consensus that Russia should not be sidelined at the summit.

Paul Guard—whose parents, Toowoomba doctors Roger and Jill Guard, were killed in the MH17 crash—said little would be achieved by Putin staying away: 'It wouldn't achieve much by uninviting him because dialogue is the way forward and I hope the G20 might be a good platform on which to strongly voice our disapproval of his government's policy and approach to Ukraine.'

Tony Abbott took a slightly different approach, saying: 'I am going to shirtfront Mr Putin—you bet I am—I am going to be saying to Mr Putin Australians were murdered, they were murdered by Russian-backed rebels.' (The rest of the world had to have explained to it what a shirtfront involved—it is a term from Australian Rules football, in which two players confront each other chest-to-chest and attempt to bump each other out of the way without using their hands.)

But before the leaders met at the G20, Australia's foreign minister, Julie Bishop, attended a summit of European and Asian leaders in Milan and took the opportunity to approach Putin, who was seated opposite her. 'President Putin, I'm Julie Bishop, Australia's foreign minister,' she told him. Her aim was to talk to him about the MH17 and Russia's lack of cooperation. As the two moved away from the tables out of range of the microphones, Bishop managed to talk to Russia's leader for about ten minutes. During Bishop's intervention, Putin's piercing blue eyes never left her face. When she was finished, he said, 'So this is what you call a shirtfront?', referring to Tony Abbott's threat. Bishop said that she wouldn't quite use that phrase and would herself refer to it as a 'diplomatic buttonholing'.

When Abbott and Putin did meet later on, there was little sign of any 'shirtfronting' by Prime Minister Abbott. The two leaders discussed matters without any apparent friction.

On 4 November 2014, the DSB at long last received clearance to visit and examine the wreckage site. It was the first opportunity that was deemed sufficiently safe. Up to now there had been criticism from the bereaved at home: why was it taking so long? Media footage showed that large groups of journalists, officials and even families of the victims had visited the crash site weeks before. It was hard for them to understand, but for the DSB the safety of their investigators was vitally important.

The first team to enter the area was to prepare plans for the team that would be charged with collecting the wreckage of Flight MH17. There were of course new delays, and the actual recovery work at the crash site began on Sunday 16 November 2014. It had been a nail-biting three and a half months for the teams, but now they could finally do the work they had been itching to do for such a long time. Although they were already in possession of valuable data—such as the flight recorders, photographs and air traffic control information—salvaging the wreckage was considered key in finding the answer to the cause of the crash.

Work at the crash site remained a risky business. Escorted by the local armed police, the investigators wore bulletproof vests and their work was restricted to daylight hours only. The time they could spend on site was highly uncertain because hostilities could flare up again at any moment. The whole mission could be aborted at any given time, and this knowledge strongly influenced the way the investigators went to work and the choices they made while they were in the field. Their priority became finding and securing the most relevant pieces of wreckage and loading them onto a waiting vehicle. A list was made of the pieces of wreckage that were most important. At the site, however, it became apparent that several relevant parts of the wreckage had by now disappeared.

Most of the cockpit could be pieced together though, and those fragments revealed that the front of the cockpit had suffered most from the impact. The explosion had struck close to the captain's seat. What exactly had hit the MH17 could still not be proven beyond reasonable doubt, but the view was firming that this could have been a Buk, or some kind of sophisticated surface-to-air missile capable of targeting an object cruising at an altitude of 32,000 to 33,000 feet.

Observed, and sometimes bullied, by the armed men who were supposed to protect them, the investigators went about their work as best they could. The guards were especially wary of why some wreckage parts that were loaded onto the trucks were considered important and constantly demanded that the investigators explain their reasons for loading certain shards of metal. When the guards wanted to know why a particular cylindrical object was being loaded onto the truck, the team only shrugged their shoulders and said it was a motor part that could be of assistance to them. In reality the investigators had just carefully loaded a piece of what they suspected was the outer shell of a Buk missile.

Securing important pieces of wreckage went on till 22 November. The investigators knew they would go back at a later stage, but for now they had enough. The parts they had now managed to salvage would be transported to the Netherlands, where they would undergo further examination and experts would try to piece the different parts of the plane together.

Two weeks later, on 9 December 2014, the first two convoys set out from Kharkiv to take the aircraft parts back to the Netherlands. Later there would be two more such convoys. Each convoy consisted of four orange-coloured trucks carrying parts of the wreckage, with each of these parts carefully wrapped in orange tarpaulin. In total, sixteen trucks had been assigned to transport the parts to the Dutch military helicopter base at Gilze-Rijen. On arrival, all the salvaged components were to be assembled in a specially safeguarded hangar.

After six long nights driving across Europe, from Ukraine to the Netherlands, the first two convoys, consisting of eight orange flatbed trucks, finally trundled into the air base under military escort. For the silent huddle of families who had come together for the arrival, it was a solemn, almost eerie sight, and it evoked memories of the repatriation of the dead weeks before. However, at Gilze-Rijen there was no ceremony to mark the arrival of the convoys, no royals or politicians, just the cluster of hushed relatives waiting to see, for the first time, what was left of the aircraft in which their loved ones died.

A sealed aircraft hangar had been prepared at Gilze-Rijen. There the components, in accordance with a fixed procedure, would be unloaded, photographed, scanned and categorised, down to the last nut and bolt. Experts would then start the extremely difficult and complex task of piecing together the components of the aircraft on a specially constructed frame. The whole reconstruction would take months to complete and a final report on the cause of the crash wasn't expected until mid-2015.

Angry and disappointed because it had taken such a long time for the investigators to reach the crash site in Ukraine, those left behind began to openly complain about a lack of urgency. Not a suspect had yet been identified and, with the prospect that a final report would once again take months to come about, most of them were losing their patience. A group of relatives called for a UN envoy to take over the investigation, claiming Dutch authorities had failed in some respects.

But it was never the DSB's task to identify the perpetrators—that was the responsibility of the Joint Investigation Team. The JIT was to find the offenders and bring them to justice. This meant there were in fact two investigations, operating under different legal frameworks and with two different purposes.

The JIT was created on 7 August 2014 after public prosecutors and investigators from the countries that were involved in the investigation into the crash of Malaysia Airlines Flight MH17 first met at Eurojust in The Hague in late July to discuss their judicial strategy. An EU agency dealing with criminal judicial cooperation, Eurojust had been formed in the wake of the 9/11 attacks in the USA. With the focus on the fight against terrorism moving from the regional/national sphere and becoming an international affair, the 9/11 attack had served as a catalyst for the formalisation of Eurojust. Twenty-seven European countries belong to this organisation and their collaboration made it easier and more possible to exchange judicial information and personal data between the countries.

Authorities from the Netherlands, Australia, Belgium and Ukraine signed an agreement to set up the JIT with the purpose of investigating the crash of Malaysia Airlines Flight MH17, with the participation of Malaysia and Eurojust.

The purpose of the criminal investigation was to establish the facts, to identify those responsible for the crash and to collect evidence which could be used in court. The criminal investigation would focus on truth finding and its ultimate goal was, and still is, tracing and prosecuting the perpetrators. Finding facts that would hold up in court was very important because the JIT would never be able to bring any person to justice if their accusations were based merely on probability. Their conclusions would have to be substantiated by legally admissible and convincing evidence. That set the bar high.

Even though, from early on in the investigation, the most likely cause of the crash appeared to be a surface-to-air missile, nonetheless the JIT investigated other possibilities. It was important for them to keep an open, unprejudiced mind and not to be blinded by what appeared to be the most probable and logical cause. If anyone was eventually brought before a court for the MH17 disaster, their lawyers might present those other options as alternative possibilities, so the JIT had to be able to prove they had solid grounds for ruling them out. Together with the DSB, the JIT dismissed two scenarios quickly. This concerned the possibility of an accident caused by technical or human failure, and the possibility of a terrorist attack from inside the aircraft. There were no facts that could substantiate either options.

Was Flight MH17 shot down by another aeroplane equipped with a weapon system, as the Russians claimed? Radar data provided by the Russian Federation showed no clear radar images of another plane flying nearby that would support that theory: there was no other aircraft flying close enough to Flight MH17 that could have shot it down. Even the Russian Federation changed their opinion and concluded that there was no second aeroplane that could have shot down MH17.

There was an immense accumulation of evidence that Flight MH17 was definitely shot down by a ground-based air defence system. There was, however, some evidence that could undermine this conclusion. Some of the upper wreckage parts—the roof and the top of the wings—contained holes. A Buk would have targeted the plane from below, so how could there be such holes in these structures?

Taking all this into consideration, the JIT would now occupy itself with finding out the make and manufacturer of the weapon, and the location from which it had been fired. Of course, at the end of the day it would always be up to a court to make the final judgment.

The question the bereaved kept asking was how long it would take to conclude the criminal investigation. But the answer was that nobody really knew. It depended on further developments and the witnesses that might one day come forth with crucial evidence. The JIT could only make one promise to the families:

whatever happened, the investigation would continue unabated until those responsible had been brought to justice.

When a Pan Am plane was blown up over Lockerbie in Scotland in 1988, it took three years to finish the investigation and another seven for the trial. In contrast to MH17, that incident didn't take place over a region wrecked by war, a fact that was considerably complicating the current probe.

Chapter 21
2015

At the beginning of March 2015, the mangled wreckage of the MH17 had made its way from the wheat and sunflower fields of eastern Ukraine to a hangar at an air base in the Netherlands. The DSB believed it was time to reveal the damaged and charred pieces to the next of kin.

During the first week of March 2015, approximately five hundred relatives from around the world were taken to the three hangars where the wreckage was located: the hangar where the investigation was taking place and the two shelters where the remaining pieces were being sorted through. That cold and clinical collection of meticulously labelled aluminium plane parts—wings, wheels, pieces of fuselage and overhead luggage bins—was an eerie, for some a slightly macabre, sight. Spread out in that immaculate hangar, it brought home to all those who stood there that these bits and pieces were in fact the gathered remains of a crime scene. The last thing the victims saw was the inside of the plane.

'I looked at this mound of metal scrap and I had to say it out loud to myself, that this was the plane in which they all perished,' said Silene Fredriksz-Hoogzand, whose only son, Bryce, together with his girlfriend, Daisy Oehlers, had been on their way to a Malaysian holiday. 'At first sight, all of it was hard to comprehend.' Some relatives were so upset that they did not even enter the hangar; they just could not handle it.

Although the debris of the misshapen metal and parts of the destroyed plane were located in three hangars, only two of them were actually available for viewings. At the prosecutors' request the most important section of the plane, the cockpit parts, were not revealed to the press just yet. Those pieces were potentially vital as evidence to help establish the truth in the future. After the experts had assembled the parts and drawn their conclusions, the press would be called in.

Dutch Safety Board chairman Tjibbe Joustra said: 'The great majority of the next of kin were pleased to have been offered the opportunity to visit the wreckage. To actually see the pieces of wreckage is important.' In the hangar where the investigation took place, the families could view the sections deemed the most relevant from a platform and were offered the opportunity to lay flowers.

The fragments of the aircraft considered important to the criminal and aviation investigators were soon to form part of an enormous 3D reconstruction. The three-dimensional reconstruction of the aircraft would begin later that month, with its focus mainly on the areas of the plane that appeared to have suffered the most damage, the cockpit and business class section.

The JIT launched a media appeal, urging witnesses who could shed light on what had happened on the day of the crash to come forward. This witness call was posted on the websites and social media outlets of police and justice systems at the end of March, via news websites and television broadcasts. The appeal was posted as a video that included pictures of a Buk missile system being transported through eastern Ukraine on a flatbed truck. Intercepted and recorded telephone conversations were also put online, and within a week 300 witnesses had come forward, 170 emails were received and 135 telephone calls were made to the Dutch justice department. One person contacted the authorities through Skype and another through the Russian social media platform VKontakte. But although this proved helpful, vital evidence pointing to the actual offenders did not surface.

Prime Minister Mark Rutte's government was coming under increasing pressure from the public to reveal all it knew about the risks of allowing passenger planes to fly over conflict-torn eastern Ukraine. Although families of victims trusted the investigators and patiently awaited the final report, they were also aware that the truth could turn out to be politically uncomfortable.

During the first months of 2015 the Dutch government released some six hundred documents concerning the aftermath of the downing of Malaysia Airlines Flight MH17. This release of documents appeared to do little to cast new light on what the government knew, mainly because much of the information had been severely redacted. The readable pages included agendas of crisis meetings to discuss the disaster and plans for the repatriation of bodies found among the wreckage. A covering letter from the government explained that the retraction of 147 pages was in order to protect the privacy of individuals, the interests of the Netherlands' relationship with other states and had been implemented to conceal details of security around Dutch personnel working near the crash site. The released documents did, however, show that in the weeks immediately after the plane was shot down in eastern Ukraine, authorities relied heavily on media reports for many details.

A few months after the disaster, in September 2014, a ceasefire protocol had been established in Minsk, but although this did significantly reduce fighting in the conflict zone for many months, minor skirmishes continued. At the start of January 2015, the separatist forces of the Donetsk People's Republic and Luhansk People's Republic began a new offensive against the Ukrainian-controlled areas, resulting in the complete collapse of the Minsk ceasefire. Successive attempts to resolve the ongoing war in the Donbas region had seen no result by the start of February 2015.

Because the renewed heavy fighting caused significant concern in the international community, a new Minsk agreement was finalised after negotiations between German chancellor Angela Merkel, French president Nicolas Hollande, Russian president Vladimir Putin and Ukrainian president Petro Poroshenko. The agreement was signed by the Trilateral (Minsk) Contact Group, which included representatives from Ukraine, Russia, the Organization for Security and Co-operation in Europe (OSCE) and the self-declared People's Republics of Donetsk and Luhansk.

The Minsk talks did not go as far as negotiators had wanted or intended, but an agreement of a ceasefire and withdrawal of weapons between all parties was signed and it assured special status for the regions of Donetsk and Luhansk.

But for the relatives the agreement contained one disturbing element. When translated, it included a sentence reading 'Providing pardon and amnesty by way of enacting a law forbidding persecution and punishment of persons in relation to events that took place in specific parts of Donetsk and Luhansk in Ukraine'. This was the area where the MH17 had been downed. Because the MH17 wasn't specifically mentioned as an exception in the agreement, relatives were now concerned that the perpetrators, those responsible for the disaster, might benefit from the amnesty and be able to avoid punishment.

'It goes without saying that the survivors of the MH17 disaster demand that those responsible for taking down flight MH17 and the murder of 298 innocent passengers be identified, prosecuted and punished,' the next of kin wrote in a letter to the new Dutch foreign minister, Bert Koenders. The relatives also asked for clarification of the agreement. The Dutch government suddenly realised the mistake that had been made. The first Minsk agreement in 2014 had contained an additional clause when it came to amnesty: 'Responsibility, however, will not be waived in a wide range of cases. These include: . . . and persons who committed a crime connected with the crash of the "Malaysia Airlines" flight MH17.'

As part of the OSCE the Dutch had indirectly signed the new agreement but had 'forgotten' to demand that the clause be included. Prime Minister Mark Rutte now scrambled to make assurances, guaranteeing the public and relatives that it went without saying that the perpetrators would be persecuted despite any pardon bargain made.

German prime minister Angela Merkel said that there was 'no general obligation' that the amnesty 'included everyone', and added that in any case the investigation of Flight MH17 had not yet produced results. The Australian foreign minister, Julie Bishop, believed the Minsk deal would have 'no impact on the ability to bring the perpetrators of the downing of MH17 to justice'.

Ukrainian president Poroshenko, at a meeting in Brussels, assured the Dutch prime minister that the amnesty to which the Minsk agreement referred would not apply to possible perpetrators, or to persons responsible for the downing of Flight MH17. His promise did not set the families' minds at rest: if anything, it fuelled their increasing doubts. There was nothing in black and white to back Poroshenko's words and, if push came to shove, a lawyer would look at the text of the agreement and not at subsequent verbal commitments. How could such an important matter have been overlooked?

However one looked at it, the MH17 tragedy presented a hornet's nest of conflicting legal implications. The case, if ever brought to trial, would be very difficult. If a suspect was accused right at this moment, the country where he was living would have to be willing to extradite one of its nationals to a foreign tribunal that had not yet been established or acknowledged. This could become a diplomatic nightmare. Far more challenging was the prospect of actually identifying individuals to prosecute as perpetrators. For an individual to be considered a suspect, the investigators would need more information about the chain of command in order to determine who gave the order. But releasing the names of suspects prematurely would impede the ongoing investigation by alerting persons of interest.

If the perpetrators were ever brought to justice, what crime would they be accused of? If it was a war crime, then the Netherlands could initiate a domestic prosecution against anyone accused of committing a war crime against a Dutch citizen. However, because the crash killed the nationals of a number of countries, the preferable approach might be a prosecution under international law. Yet, if Russian citizens were eventually named as suspects, the legal process of bringing them to trial would not be easy or straightforward. Russia was a signatory of the European Convention on Extradition in 1996, which facilitated extradition of wanted criminals between member states, but this convention explicitly excluded military personnel, and every signatory could opt not to extradite its own citizens.

At the beginning of the Minsk treaty the level of fighting in eastern Ukraine decreased significantly, though not entirely. Fighting along the frontline basically ceased, but pro-Russian and Ukrainian forces continued to shell each other. The nation of Ukraine appeared to be at a crossroads, with little hope of stability until the shelling stopped altogether. In March President Obama's administration announced that thirty armoured humvees and an additional three hundred non-armoured humvees, plus counter-mortar radar, drones, radios and medical equipment would be sent to Ukraine. One year after Russia had formally annexed the Crimean peninsula, or, as the Kremlin would say, after Crimea had been rightfully returned to the Russian Federation, the anniversary was marked in Moscow with a triumphant celebration.

The first anniversary of the Donbas uprising was marked by violence, with three Ukrainian government soldiers and another six Ukrainian troops killed in two separate incidents. Their cause of death was highly contested. The interior ministry accused the rebels of firing upon its soldiers, whereas the leaders of the self-proclaimed Luhansk People's Republic argued that the men had succumbed to a landmine.

Tensions mounted when US troops started training the Ukrainian infantry and Russia immediately undertook a build-up of forces along its border with Ukraine. A day later President Petro Poroshenko stated that Ukraine was 'still under a threat of war' from pro-Russian separatists and that 'war could start at any moment'.

As the first anniversary of the downing of MH17 approached, the international partners in the criminal investigation put forward a draft UN Security Council resolution aiming to establish a specialist independent war crimes tribunal. But a year down the road, many of the most important questions had still not been answered.

On 17 July 2015, the next of kin gathered together at a congress centre in Nieuwegein. Dutch prime minister Mark Rutte attended the private memorial and flags on government buildings in the Netherlands were lowered to half-mast. Not a day had gone by during that year without each of these people being reminded in some way of the death of the loved one that they had lost on that flight. They knew they would carry that burden for the rest of their lives. There were songs, poems and speeches from the relatives to commemorate their loved ones.

Sharifah Asma'a Syed Alwi Al Junied, the widow of one of the copilots, stood to give a speech. She told the audience that she felt compelled to finish the job her husband Ahmad had set out to do exactly one year ago. She ended her speech with the words her husband would have said after the plane had landed: 'We appreciate you flying with us. Thank you and have a nice day.' Her words prompted tears and a standing ovation.

In Australia, a plaque honouring the victims was unveiled. At Kuala Lumpur International Airport a memorial service was held, at which the families and friends of the crash victims gathered to remember the tragedy and repeat their demands for justice.

At the commemorations marking the anniversary of the shooting down of Flight MH17 at the crash site in eastern Ukraine, a flag-waving protest by pro-Russian separatists attempted to politicise the mourning. After a church service in the village of Hrabove, residents joined a procession across an open field to a gravestone placed near the charred area where twisted metal and body parts came crashing down on 17 July. Pointing their fingers at the Ukrainian authorities, young DPR loyalists waved signs proclaiming 'They killed you, they continue to kill us'.

According to the men and women of Hrabove, this part of Ukraine had changed forever due to the crash. A year on, the smell of kerosene and death still lingered in the air. Further down the road in Petropavlivka, a large part of the plane's hull could still be found. No one had come to collect it.

On 29 July, the UN Security Council held a meeting that was intended to establish an international war crimes tribunal. Of the countries whose nationals had perished on the flight, five sent government ministers, and there were representatives of the others. The meeting began with a moment of silence in tribute to the victims.

As voting began, Russia used its Security Council veto to block the draft resolution. Angola, China and Venezuela refrained from voting. As the only nation at the fifteen-member UN Security Council to oppose the resolution, Russia attracted widespread condemnation. Their veto left the bereaved feeling they were at the receiving end of a political power game. Explaining his negative vote, the representative of the Russian Federation said his country did not support the creation of an international tribunal under Chapter VII of the Charter, because a previous Security Council resolution had not considered the downing of the aircraft a threat to international peace and security. An alternative draft put forward by his government had sought to promote a genuine international and independent investigation, and it remained on the table.

A bitterly disappointed Dutch foreign affairs minister, Bert Koenders, told the members: 'We came to the Council with a desire to see justice done in the most effective, impartial and legitimate way, with the greatest possible chance of success.' He expressed his deep disappointment that the Russian Federation had used its veto to stop the council from actively ensuring that justice was served.

Julie Bishop let the council know that her country was determined to bring the perpetrators to account and, with the other members of the joint investigation team, would decide on an alternative prosecution mechanism.

From the moment a Malaysian aeroplane carrying people from many different countries crashed on Ukrainian territory amid pro-Russian rebels, the Netherlands and Australia had found themselves caught up in a diplomatic game of chess that involved more than a dozen world leaders. There was so much at stake and there were so many interests to take into account that the Netherlands, as leading investigative country, had been forced to move very cautiously. By mid-2015 DSB's chairman, Tjibbe Joustra, wondered if the Russians would even show for the next briefing about the investigation of the crash.

According to the protocol that had been set up just after the crash, Malaysia, Ukraine, the United States, United Kingdom, Australia and also Russia were invited to participate in the investigation. But Russia was becoming reluctant to take part as increasing evidence gathered by the DSB investigators irrefutably pointed in their direction. Moscow flatly denied any involvement and instead pointed the finger at the Ukrainian military.

The Russian foreign minister, Sergej Lavrov, claimed that the MH17 investigation was anything but transparent. The

Americans still had not revealed their satellite footage and images. The Russians wondered why. What was on those images that no one was allowed to see? Could they prove the presence of Ukrainian planes nearby at the time when the disaster happened, just as Moscow was claiming? The Russian state network Channel One aired footage from the country's own satellite, showing a Ukrainian jet fighter following the aeroplane and firing a rocket at it. Russian media and officials accused Ukrainian Captain Vladyslav Voloshyn, an Su-25 attack jet pilot, of shooting down the Malaysia Airlines flight.

This 'evidence' immediately came under scrutiny. Among other things, the letters on the hull of the plane being shot at did not match with MH17, and the date of the footage proved that it had been taken before 17 July. Ultimately the Russians were accused of producing false satellite imagery.

By now Moscow had become very sceptical about the DSB investigations and accused the Western investigators of being biased. Keeping the Russians on board was a painstaking task for Joustra. Russia could walk away from the investigating table at any moment and reject the conclusions established by the DSB board. Without the Russians on board, any attempt to bring possible Russian perpetrators to justice would be destined to fail. But working together with the Russians had proved to be very disillusioning. Once the DSB presented its final report, Moscow would surely reject any conclusions. The diplomatic tension between Russia, Australia and the Netherlands had reached boiling point.

In the meantime, victims' families from Australia, New Zealand and Malaysia went to the European Court of Human Rights to sue President Vladimir Putin and Russia for $10 million each. Russia again denied any accountability. The compensation claim was filed with the Strasbourg-based court by Sydney legal firm LHD Lawyers, who alleged that Russia had worked to keep its involvement hidden.

All through 2015 the DSB forensics experts had been working hard at piecing together large parts of the cockpit and hull of MH17. The reconstruction hadn't been easy. It was a meticulous process with thousands of parts recovered from the retrieval efforts in Ukraine shipped to the hangar. The forensic researchers at Gilze-Rijen Air Base had to search through a proverbial haystack of wreckage parts.

An outline of the aircraft had first been drawn on the floor of a hangar at Gilze-Rijen and pieces of wreckage placed on or near the outline, where it was thought they belonged. Positioned on the floor, the pieces resembled a giant jigsaw puzzle with just the image on the box to help find the places where they fitted. Eventually the parts were transferred onto a black skeletal three-dimensional frame, where the pieces of wreckage were held in place. Because many parts of the wreckage were badly mangled, the frame was slightly bigger than the original model of a Boeing 777-200. Some parts had to be twisted back into shape and wrapped over the frame.

The assembled reconstruction clearly showed the damage and impact the plane had been subjected to. It also showed from which direction the impact had come, slightly to the left just above the cockpit, and how the plane had fallen to earth in separate parts.

It was October 2015 and the DSB was ready to present its final report. Not only had it become evident that the plane had been struck by a missile, but the forensics had found fragments in the body parts of the cockpit crew members that backed this assumption. More than a hundred objects were found in the body of one of the flight attendants and literally hundreds of metal fragments were found in the dispersed body of one of the captains. The fragments all pointed in one direction: 'Based upon the damage examination it is concluded that the impact damage on the wreckage of flight MH17 is caused by a warhead with various types of preformed fragments in the 6–14mm size range, including one type with a bowtie shape detonating to the left of, and above, the cockpit.'

The report stated that the front of the aircraft was destroyed by a missile, killing two of the pilots and a flight attendant instantly, and causing the rest of the plane to break apart. Bow-tie-shaped fragments in the debris and traces of paint were crucial in determining the precise model of warhead involved.

'The damage observed on the wreckage is not consistent with the damage caused by the warhead of an air-to-air missile in use in the region in amount of damage, type of damage and type of fragments. The high-energy object damage on the wreckage of flight MH17 is therefore not caused by an air-to-air missile.'

The report concluded that MH17 was shot down by a Buk surface-to-air missile, which exploded less than a metre from the cockpit. The report named the missile used as a 9N314M warhead as carried on a 9M38-series missile and launched by a Buk surface-to-air missile system.

'Of the investigated warheads only the 9N314M contains the unique bowtie shaped fragments found in the wreckage. The damage observed on the wreckage in amount of damage, type of damage, boundary and impact angles of damage, number and density of hits, size of penetrations and bowtie fragments found in the wreckage, is consistent with the damage caused by the 9N314M warhead used in the 9M38 and 9M38M1 BUK surface-to-air missile.'

The Russian government immediately challenged the finding that a Buk missile shot down the plane. The DSB noted Russia's objections, but issued a point-by-point rebuttal.

Days after the report was presented, former Ukrainian president Viktor Yanukovych suddenly surfaced again. The former president, who now lived in Russia, was going to take Ukraine to court for violating his human rights, he told the press. Ukraine had 'repeatedly breached his human rights', denying his right to a fair trial and the right 'not to be discriminated against because of his political status and opinions'.

In November 2014 the surviving relatives of the victims formed the MH17 Disaster Foundation to commemorate the victims and guard the interests, in the broadest sense, of the surviving relatives. In a statement they let the press know that: 'After a period of disbelief, pain, sadness and mourning all surviving relatives have been able to say goodbye to their loved ones. Now that the investigation of the DSB (OVV) has come to an end and we know what has happened we feel the emphasis must shift to locating and prosecuting the guilty.'

Despite a truce intended to last through the holiday season, Ukraine and pro-Russian rebel forces continued hostilities in December 2015. The village of Zaitseve was the centre of the fighting, which claimed the life of a soldier and a civilian and wounded many more. The OSCE reported that a group of observers came under fire near the city of Mariupol in south-eastern Ukraine, but there were no casualties.

Chapter 22

2016

By the end of 2015 Russia and the United States were extending their sanctions on each other's goods and businesspeople. This had begun with American sanctions against those involved with the Ukrainian conflict, which was followed by Russian retaliation. In January 2016 a British-based group of citizen journalists called Bellingcat named twenty suspects they had tracked down and who they claimed were involved with the downing of MH17.

Based in Leicester, Bellingcat specialised in trawling through data on social media. Its founder, Eliot Higgins, had started a blog in March 2012 under the pseudonym Brown Moses, where he had published his research of online video footage of the Syrian civil war. He had examined hundreds of short clips on the internet, focusing on details of the weapons used. As a result, he was able to establish that the Syrian regime was using cluster munitions and chemical weapons.

On 15 July 2014, just two days before the downing of MH17, Higgins had launched the Bellingcat platform with the help of private donations. After the downing, Higgins's band of citizen journalists began conducting their own investigation into what caused the MH17 to crash. They followed the progress of a Russian missile launcher that had been noticed in the area where the plane had come down. The Bellingcat team—which at the time was formed by an American, a Russian, a Dutchman, a Finn and its founder, Englishman Higgins—were all volunteers and were not being paid for their work. The MH17 disaster had left a trail of digital data, before and after the disaster, and the team members were experts at finding this data and piecing the puzzle together. The evidence they uncovered online and on social media seemed to point to this particular Russian missile as being involved.

Throughout their investigation, Bellingcat shared their findings with the JIT investigators from the Netherlands, Belgium, Malaysia, Ukraine and Australia. The JIT was very well aware of the importance that social media could have in uncovering what had happened and in the ultimate arrest of any suspects, so they took the information that Bellingcat shared with them seriously. When Russian officials blamed the flight's destruction on Ukrainian forces and presented radar data, expert testimony and a satellite image, it was Bellingcat that exposed the photo as being a composite of Google images, with even the Malaysian airline logo being misplaced.

Now the Leicester-based investigative journalists were revealing to the world that a Russian unit had transported to

Ukraine the Buk missile system that eventually brought down MH17. The unit was identified as the Second Battalion of the 53rd Anti-Aircraft Missile Brigade, coming from the area of Kursk.

The battalion consisted of about a hundred soldiers, but Bellingcat's analysis narrowed the number of suspects involved with the MH17 down to approximately twenty soldiers. The Dutch Safety Board had concluded in October 2015 that the aircraft crashed due to the impact from a surface-to-air missile, most likely a Buk, which suggested that the type of weapon had been clearly established. Using the internet and social media, Bellingcat was able to piece together that the Russian 53rd air force brigade had Buk weaponry at their disposal. Although the journalists did not claim to know who pushed the button or who gave the order, they were pretty sure that someone serving on the 53rd brigade could reveal that information. Difficult as it would be, if any perpetrators were tracked down, finding reliable witnesses would prove much harder. It was expected that no one in that battalion would stand up voluntarily to give evidence.

There were people in Russia and in the West who thought that Bellingcat's claims were based on flimsy and biased evidence; hardly anyone appeared to be checking if the information supplied by Bellingcat was correct. When other experts took a close look at their claims, they discovered that the flatbed truck that was supposed to be transporting the Buk took a route that led under an overpass. The flatbed with the Buk on it could never have been driven under it because the underpass was not high enough to allow clearance. There was no detour route, although it was later claimed that the Buk could have been taken off the flatbed and driven under the underpass and into a paddock on its own wheels.

A civilian journalist platform, of course, is under no obligation to be unbiased and it can offer plausible, but unproven, hypotheses. The increased public scrutiny did not deter Higgins, who remained confident about his conclusions, explaining that: 'People who say I am biased will say that anyway. The methods we use are transparent and anyone who invests some time can validate what we do.'

In May Bellingcat unveiled new Buk footage, which had been shot from a moving car on 17 July. It was the first time that the Buk was clearly visible on top of the flatbed.

Russia rejected Bellingcat's report. In a separate probe into the crash, Russian arms manufacturer Almaz-Antey said the missile had exploded near the left side of the aircraft. Almaz-Antey considered this to be proof that the projectile could only be a missile from a Buk system launched from the region of Zaroshchenske, controlled by the Kiev forces at the time of the incident.

In March 2016 the Dutch-led JIT stated that they would soon be able to determine the exact launch site of the missile that destroyed the plane. Fred Westerbeke, the prosecutor leading the international probe, warned that it would take much longer than the JIT had previously expected to complete the whole investigation. He pledged to finish the investigation 'as quickly as possible, if only because of the frustration among the families', but declined to offer a possible date. Two years after the disaster, the survivors were still facing much uncertainty and frustration.

There were still two Dutch victims who had not been identified; one of them was sixteen-year-old Gary Slok, who had left for a holiday in Borneo with his mother. His father, Jan Slok, was slowly losing hope that any remains of his son would ever be found. His ex-wife, Petra van Langeveld, had been identified months ago. Every time fragments or remains were found at the crash site, Jan Slok had hoped some part of these remains would be confirmed as being Gary's. But after two years the boy still had not been found.

As time passed it became ever harder for Jan to accept that his son would probably never come home. 'I even asked them [the family counsellors] to lie to me and tell me that he had been identified. Just for the sake of my own peace of mind.' Jan did receive Gary's backpack with his things inside and, in the absence of any physical remains, Jan and his wife, Louise, symbolically buried that backpack in a coffin next to his mother's.

The downing of MH17 was becoming such a complex issue that now even the truth was becoming difficult to recognise. With all the different versions and stories, the obvious question arose as to who to believe or who not to believe.

Nineteen months after the crash, the next of kin were becoming exceedingly impatient with the drawn-out process of investigation. It was taking way too long. Eighteen families combined forces and sent a letter to Russia, Ukraine and the

United States, asking them to disclose any satellite or radar images connected to the downing of MH17. The Russians were quick to engage with the families, who asked Putin if he could find out if there were backups of the imagery; they wanted to know if Russia possessed footage of the actual downing.

Deputy chief of Russia's Air Transport Agency Oleg Storchevoi informed the families that Russia had already offered their imagery to the Dutch Safety Board in August 2014, right after the crash. Russia still had the images and was willing to offer them to the DSB or any other organisation responsible for investigating the MH17 tragedy. But the DSB claimed that Russia had only sent video footage of the radar screen combined with the footage from the primary and secondary surveillance radars. Storchevoi answered that: 'The Russian primary [a radar system that is situated on the ground and traces the skies for any movement] radar footage is only kept on video format which is not against any international civilian air force rule.' He went on to say that this data 'was ignored by the DSB in its work and was not even mentioned in their report on the results of the investigation'.

It took Ukraine six months to respond to the letter requesting radar recordings. Only after Dutch prime minister Rutte demanded a response from Poroshenko did Ukraine feel compelled to reply. To the astonishment of the families, Ukraine let them know that there was no radar imagery for 17 July—Ukraine radars had all been offline that day due to maintenance.

Ukraine had three radar systems and apparently on 17 July 2014 all three had been turned off. One of them had been badly damaged during the hostilities in 2014, but Ukrainian officials claimed the others had been switched off because no military flights had been planned for 17 July. It was a dubious explanation. The country was at war, so it would be very unlikely for it to turn off all its radar systems. Just before 17 July, many military flights had been operating and eyewitnesses told journalists that they had seen a number of military aircraft flying over the area where the plane was brought down on 17 July.

If Ukraine had turned off their radars, this should have been reported to Eurocontrol, the organisation responsible for the air safety of forty European countries. But no such report was received by Eurocontrol. Later on, Ukraine's failure to produce radar images became even more confusing when its former minister of transport, Vladimir Shulmeister, visited the Netherlands and, during a press conference, said he had been very surprised when he read the DSB report; he claimed that the Dutch had never asked Ukraine to share their radar images. Shulmeister had served on the board of the Ukrainian committee that handled all matters concerning the MH17; he said he would have known if the Dutch had asked Ukraine for their radar data. Ukraine, as a member of the Joint Investigation Team, was actively participating in the investigation to identify the murderers, so it would have been hard for the Dutch to put any political pressure on them. But it was an astonishing level of miscommunication between these two members.

United States secretary of state John Kerry had indicated just three days after the crash that the US government possessed data that pinpointed the exact location of the suspected missile launch that downed the airliner. But in its October report, the Dutch Safety Board placed the likely firing location within a 320-square-kilometre area that covered territory under both government and rebel control. Apparently, the Dutch at that time had not yet received the US imagery, or else their location details would have been much more precise.

In a statement, the Dutch diplomatically blamed technicalities in US laws for the lack of American cooperation. The Dutch government in an official letter to the parliament advised that, under the American legal system, it is juridically complicated to pass intelligence information on to the criminal justice system; furthermore, if it made the satellite imagery public, the USA would reveal important military information, such as where their satellites were positioned and the quality of their imagery.

Weeks later, the Dutch minister of justice, Ard van der Steur, claimed that the Americans had in fact shared their imagery with the Netherlands. This was an important statement because John Kerry had at an earlier stage claimed that: 'We saw the launch, we saw the impact and we saw the plane disappear from our radar. So it's no mystery where it came from and where these weapons came from.' Clearly, the imagery shared with the Netherlands could be of vital importance in arresting the suspects and charging them before a court.

Fred Westerbeke, the Dutch prosecutor and coordinator of the Joint Investigation Team, said that all requested data had been handed over by the US to the Dutch Military Secret Service, but that there was a public misunderstanding about the imagery. 'There is no footage showing a rocket being launched.

The intelligence services don't have footage that answers every question.' This was in stark contrast to what Kerry had claimed.

As 2015 had worn on and conflicting reports concerning the US satellite images had surfaced, it became very doubtful as to whether the Americans had actually shared their satellite information with anyone. Ukraine certainly had not, and the Russians had only shared their video footage of the radar. Still, in March 2016 the Dutch minister of justice, van der Steur, claimed there was no further need for any radar imagery. There was enough to satisfy those working on the case. Nonetheless, two family members of victims, Silene Fredriksz-Hoogzand and Thomas Schansman, together with sixteen others, wrote a letter to Rutte asking for the satellite images to be released and asking him to explain why it was taking so unbearably long to sort it all out.

People were afraid that the truth was being swept under the carpet for some reason and were getting the impression that the government and the investigators were deliberately creating a cover-up. Thomas Schansman, because of his son Quinn's dual nationality, also wrote to John Kerry asking him about possible radar or satellite data. In his answer Kerry replied: 'We continue to work together with the Joint Investigation Team to find the cause of the attack and identify those responsible.' But Kerry did not specifically mention radar or satellite images in his reply.

Questions arose in the Dutch parliament concerning the issue of raw radar data and satellite imagery that the United States claimed to have in its possession and which the US described as strong evidence. But in Washington officials failed to clarify to what extent the US intelligence had shared their data: 'I believe we have collaborated with the Dutch in their investigation,' State Department spokesperson Mark Toner said. 'I just don't know to what level we shared information with them, I'd have to look into that.'

Nonetheless, the DSB claimed that the missing images were not vital to the investigation and that it would be very unlikely for the images to show a rocket, which was also in stark contradiction to what US secretary Kerry had claimed. The DSB wrote that if they had had such images, it would have done nothing to change their conclusion that a Buk rocket made in Russia had been responsible for taking down the plane.

In a letter to the relatives, the Dutch prosecutor explained the status of the investigation. The letter stated the following on satellite data: 'To date the JIT has no satellite images of the launch of the missile. Because of clouds usable images are not available from the firing location at the time of day when the MH17 was shot down.' Maintenance requirements, legal issues, fuzzy video footage and now even the clouds had been brought into the equation.

Twenty months after the downing of Flight MH17, the White House announced a new package of US$335 million in security assistance for Ukraine, but yet the public still did not know what had happened and who was responsible for the deaths of 298 innocent people.

On 6 April 2016 a plebiscite was held in the Netherlands on a proposed EU–Ukraine Association Agreement. Dutch voters rejected this proposal by a margin of 61.1 per cent to 38.1 per cent and turnout for the vote was 32.2 per cent, higher than the 30 per cent that was required for the result to be considered valid. The vote was non-binding, but it would have been difficult for the Dutch government to directly contravene the expressed will of the voters and approve the agreement. Mark Rutte stated that his government, which had supported the agreement, might have to reconsider because 'with such a victory for the "No" camp, ratification cannot go ahead without discussion'.

Doubt and suspicions about Ukraine's role in the MH17 disaster underpinned the 'No' campaign's efforts to convince the Dutch that an already ratified, 1200-page treaty with Ukraine was a bad idea. While the European Commission formally issued its support for a visa-free travel arrangement for Ukrainian citizens, this did not guarantee that the proposal would be adopted. All of the EU's member states and the bloc's parliament would have to vote.

By the end of April, the casualty count of the ongoing war in Ukraine was estimated by the UN to be almost 9500 and the injured totalled 21,000. In April 2016 the level of violence rose dramatically and could be compared to that of August 2014. All through the Easter ceasefire deaths were reported due to hostilities. A new report by the United Nations found both sides of the conflict were responsible for multiple human rights abuses, including carrying out summary executions of combatants and civilians, as well as indiscriminately shelling civilian areas.

Two months shy of the second anniversary of the disaster, seven Australian families who lost loved ones on board MH17 initiated legal proceedings against Malaysia Airlines for flying over a known conflict zone. The claims accused the airline of failing to monitor the situation in eastern Ukraine in the months leading up to the disaster and failing to perform its own risk assessment of the worsening conflict.

On 17 July 2016, two years after the plane was brought down, Malaysia Airlines struck a deal to settle the damages claims relating to most of the victims. Soon afterwards, relatives were invited to attend an official press conference to be held by the JIT on 28 September, at which the initial results from the team's criminal probe would be revealed.

According to the JIT, there was now irrefutable evidence that Flight MH17 had been downed using a Buk rocket of the 9M38 series. They had also been able to pinpoint the launch area, a farmer's field near Pervomaiskyi that had been under the pro-Russian separatists' control at the time. Witnesses at the launch site near the village of Pervomaiskyi reported hearing 'a very loud noise' and 'a high whistling sound', but they were unsure whether this sound had come from the falling debris of the MH17. Afterwards, the Buk was said to have been transported back to Russia.

Around a hundred people had been identified who could be linked to the downing of MH17 or the transport of the Buk; the JIT did not name any suspects but said they would try to find out who gave the order to smuggle the Buk system into Ukraine, and who gave the order to shoot down MH17. The investigators—which included representatives from Australia, Malaysia, Ukraine and Belgium—said their conclusions were based on a wealth of supporting evidence, such as forensic examinations, witness statements, satellite images, radar data and intercepted telephone calls.

A video reconstruction of the Buk's alleged journey was shown at this JIT press conference. It was seen leaving rebel-held Donetsk on a low-loader, heading east. After arriving in Snizhne on the afternoon of 17 July, it was offloaded and driven into a field south of the town. Early the next day it was taken back across the Russian border via the rebel-held city of Luhansk.

The one question that was not answered was this: if the separatists or the Russians were responsible, what were they aiming at? Surely not a commercial aircraft. A Ukrainian airforce Su-25 jet maybe? But the difference in shape, size and speed between a commercial plane and an Su-25 is quite significant, so how could a mistake like this have been made? Such questions could only be answered by the perpetrators.

Russia immediately dismissed the findings. Dmitry Peskov, Vladimir Putin's press spokesman, said the 'whole story is unfortunately surrounded by a huge amount of speculation and unqualified, unprofessional information'. Attempts to extradite Russian citizens to stand trial would be difficult if not impossible if Russia continued on its course of dismissing all findings and allegations.

For the relatives it was a disappointment because investigators were unable to say how long their inquiry into the suspected criminals would take. Were they looking at months, or would it be years? The chief Dutch prosecutor, Fred Westerbeke, said he could not make any promises in that respect, but he expected it to be a 'long haul': 'The work is going on with all countries, and our best people,' he said.

In a surprising interview with *The Guardian*, Igor Girkin surfaced in June 2016 and criticised Russia's role in Ukraine. Portrayed as a hero in Russia and as a criminal in Ukraine, Igor Girkin had been a key actor in the pro-Russian separatist movement in Ukraine over the course of 2014. Girkin's main criticism of Putin was that the Russian president had not gone far enough; he claimed that Putin had got himself 'stuck in the middle of a swamp' by stopping at the annexation of Crimea.

The Netherlands, in anticipation of suspects being arrested, had discussed the prospect of an international tribunal with Australian foreign minister Julie Bishop. It was to be similar to the one following the 1988 Lockerbie bombing, when Pan Am Flight 103 was blown up while flying over Scotland. In that special case a Scottish court had been set up in the Netherlands to facilitate the trial of the two Libyans charged over the disaster. A special court to preside over the trial of the MH17 accused would not need UN approval, and this meant the countries involved would not have to deal with a Russian veto. The court could be established through a treaty with all the countries that lost citizens and residents in the disaster.

But the Lockerbie example cast serious doubts on this plan of action. In that case, the two men accused had been eventually extradited 'voluntarily' by Libya and tried in the special Scottish court in the Netherlands. But it was highly unlikely that Russia would surrender any of its citizens for trial elsewhere. Due to Russia's power of veto there, the Security Council would lack the capacity to impose the same amount of pressure as was brought to bear on Libya. In the Lockerbie case only one person was ever convicted for the bombing and today, more than thirty years after the downing of Pan Am 103, many questions still persist over his guilt. It was a highly unsatisfactory outcome.

For the MH17 relatives it was important that first and foremost the individual perpetrators were identified and tried. But they wanted more than just that. To be able to feel that any kind of justice had been done, they wanted Russia to be held accountable for 'wrongful death' and Ukraine for 'gross negligence'.

But in the face of Russian obstinacy the question arose as to whether the Western powers would be willing to risk a major conflict with Russia over the MH17 disaster. And in August 2016 Ukraine celebrated its twenty-fifth year of independence with a grandiose military parade through downtown Kiev. 'Our parade is a signal to the enemy: Ukrainians are seriously ready to fight for their independence,' said Petro Poroshenko, the president of Ukraine.

Chapter 23
2017

All through January 2017 hostilities between the separatists and Ukraine's military forces continued. Some thirty incidents of shots being fired were reported each day, especially around the Donetsk area, causing casualties on both sides as well as civilian deaths when villagers were caught in the crossfire. But the greatest cause of death were the landmines.

By now the ongoing war in Ukraine had become once again almost invisible to the rest of the world. In this strange war no party appeared to book any gains and both parties appeared to be just shooting intermittently at each other. The world had turned away and lost interest in the simmering war that neither side had declared. Every day sniper rifles, machine guns and loud booms from grenade launchers could be heard reverberating across the fields in the Donbas region.

The war also wasn't always prominently visible. In fact, the towns and cities involved seemed to be going about their everyday business: buses drove through the streets, shops were open, and the garbage was being picked up. But the sound of war could be heard almost everywhere in the region.

Despite almost 1.8 million people having fled the conflict area, some 800,000 civilians still remained in their houses close to the battlefields, facing the risks involved on a daily basis. The elderly didn't want to lose what little they possessed and stayed home to guard it; some stayed because they had nowhere else to go; farmers still worked the fields and miners still entered the mineshafts every morning.

On 17 January 2017, Ukraine went to the International Court of Justice in The Hague to file a suit against Russia. But the news around President Donald Trump taking office, and the mass protests, controversial executive orders and pending lawsuits that followed, meant that news of the Ukrainian suit escaped almost everyone's attention.

The International Court of Justice was established in 1945; it is the main judicial body within the United Nations and is located in the Peace Palace in The Hague. The court has fifteen judges who rule on legal disputes between countries. Ukraine's application to the court presented a mix of overlapping claims: it covered all at once allegations of Russia's financing of terrorism in the region, as well as its persecution of ethnic minorities within Ukraine. Ukraine also wanted the ICJ to declare Russia responsible for the MH17 tragedy.

'Russia must pay its price for the aggression,' Ukrainian president Petro Poroshenko said after Kiev launched the proceedings on his orders. Ukraine requested the court to declare that the

Russian Federation 'bears international responsibility, by virtue of its sponsorship of terrorism and for the acts of terrorism committed by its proxies in Ukraine, including: the shoot-down of Malaysia Airlines Flight MH17, the shelling of civilians, in Volnovakha, Mariupol, and Kramatorsk and the bombing of civilians, in Kharkiv'. Ukraine demanded that Russia make 'full reparation' to all the victims.

But first and foremost, Ukraine accused Russia of financing acts of terrorism within Ukraine and violation of treaties that had been signed by both countries. The International Court of Justice had now to decide whether to take up the case. The outcome would be binding on all parties and there was no possibility of appeal.

The Dutch foreign minister, Bert Koenders, did not back Ukraine's rush to the ICJ as far as the MH17 was involved. He explained that parties must maintain discipline in their approach to the prosecution of those involved in the downing of MH17. It was 'too early', he urged. The relatives of MH17 victims said they would follow the trial, but at a distance; they stressed through their spokesman that they were not a party to Ukraine's move. Together with the Dutch government, they were carefully taking their own steps against Russia.

At their press conference in September 2016, the Joint Investigation Team had stated that the plane was shot down from pro-Russian rebel-controlled territory by a missile that had been recently transported from Russia. But the Russians subsequently claimed that no such missile appeared on radar images from their Ust-Donetsk radar station. The JIT and radar experts confirmed that a Buk missile launched from the location established by the JIT need not be visible on the radar images from Ust-Donetsk at all: the speed of such a missile is much higher than the speed of civil aircraft, so a civil radar station will generally not show any visible trail on the radar images. This prevents 'clutter' on the radar image.

The JIT investigators, who were carefully compiling a case for possible future criminal prosecutions, stopped short of saying that Russians, or the Russian state, were responsible for the downing; it was a matter for ongoing investigation in their opinion. The countries working together on the JIT, including Australia, had agreed to delay taking action until the criminal investigation had concluded later in the year.

Meanwhile Moscow, which had always denied arming the separatists in Ukraine, shrugged off the whole MH17 downing, as well as Ukraine's other accusations, as simply 'political'. 'Russia has always condemned in the strongest manner any signs of terrorism and actively fights against it,' Russia's foreign ministry once again stressed.

In this same January a journalist caused a stir when he recovered some victims' remains from the site. Dutchman Michel Spekkers returned from a two-week stay in eastern Ukraine where he and his colleague, Stefan Beck, also Dutch, had been gathering firsthand accounts of the locals' attitudes toward Moscow and Kiev. On the last day of the trip, Spekkers went to the crash site of MH17, from where he said he retrieved parts of the wreckage as well as what was later established by Dutch prosecutors as human remains of one of the passengers of the downed Boeing. Spekkers was surprised to see numerous parts of the ill-fated plane still lying around.

His seemingly lighthearted tweets about what to do with the items he had found at the crash site offended the survivors of the MH17 victims. He did, however, establish that after almost three years, there were still human remains as well as personal belongings scattered around the crash site. The relatives were shocked and wanted the Dutch minister of security and justice, Ard van der Steur, to conduct further investigation at the crash site. Some next of kin had only received a small quantity of body parts from the crash site, and two victims—Gary Slok and Alex Ploeg, both of them Dutch—had not been identified at all. The journalist himself said he had been appalled when he found what looked like human remains at the site. 'It's been more than two and a half years ago. I find this disgraceful.' On Spekkers' return to the Netherlands, police confiscated everything the reporter had discovered, as well as both his and his friend's laptops and mobile phones.

In February, Daniel Romein, a member of the Bellingcat team, published a new report on MH17. His conclusion was that the man whose telephone was tapped by the Ukrainian Security Service on 17 July 2014 was involved in the transport of the Buk missile launcher that downed MH17. His name was Sergey Nikolaevich Dubinsky, nicknamed 'Khmuryi'. In July 2014 Dubinsky had been a Russian war veteran and a colonel. He had taken up arms in the Soviet–Afghan war and later in Chechnya, and later again served in the 22nd Spetsnaz brigade. Investigators claimed that Dubinsky had later been expelled from the ranks of the pro-Russian militants for alleged financial crimes.

This was the first time that a Russian had actually been named and identified as being connected to the MH17 downing. It had always been the general assumption that the pro-Russian separatists had been responsible. The independent Russian newspaper *Novaya Gazeta* also confirmed that the voice on the recorded tape was that of the former Russian colonel Sergey Dubinsky. His voice had been recognised by a former soldier who had fought alongside Dubinsky in the Russian war in Afghanistan in the eighties. The former comrade-in-arms who had given the interview, Serhiy Tiunov, said that he did not believe Dubinsky was the main culprit. 'He is the key witness, but not the killer. And also, he is my colleague. I want him to stay alive. I think he didn't press the button of that Buk, only coordinated its transportation.' Dubinsky himself was quoted as saying 'the bastards in Moscow' were responsible for the tragedy. Official Moscow sources dismissed the tapes with Dubinsky's voice as 'internet fakes'.

In February the Dutch investigators were still trying to make sense of the Russian radar data. The Dutch national prosecutor's office said 'many uncertainties' remained about the radar images supplied by the Russian authorities. The issues centred on the differing formats in which the radar data had been presented. It couldn't be determined with certainty whether the images were authentic and what precisely they showed, the prosecutor claimed. The Russians were surprised that it had taken the investigators so long to acknowledge that there was a problem in deciphering the Russian data; Russia was willing and ready to help the international investigators 'translate' the radar data, but the Dutch had so far not requested any help and had only asked for additional data. 'If Dutch investigators couldn't decipher data from Russia, they could have asked for help,' military expert Aleksandr Tazekhulakhov said. 'The problem here is that the Dutch have attempted to keep Russian representatives out of the MH17 probe,' he added.

Three months after Ukraine launched its allegations against Russia at the International Court of Justice in The Hague, that court said that it would not impose measures ordering Russia to stop funding and equipping pro-Russia separatists as sought in the case brought against Moscow by Ukraine. The court said it was refusing the request by Ukraine to issue a provisional measure to block what Kiev said was Russian monetary and military support for separatists in eastern Ukraine. Even if Ukraine's other accusations were to be upheld by the ICJ, taking action on such a ruling would be a difficult matter given that the court has no means of enforcement. The MH17 was not mentioned.

By the end of April, the relatives were caught up in a legal battle to obtain the images captured by Schiphol airport's security cameras on 17 July 2014. The victims had been caught on camera and these moving images were the last recordings of the MH17 passengers. For three years the relatives had begged the prosecution, which had this footage in its possession, to let them see what the security cameras had filmed. But the prosecution had bluntly refused to share the footage from the thirty-four security cameras that had been operating in the departure hall and lounge. The prosecution claimed that the images were not clear enough for anyone to be recognisable.

However, two families had received footage during the first days after the crash. They had obtained this through the efforts of the family counsellor. As part of a help program for the relatives, counsellors had been appointed to each family who had lost a loved family member. These two families had been able to witness the last moments of their loved ones before they boarded the plane, and now the other relatives wanted the consolation those last images had brought to the two families—they wanted to see their loved ones alive and strolling around the departure hall, happy to be going on holidays.

Important as this was, it raised a question of privacy, as is always the case whenever footage is shared, as there were also images of other passengers at Schiphol, passengers who had nothing to do with MH17. Nonetheless, many relatives expressed their wish to view the footage, indicating they would be willing to sign a privacy statement. They were not going to back down.

In May 2017, as the war dribbled on, Kiev hosted the Eurovision Song Contest. Russia had at first declined to send an entrant but then at the last moment it changed its mind. But Ukraine barred Russia's contestant—Yulia Samoylova, who uses a wheelchair—from entering the country because she had once visited Crimea and sang for an audience there. Travel to Crimea by foreign nationals without prior authorisation from the Kiev government had been regarded as a crime in Ukraine since Russia's 2014 annexation of the region. The year before in 2016, Russia had accused Ukraine of politicising the song festival by choosing a Crimean Tatar as its contestant. Russian foreign ministry official Grigory Karasin, speaking to Interfax news agency, called the decision to bar Samoylova 'another outrageous, cynical and inhuman act by the Kiev authorities'.

In the meantime, Ukraine's claim that Russia had violated two UN conventions was considered by the chairman of the UN International Court of Justice, Ronny Abraham. Ukraine was now given a further thirteen months to submit evidence of Russia's violations, with that opportunity expiring on 12 June 2018. After that, the Russian side would have exactly the same period of time to submit objections and counter-arguments. Thus the complete position of both parties would come before the court no earlier than 12 July 2019.

Just days before the third anniversary of the MH17 tragedy, the G7 foreign ministers of Canada, France, Germany, Italy, Japan, the United Kingdom and the United States, as well as the high representative of the European Union, called on Russia to cooperate with MH17 investigators. They found the JIT's findings on Russia's role in the downing of MH17 compelling, significant and deeply disturbing. The G7 recalled that UN Security Council Resolution 2166 demanded that all states cooperate fully with efforts to establish accountability.

As 17 July approached, suspects were being named and traced. The five countries that were working together in the investigation of the shooting chose the Netherlands as the country where suspects would eventually be prosecuted. 'With this decision we are taking a next step on the way to uncover the truth, the prosecution of suspects and satisfaction for the bereaved,' Dutch prime minister Mark Rutte said in a statement posted on Facebook. 'This remains the highest priority for the Dutch government.'

Announcing a venue for a future trial without felons to try as the disaster's third anniversary approached was nothing more than a sign of recognition that closure was needed and that the relatives needed to know a resolution was still being pursued. Whether it would ever be reached was still very uncertain. The whole inquiry had been grinding forward at a glacial pace, thanks to the difficulty in ascertaining who exactly directed the missile system from the battlefields of eastern Ukraine.

To back the choice of the Netherlands as the country where a trial would be held, Australian prime minister Malcolm Turnbull and Australian foreign minister Julie Bishop issued a joint statement: 'The investigation team's decision to support a Dutch national prosecution will ensure that results from the investigation are taken into account and that justice for the victims and their families, including the 38 people who called Australia home, is delivered. While we cannot take away the grief of those who lost their loved ones because of this atrocious act, we are committed to holding the perpetrators to account and achieving justice for all the victims.'

As far as Australia was concerned, the choice for the Dutch legal system was an 'important step' in the prosecution process.

The probe into who could be held responsible was extensive although still no suspect had been officially identified so far. Washington also welcomed the decision to grant jurisdiction to the Dutch courts for the prosecution of those responsible for the tragedy. The US had full confidence in the ability of the Dutch criminal justice system to conduct a prosecution that would not only be comprehensive but also objective and just.

The memory of the crash remained an open wound for the people of the Netherlands. Three years after MH17 was shot down, the disaster's memorial day in Amsterdam brought together families from around the world. Some two thousand people attended the opening of a new memorial at Vijfhuizen, near Schiphol airport. The monument—a curved steel wall and an eye-shaped sculpture engraved with the victims' names—was placed in an amphitheatre surrounded by 298 trees, still saplings, planted in the form of a commemorative ribbon. The memorial was attended by the Dutch King and Queen. All 298 names of the victims were read out during the ceremony.

Earlier in March families had come together to each plant a sapling to commemorate their loved ones. The forest was to take on the shape of the black memorial ribbon that is often worn as a symbol for the disaster. Relatives were asked to choose a tree to represent their loved ones from ten different species. Around the forest thousands of sunflowers were planted.

Fifteen lime trees were planted for the Malaysia Airlines crew members, and in the following months family members of the victims each planted their own trees for their missing relatives. Some buried their loved one's ashes at the base of the tree. Some relatives planted just one tree, but those who had lost more than one family member would plant a tree for each of the family's victims. All 298 saplings had a plaque bearing the name of a MH17 passenger. Many branches of the different trees bore cards and ribbons sent by grandparents, friends, cousins and brothers and sisters.

Jon and Meryn O'Brien, who lost their 25-year-old son, Jack, in the disaster, had come to Amsterdam from their home in Sydney to attend the memorial. Jack's mother shed tears as she looked at the photograph pinned to the tree of her only son, his smiling face looking out over the memorial park. Three years down the track, the O'Briens, like many others, had still not come to terms with their son's death. There was a life before Jack died, and another after Jack died.

Their son had been on a seven-week trip through Europe that also included trips to Moscow and St Petersburg, but he had never made it home. Their only consolation was that Jack had sent messages about how much he was enjoying his trip. The photos he had forwarded to his sister and parents showed him standing in an eerie twilight in midsummer Iceland, running with the bulls in Pamplona and the different meals he had managed to devour along the way. Jack had been so close to coming back to his parents, but fate had chosen differently that day. And now they were placing trinkets from Jack's family and friends in Australia—ribbons and knitted scarfs in the colours of his Winston Hills football team—on the branches of a tree more than ten thousand kilometres away in the Netherlands.

Jon and Meryn O'Brien realised that the investigative and prosecution process would probably take years to play out, but their son had lost his chance to live so the truth mattered. They had sent letters to Putin pleading with him to reveal all he knew. The relatives all felt that some responsibility must lie with Ukraine for not closing its airspace during the conflict, and with Malaysia Airlines, which had continued to fly over Ukraine.

By now most relatives realised that justice for this tragic incident was not going to be a two-year process but more like a ten-year process. The JIT would only get one chance to do this right and, in the meantime, everybody was asked to remain patient. Family members were motivated to keep the publicity pressure on, because that was what would finally make the case move forward. They would keep what happened on 17 July 2014 alive and they would keep the victims in the public eye until those who were responsible were brought to justice.

By now most of the relatives assumed that the chance of suspects actually being tried was very small. Mostly they just wanted to have the whole story set out in front of a judge. They wanted names, what happened, who was responsible, including the chain of command that had been in charge of this strategy. They of course wanted to see those responsible tried and sentenced in the Netherlands, but they also realised this was something that wasn't going to happen any time soon. Some wondered if the MH17 case would ever come to any satisfying end.

In Australia a memorial was unveiled outside Parliament House in Canberra. A large contingent of the victims' relatives attended the ceremony along with Australia's ambassador to the Netherlands. And earlier that day, more than ninety family members attended a memorial in Malaysia for victims and a briefing about the ongoing probe. Malaysian transport minister Liow Tiong Lai told reporters after the event that the investigation was 'very detailed and we are quite convinced that we will be able to find the culprits'. But foreign minister Julie Bishop said in a statement that those behind the shooting down of MH17 may have to be tried in absentia. Bishop promised to use every legal avenue to bring those responsible to justice.

Every year the people of Hrabove, where the plane had come down, conducted their own memorial at the site where a shrine had been erected. A number of villagers had been badly traumatised after they confronted the enormity of the body count. Bodies had fallen into their gardens and in one case a body had fallen through a kitchen roof. Many villagers were still suffering from these vivid memories, which kept them awake at night and made them anxious about any loud noises.

Near the end of 2017 Bellingcat identified one of the high-ranking military that the JIT had been searching for over quite some time. In September 2016, the Joint Investigation Team had announced the preliminary results of its MH17 investigation and asked researchers to help identify the voices of two people captured in a radio transmission about the delivery of a Buk missile to the separatists. In the conversation, intercepted and released by Ukrainian national security officials in July 2014, the men address each other only by call signs and names that could easily have been invented. One was 'Delfin' or 'Dolphin', the other 'Orion'.

The JIT had been attempting to identify the two people behind the voices on these tapes as both were suspected of having played a significant role in the downing of MH17. Bellingcat now said it had reasonable evidence to link one voice on the tape, that of Delfin, to a Russian general. On the tapes a man's voice can be heard talking about a convoy heading for Snizhne, the village near which people claimed to have seen a Buk launching system. After analysing the voice on the tape, Bellingcat concluded that the wanted man called 'Delfin' must be Colonel General Nikolaj Fjodorovitsj Tkatsjov. Bellingcat admitted that the evidence was circumstantial, but they still referred it to the JIT. They continued searching for the other voice on the tape, that of a man with the code name 'Orion'.

In November Dutch forensic experts received more fragments of human remains found in east Ukraine. Freelance journalist Patrick Lancaster had collected twenty-three fragments and handed them over to the Ukrainian authorities, who sent them to the Netherlands to be tested. First it was assumed that the fragments had come from animals but, after testing, fifteen of the twenty-three fragments were found to have human DNA, and eight of those were traced to people who had died in the disaster.

Chapter 24
2018

At the beginning of 2018 one of the most persistent rumours about the MH17 tragedy was exposed as being a lie. Over the years, the Kremlin and its media—and occasionally some of the Western media—had put forward a number of contradictory and sometimes highly implausible alternative theories on MH17, such as:

'MH17 was blown up by a missile intended for the Russian president's plane.'

'It was already full of dead bodies and deliberately crashed.'

'It was shot down by a Buk missile, but not one of Russia's.'

'MH17 was shot down by a Ukrainian jet.'

This last theory in particular ricocheted around Russian state media and on Twitter; according to this account, two Ukrainian fighter jets had flown close to the Boeing 777 shortly before it disappeared from the radar. But beyond this claim it had always been clear what Russia's guiding position on the tragedy was:

Ukraine was to blame. 'The state over whose territory this occurred bears responsibility for this awful tragedy,' Putin told a meeting of economic advisers just after the crash.

So the theory that a Ukrainian jet had been responsible for the downing was the one that Moscow persistently clung to; it even named the pilot and offered a witness. This theory, so strongly advocated by Russia, initially caused doubt in the West, especially because Ukraine had not closed its airspace even though in the days preceding the disaster there had been several air battles in the area, including the downing of a Ukrainian military cargo plane from a high altitude. When a 'Spanish air traffic controller', who went by the name of 'Carlos' and allegedly worked at Boryspil airport in Kiev, reported on Twitter that he had noticed two Ukrainian fighter jets flying close to Flight MH17 just before the crash, it had increased the degree of doubt in the West.

But after people began to investigate the identity of this mysterious 'Carlos', some major questions were raised. Jose Carlos Barrios Sanchez, a Spaniard by birth, claimed he had worked for several years as a traffic controller. Kiev airport stated that all their air traffic controllers were and always had been Ukrainian, and that they would never employ a Spaniard to do this kind of work at the airport.

Sanchez turned out to be a conman who was wanted in Spain for forgery and misappropriation of property. As the chairman of an apartment cooperative association near Madrid, Sanchez had pocketed thousands of euros that belonged to the association. After a court in Madrid sentenced him to six months in prison, he fled to Bucharest, where he was extradited for duping eight Romanian citizens and sent back to Spain. Carlos soon disappeared from Russia's account as a swirl of speculation rose about the veracity of his claims.

After Carlos was disclosed as a fraud, Russian media outlets published reports of a new key witness who could back the Ukrainian jet theory. This new anonymous witness said that on 17 July he was staying on the air base in the village of Aviatorskoe, near Dnepropetrovsk, and claimed to have seen a Su-25 jet that had previously been loaded with air-to-air missiles returning to base with one missile missing. The pilot of the aircraft, Captain Vladislav Voloshin, had been exceptionally nervous after landing, and talked about the 'wrong plane'.

Questions about the feasibility of a Su-25 downing MH17 were again raised. Were the Russians telling the truth? It would seem that an experienced pilot like Voloshin would have noticed it was the wrong plane before he fired a missile at it. Flight MH17 was a big aircraft and not one that could be mistaken for a Russian spy aircraft.

If it had flown so close to the civilian aircraft, the MH17 pilots would have noticed the jet on its radars; but the Dutch Safety Board report states that: 'No aural warnings or alerts of aircraft system malfunction were heard on the cockpit voice recording, which ended at 13.20.03 hours. Crew communication gave no indication that there was anything abnormal with the flight.'

The DSB also concluded that only a rocket fired from the ground had the explosive power displayed in the destruction of

MH17 and that the missile of a Su-25 would have left a very different damage pattern.

Captain Vladislav Voloshin had from the start called the Russian allegation a lie. He denied that he had been carrying air-to-air missiles and said that he had never flown his jet on 17 July. He had however flown his aircraft on 23 July and his load had been air-to-surface weapons for ground targets.

After the Russian accusations in December 2014, Voloshin quit the Ukrainian Air Force and became acting director of Mykolaiv International Airport in 2017. In Ukraine he was a war hero who had flown thirty-three combat missions in a low-flying Su-25 ground attack jet against Russian-backed separatist rebels in eastern Ukraine and had been awarded a medal for bravery. But after he left the army, his colleagues at work reported that he had been feeling depressed. Voloshin took his own life at his home in Mykolaiv, near the Black Sea, in March 2018.

On the day the pilot took his life, his wife heard a gunshot and ran to him. She immediately called police and an ambulance, but a team of paramedics arriving on the scene was unable to save him. Voloshin's father said: 'The reason for his death was obviously the war—and everyday problems.'

After MH17 was shot down, the International Civil Aviation Organization (ICAO), among its other responses, set up a Conflict Zone Information Repository as a means of sharing relevant information among states and air carriers about the routes they fly.

The Dutch Safety Board, which had issued eleven recommendations about flying over conflict zones in its October 2015 final report on the downing of MH17, in early 2018 launched an investigation to assess what follow-up there had been to its recommendations. The board said it wanted to determine the measures that parties had taken regarding airspace management in conflict zones and the sharing of information about threats. The board also said it would look at how operators consider flying over conflict zones in their risk analyses. According to the report: 'The investigation shows that a range of measures has been implemented. However, the effect on flight safety is difficult to measure. States and airlines around the world are aware of the issue at stake and devote more attention to it. Stakeholders no longer assume that open airspace over a conflict zone actually guarantees safe passage. Airlines are taking a more structured approach to analysing the risks and uncertainties, scaling up to a higher risk level at an earlier stage. Some airlines state that they now decide more quickly to refrain from overflying specific areas if no clear information relating to such areas is available.'

At the beginning of March 2018 former Russian double agent Sergei Skripal and his daughter Yulia became the victims of a nerve-gas poisoning in Salisbury, England. England immediately pointed the finger at Russia, saying that their involvement was very plausible, even though there was no hard evidence. But the outrageous use of a banned Russian nerve agent on British soil was the first chemical weapon attack in Europe since the Second World War and, in retaliation, Great Britain immediately expelled Russian diplomats. Australia, the United States and several European countries, including the Netherlands—did the same. Twenty-eight nations together expelled a total of 153 Russian diplomats in an unprecedented demonstration of global solidarity with the United Kingdom.

Relatives of the MH17 victims, however, were furious. No diplomats had been ordered to leave the country after their loved ones were murdered. Why were the Netherlands and Australia so eager to take measures in this case? Prime Minister Mark Rutte hurried to explain that the two cases were totally different and could not be compared. 'The Netherlands must be neutral in the MH17 case, because otherwise the investigation will be discredited,' he said. 'If we point the finger at one country then the chances decrease that we will ever get the perpetrators to court.'

On 26 May the JIT held a press conference. The team presented evidence about the origin of the Buk TELAR (transporter erector launcher and radar) that was involved in the downing of MH17, saying it had belonged to the 53rd Anti-Aircraft Missile Brigade based near the city of Kursk, Russia. The JIT also presented seven unique characteristics of the Buk owned by that anti-aircraft brigade.

As long ago as May 2016 Bellingcat had published its report on the unique characteristics of the Buk. The JIT report now was mostly based on what Bellingcat had presented in 2016, but this evidence had now been thoroughly investigated so that it could stand up in court. They also claimed to have irrefutable evidence that a Russian-based brigade was responsible for the crime. The

JIT had asked the Russian Federation to provide information on the whereabouts of the 53rd brigade in July 2014, but Moscow had not responded to these requests. Although presented as new information, most people who had followed the news about MH17 over the years had heard it all before.

The Joint Investigation Team found itself forced to seek other avenues to obtain information about the perpetrators and once again requested help from the public so it could finalise its investigation into the 53rd brigade. Answers to a number of questions were needed:

Who were the members of the Buk crew?

Who gave them instructions, and what were they?

Who was responsible for the operational deployment of the Buk?

Who can provide information on the 53rd brigade?

The next day on 25 May, Bellingcat, jointly with *The Insider*, the Moscow-based investigative website run by Roman Dobrokhotov, and the Washington bureau of the US newspaper company McClatchy, held a press conference in the Netherlands. Researchers claimed 'with very high certainty' that they had located the man who went by the code name 'Orion'. Together with 'Delfin', he was suspected of having coordinated pro-Russian separatists in the region and he had most likely played a role in the MH17 tragedy. The man in question turned out to be a Russian military intelligence officer named Oleg Ivannikov, who previously served (under a different name) as defence minister for the breakaway republic of South Ossetia. Oleg was a missile specialist who was in charge of military operations in eastern Ukraine during an 'undercover deployment' by Russia at the time of the downing of the MH17.

When the researchers called his home number and recorded the Russian officer's voice, it turned out to be very similar to the voice of 'Orion' in the radio transmission intercepted by Ukrainian officials in 2014. The voice was unusually high for a man; at the press conference it was described as 'womanish'. Even though both audio fragments were too short for forensic computer-assisted audio analysis, a linguistic and acoustic comparison of the two voices compellingly pointed to the voices belonging to the same person.

As a result, on 25 May 2018, Australia and the Netherlands put out a statement. They were officially holding Russia responsible for its part in the downing of MH17. The Netherlands and Australia were now convinced that Russia was responsible for the deployment of the Buk installation that was used to down MH17 and were finally taking the next step by formally holding Russia accountable. Holding the Russian Federation responsible under international law was separate, but complementary, to the prosecution of individual suspects. It was up to the Dutch Public Prosecution Service to decide if and when individuals would be identified as suspects and indicted. Locating these suspects was still an ongoing JIT investigation.

President Putin rejected these accusations by the Netherlands and Australia. When asked if a Russian missile had shot down the aircraft, Putin replied: 'No, of course not.' He added that Moscow did not trust the Dutch-led MH17 inquiry, because Russia wasn't given full access to its work. Russia's defence ministry also denied supplying the Buk. Experts in Moscow were still in the process of analysing videos presented by Dutch investigators, the ministry said. According to the Dutch JIT coordinator Fred Westerbeke, the investigation was in its 'final phase' and it wouldn't take many more years to find missing information. Australian foreign minister Julie Bishop called for international support for the Dutch–Australian legal initiative.

That same month the world turned its focus to Russia for a totally different reason: Russia was to host the football World Cup. On the eve of the World Cup, eleven MH17 relatives wrote a compelling and heartfelt letter to the Russian people. The letter began: 'In June the world will turn its eyes toward Russia for the Football World Cup. It will be a long awaited and joyous event. For most Russians it will also be an occasion of deep national pride. Some of us who write these words are passionate followers of football, others are not. But none of us will be able to share in this World Cup in the way we would have done before. We have something in common that gives this event and the place in which it is held, a different, darker meaning.'

The letter went on to explain how their lives were shattered and how three years on they still struggled to comprehend what happened that day. That their children, parents, brothers, sisters and partners were killed in a war, but that they were aware their loved ones were not the only ones who had lost their lives.

'More than 10,000 people have been killed, most of them civilians. Their families are grieving like ours, not understanding why the people they love have been snatched from them.

It is the finality of death that is so painful. We could live with a separation, even of years, if we knew it had an end.

'We are not the same people we were before. The world we live in is darker and less hopeful. We have struggled to maintain faith in human goodness. It may be that some of us will find some sense of purpose and happiness again. But we will always be marked by the brutal and sudden death of those we love.'

The open letter to Russia sought to hold 'the chain of command that led to the shooting down of MH17' accountable for the incident, whilst accepting the innocence of 'ordinary Russian people'.

'Like all who have suffered the violent death of people we love, we are tempted to respond with hate. But we have to separate ordinary Russian people from the individuals responsible—the chain of command that led to the shooting down of MH17. Most of us don't know Russian people well. Hate and distrust come partly from ignorance and when we know more of a person's story, that can change how we see things.' The letter went on to ask the Russian government to cooperate fully with the international investigation into MH17.

'It will not bring our families back, but the truth does matter, the truth does exist and we want those responsible for MH17 to be identified and held accountable. We have confidence in the thoroughness and impartiality of the work conducted by the Joint Investigation Team. The same cannot be said about the reporting on MH17 coming out of Russian state media channels.' The letter questioned whether the Russian people really wanted to live in a country where the truth does not exist.

At the end of the letter the writers commemorated Flight 9268, an international chartered passenger flight operated by Russian Metrojet. On 31 October 2015 the Airbus carrying 224 passengers and crew was destroyed by a bomb above the northern Sinai following its departure from Sharm El Sheikh International Airport, Egypt, en route to Pulkovo airport, St Petersburg, Russia, killing everyone on board. The plane was mostly filled with tourists.

'In 2014 our children and families lay lifeless amidst the fields and sunflowers of Eastern Ukraine. In 2015 Russian children and families lay lifeless on the stones and sand of the Egyptian desert. In death we are not so different. Barriers of language, culture, differences in race or religion no longer matter. What remains is loss and love. Human loss and love.'

The letter was signed by:

Jon and Meryn O'Brien (Jack O'Brien, 25), Australia

Jeremy and Louise Pocock (Ben Pocock, 20), United Kingdom

Rob Fredriksz and Silene Fredriksz-Hoogzand (Bryce Fredriksz, 23, Daisy Oehlers, 20), Netherlands

Joanna Anderson (Stephen Anderson, 44), United Kingdom

Claudio Villaca-Vanetta (Glenn R. Thomas, 49), United Kingdom

Hans de Borst (Elsemiek de Borst, 17), Netherlands

Paul Guard (Roger Guard, 67, Jill Guard, 62), Australia

Every year since the downing of Malaysia Airlines Flight MH17 over Ukraine on 17 July 2014, the US State Department had issued a statement to mark the anniversary. But on the anniversary of 2018 the State Department was conspicuously silent about it.

Officials had prepared a draft statement that was sharply critical of Russia for its alleged role in the attack. The statement was to be issued a day after Donald Trump met with Vladimir Putin in Helsinki but, for reasons the State Department did not explain, it never was. Based on a cached version of the US embassy's website in Moscow, it appeared on the home page briefly on Tuesday 17 July, but then it was quickly taken down.

Trump lavished praise on Putin in Helsinki and stunned US lawmakers and national security experts by siding with Russia against the US intelligence community's assessments of Russian interference in the 2016 presidential campaign. Trump later claimed he misspoke regarding Russia's interference, when he said the word 'would' instead of 'wouldn't'. The sentence Trump referred to was: 'I don't see any reason it would be Russia.'

Rin Norris and Anthony Maslin, who had lost their three children and the children's grandfather, were beside themselves with rage. Anthony delivered a scathing attack on Donald Trump over his attitude towards Russia. He took his anger to Facebook, posting an open letter addressed to Trump, saying the MH17 tragedy 'destroyed our life and many other lives in the process'.

'Mr Trump, you invented and speak a lot about "fake news". But let's try talking about something that is not fake,' he wrote in his Facebook post, 'let's call them irrefutable facts. That passenger flight MH17 was shot out of the sky and 298 innocent people were murdered is an irrefutable fact,' he wrote alongside a photo of his children Mo, Evie and Otis. Anthony Maslin went on to accuse Trump of kissing Putin's arse, also describing this an irrefutable fact; he said he did not feel anger toward the two men, but something much worse—pity. 'You have no empathy for your fellow man, and you clearly have no idea what love is. So you have nothing.'

In September 2018, Russia's defence ministry claimed it had 'newly discovered evidence' that potentially pinned the attack on Ukraine. According to the defence ministry, the serial number found on debris from the Buk missile was cross-referenced with a logbook purporting to show it was produced in 1986. The missile was then delivered by rail to a military unit in western Ukraine and, to their knowledge, had not left Ukraine since. Russia was implying that the missile was fired by Kiev's forces. Ukraine's defence minister, Stepan Poltorak, dismissed Russia's claims as an 'absolute lie' and 'another fake story'. In a statement on 17 September, the JIT said it would 'meticulously study the materials presented as soon as the Russian Federation makes the relevant documents available to the JIT as requested in May 2018' and required under a UN Security Council resolution.

At the end of September, the Dutch minister of foreign affairs, Stef Blok, let his Russian counterpart, Sergey Lavrov, know that he would like to talk to him about the MH17 disaster. The Dutch minister had bumped into Lavrov in New York, where the general meeting of the United Nations was being held. Blok urged Lavrov to join him at the negotiating table to try to come to some kind of understanding. Lavrov said it was too early to come to any conclusion about the MH17, simply because the investigation was ongoing. And he certainly did not see any reason why Russia should express apologies in the matter.

In October the Dutch authorities revealed that they had expelled four Russian spies in April after they were caught trying to hack into the Organisation for the Prohibition of Chemical Weapons. Dutch investigators said the spies also intended to travel onwards to the Spiez Laboratory in Switzerland, which was at that time testing novichok samples from the Skripal poisoning in Salisbury. Among the men arrested in The Hague was one officer accused of conducting 'malign activity' targeting Malaysian institutions investigating the downing of flight MH17.

Chapter 25

Empty chairs

In July 2019, five years will have passed since the MH17 plunged into a sunflower and wheat field in eastern Ukraine. If anything, the disaster has made clear that international peace and security cannot be taken for granted and that, if we turn our heads away from what is happening in the world, disasters will continue to happen. International and internal terrorism, as well as the unrestricted flow of conventional and high-tech weaponry, have no regard for state borders, national sovereignty or human lives. Worldwide, foreign policy should be more than just a short-term national interest. The fate of Flight MH17 has taught us that problems other countries face can quickly become disastrous for all of us.

The war in Ukraine is still raging. Despite the focus on Ukraine's problems in the aftermath of the MH17 tragedy, the ongoing civil war has once again faded into the background—a forgotten war in which every day people still lose their lives.

The dead are reduced to little more than anonymous statistics in a conflict that has taken well over ten thousand lives. On an international scale little has been done to ease the plight of the people in eastern Ukraine. Russian 'humanitarian' convoys trundle into the area regularly, but no one really knows what exactly is being transported in those trucks. The USA claims it is 'aiding' Ukraine, but this 'aid' is only meant to be used for boosting defence resources. Kiev has said it will use the funds to buy anti-tank weapons. And so the fight for power in a dilapidated industrial area in an unassuming part of the world rattles on.

For the MH17 families, there was a life before 17 July 2014 and a life after it. The initial shock and grief of losing family members was followed by a period of almost unbearable uncertainty before the bodies were returned. When the remains were finally brought home, the slow process of identification began. To help with identification, relatives were asked to donate DNA and to answer countless questions about the victim's external characteristics—whether they had tattoos, or were ever operated on, or about the underwear they had worn that day. The forensic specialists asked for clothes, jewellery, toothbrushes, all dental records as well as family photos showing the victim's teeth. The long process of identification, returning possessions and dealing with practical matters was excruciatingly hard.

When the redeeming news of a victim's identification was finally passed on to their families, the sad ritual of the burial followed. For some this brought closure; for others it was an agonising reality that truly brought home what had happened on that devastating day.

Some relatives received bodies that were fully intact while others were almost intact. But many relatives only received body parts to bury—some only a finger or bone fragment. A few families had already conducted a funeral and buried what they thought was left of their loved one's remains, only to have forensics tell them that more body parts had been found. It forced them to choose to either organise another funeral ceremony or have the additional remains buried or cremated without commemoration.

Two victims remained totally missing. No body part was ever found of sixteen-year-old Gary Slok or Alex Ploeg (fifty-eight), both Dutch. Gary Slok's father, Jan, went to Eindhoven airport eleven times, hoping every time that remains of Gary, however small, would be in one of the caskets unloaded from the plane. After these arrivals both Jan Slok and Alex's brother Piet Ploeg would wait anxiously to hear from the forensics, but neither ever received that telephone call.

Although many relatives and friends felt their lives had ended that day, life went on regardless. Everyone dealt with their loss differently and in their own time. At the end of 2016, relatives and friends planted the trees for their loved ones at the National Monument MH17 in Vijfhuizen. The Australian parents of Jack O'Brien, Jon and Meryn, found it somehow helped to plant the tree and place small trinkets from family members on its branches; however, for Silene Fredriksz-Hoogzand, the act of planting the sapling had felt like betrayal, as if she had replaced her son, Bryce, and his girlfriend, Daisy, with a tree. 'I had a son. Now I have a tree.' It had made her all the angrier for her loss.

Viewing the wreckage also evoked mixed emotions. Before this, the victims' deaths for some remained an abstraction, something they had heard about but had no actual physical proof of. But when they were confronted by the wreckage, all hope ended at the sight of those scattered plane parts in that cold hangar.

While the downing of MH17 was shocking, it is rare, but not unprecedented, for civilian airliners to be shot down. On 4 October 2001 the Ukrainian military accidentally shot down a Russian civilian plane while carrying out exercises on the Crimean peninsula. They had launched a surface-to-air missile that struck a Siberia Airlines plane as it was travelling from Tel Aviv to Novosibirsk, Russia: all seventy-eight people on board were killed, and the plane disintegrated over the Black Sea. Much earlier, on 3 July 1988, Iran Air Flight 655, en route from Bandar Abbas in Iran to Dubai, was shot down by surface-to-air missiles from the US warship USS *Vincennes*, killing all 290 passengers, including sixty-six children and sixteen crew members.

On 1 September 1983 Korean Air Lines Flight 007, travelling from New York City to Seoul, was shot down by a Soviet fighter plane. The plane had deviated from its original planned route and flown through Soviet prohibited airspace; the Soviet Air Forces mis-identified the aircraft as an intruding US spy plane and proceeded to attack it with air-to-air missiles. It disappeared in the Sea of Japan, killing all 269 passengers and crew. And on 27 June 1980, Itavia Flight 870 from Bologna to Palermo crashed in the Tyrrhenian Sea, near Sicily, killing eighty-one passengers and crew members; although initially there was doubt as to how and why the plane had crashed, investigators concluded that it was 'abundantly clear' that the plane was downed by a missile strike. The history of civilian planes being shot from the skies in fact goes back as far as 1955, when El Al Flight 402 travelling from Vienna to Tel Aviv was shot down by two Bulgarian MiG fighters. Bulgaria admitted to having shot the plane down 'in error'.

With all these cases having disappeared from our collective memory, it is puzzling why, five years down the track, the MH17 downing is still firmly anchored there. Like the above examples, the MH17 disaster was more or less an intentional attack, although the plane itself may have been mistaken by the perpetrators for an enemy aircraft. But the downing of MH17 was never just another plane crash: what made it truly different was that for the first time in history an aircraft disaster left a long trail of digital information, and users of social media were quicker to gather information about what had happened than the regular news organisations.

The rise of the internet and social media has undoubtedly been a contributing factor to the global awareness of this tragedy. On the evening after the disaster, followers of Facebook and Twitter said they had discovered more news about the downing on social media than through regular media outlets such as newspapers and television. People on the scene immediately took to social media with photos and film, even showing the burning parts of the plane just after it had landed in the Ukrainian fields. The stunningly abundant and constant stream of news and footage flooding the internet increased worldwide awareness of the disaster. At the time of previous similar aircraft disasters, social media was non-existent or in its early stages, and so these events slipped quickly into oblivion, sometimes within just days or weeks.

What distinguishes Flight MH17 from other plane crashes is also due to the incredibly complex nature of the disaster. Often in crisis situations the cause surfaces relatively quickly after the occurrence. The story surrounding a disaster, although often not fully coherent, will be pretty much clear within a week of it happening. This was not the case when it came to MH17. Because the plane was shot down in a war zone, it took a long time for experts to access the area, and the cause of the crash and the identity of the perpetrators are still subject to ongoing investigation.

The perception of the disaster was, and still is, dominated by the information presented by politicians, the media and the internet. Because of its international dimension, the MH17 disaster is a highly political affair. Over time the disaster turned into an international crisis that brought back memories of the Cold War, with Russia on one side and the West on the other. Some say that Russia's constant refusal to show any accountability for its role in the disaster is one of the most shameful demonstrations ever of refusing to accept blame where a major international incident is concerned. Others say Ukraine, as one of the possible suspects, should never have been given membership of the JIT, where it can influence the investigation and exert veto power over the dissemination of findings.

Many facts surfaced after a long period of time, so insights as to the how and why of the downing had to be continually adjusted. After the first hours, people roaming the disaster area were accused of looting; but later, when wedding rings and other items, such as a wallet smelling of smoke and kerosene but with 300 euros still tucked inside it, were returned, relatives mellowed and their judgement became less rigid and more realistic.

No one has officially been accused of the act of downing the MH17. While investigators have called for information on two possible suspects, no charges have yet been brought and no one has appeared at the high-security court based in the business area close to Schiphol airport where any future trial will be held. The ongoing investigation helps keep the story alive, with regular feeds to the media keeping the public informed.

There are still many questions left unanswered concerning Flight MH17 and many of them will most likely stay unanswered for a long time to come. For the relatives and friends of the MH17 victims the wait is by no means over.

Jan Slok is still waiting for his son's remains. Many relatives are waiting for the right party to be held accountable. Piet Ploeg, the brother of Alex Ploeg, is still waiting for answers, but he isn't pointing the finger: 'I'm not very interested in who pushed the button, but [I want to know] who was responsible, which organisation, which country. It could be Russia, it could be Ukraine, it could be the separatists.'

Some families are still waiting for compensation from the airline company, for full cooperation from Russia, for an apology from the separatists ('Even if they didn't mean to shoot down a commercial airliner, there is one word we want to hear: and that is "sorry"'), all of them are waiting for the truth.

Quite quickly after the crash, relatives came together and formed a group, the MH17 Disaster Foundation. Many victims were relatively young; they were well-educated and socially and or politically active, as were many of their relatives. The Disaster Foundation has been instrumental in keeping the memory of the victims of the MH17 alive. Every year on 17 July they organise a memorial and they helped found the memorial in Vijfhuizen.

Over the years the MH17 Disaster Foundation has kept the story of their murdered loved ones alive in the media by using Twitter or Facebook accounts, by speaking about the disaster on television and in newspapers, and by sending letters to politicians as well as world leaders, seeking attention on a regular basis.

Many victims have been commemorated with scholarships, institutes, boats, park benches and plaques in their name. An AIDS institute in Amsterdam was named after Joep Lange, the prominent AIDS specialist who died on the flight. The institute will focus its attention on the poorest people in developing countries, to ensure they get adequate medical treatment. The establishment of the institute was funded by the Dutch government as well as by an American contributor.

A local football field was named after Stefan van Nielen.

Gary Slok's football club, Excelsior, initiated the Gary Slok award for goalkeeper of the year.

Newcastle United announced a new community award to be named after Liam Sweeney and John Alder.

AFEW (AIDS Foundation East-West) International set up the Martine de Schutter Scholarship Fund, which allows participants from Eastern Europe and central Asia to attend the International AIDS Conference.

Four years down the track families still struggle to come to terms with their grief. Hans de Borst, the father of Dutch victim Elsemiek de Borst, posted a heartbreaking tweet about his daughter on the eve of the fourth anniversary of the downing: 'Every time I think I cannot miss you more than I am missing you now, it appears that I can!'

Most relatives have a photo of their lost loved ones on them, on their mantelpieces, hanging in their homes or in photobooks. They are precious relics; the dead will remain as old as the last picture that was taken of them, there will never be a new photo added to the collection.

Although gone, family members are reminded of them almost every day, sometimes in unexpected ways. A few days after the MH17 crashed, a letter found its way to the home of Stefan van Nielen, the young victim whose brother, Martijn, had escaped the disaster because he had taken a different route to Kuala Lumpur. Stefan had envisioned a life in the tropics and the letter to him was from the Bali company to whom he had applied for a job: his job application had been accepted, the letter said.

Their loved ones no longer being present in their everyday lives is obviously the hardest outcome for the families to cope with. Quinn Schansman's father says that he still expects his son, who travelled a lot, to come through the door any minute: 'I keep thinking, well this time he's been gone for so long . . .' A mother of a MH17 victim claims that 'there is nothing more prominently present in one's life than a child that isn't there anymore'. A father wonders if he will one day be strong enough to be able to remember his son's life, instead of always thinking of his son in terms of his death.

Anthony Maslin and Marite Norris lost their three young children and Marite's father in the MH17 disaster. Their lives were torn apart by the deaths. Two years after that horrific event the couple showed the world that, although hatred has the power to destroy life, it is love that possesses the unique ability to create it. Their daughter, Violet May Maslin, came into the world on 10 May 2016. 'We still live with pain, but Violet, and the knowledge that all four kids are with us always, brings light to our darkness. Violet's birth is a testament to our belief that love is stronger than hate.' The message was signed by Anthony Maslin and Marite Norris.

In June 2018, 298 empty chairs were placed in front of the Russian embassy in The Hague, Netherlands. It was meant as a silent protest in the name of those who were no longer there and no longer had a voice. The year before, in the same park opposite the embassy, the same group had installed a remembrance bench carrying the following message to Russia: 'Take responsibility and be transparent.' The message the activists conveyed to the president, government and people of Russia in June 2018 was: '298 people, 80 of them forever children, have nothing to celebrate today. Their seats remain empty. Those who sealed their fate are silent and look away.'

Today the chairs have gone, but the memorial bench is still there.

Appendix

List of victims

MH17 technical and cabin crew in order of rank as supplied by MAS

CAPTAIN	WAN AMRAN BIN WAN HUSSIN	MALAYSIA
CAPTAIN	CHOO JIN LEONG, EUGENE	MALAYSIA
FIRST OFFICER	AHMAD HAKIMI BIN HANAPI	MALAYSIA
FIRST OFFICER	MUHAMAD FIRDAUS BIN ABDUL RAHIM	MALAYSIA
IN-FLIGHT SUPERVISOR	MOHD GHAFAR BIN ABU BAKAR	MALAYSIA
CHIEF STEWARDESS	DORA SHAHILA BINTI KASSIM	MALAYSIA
CHIEF STEWARDESS	AZRINA BINTI YAKOB	MALAYSIA
LEADING STEWARDESS	LEE HUI PIN	MALAYSIA
LEADING STEWARDESS	MASTURA BINTI MUSTAFA	MALAYSIA
FLIGHT STEWARDESS	CHONG YEE PHENG	MALAYSIA
FLIGHT STEWARD	SHAIKH MOHD NOOR BIN MAHMOOD	MALAYSIA
FLIGHT STEWARD	SANJID SINGH SANDHU	MALAYSIA
FLIGHT STEWARDESS	HAMFAZLIN SHAM BINTI MOHAMEDARIFIN	MALAYSIA
FLIGHT STEWARDESS	NUR SHAZANA BINTI MOHAMED SALLEH	MALAYSIA
FLIGHT STEWARDESS	ANGELINE PREMILA RAJANDARAN	MALAYSIA

MH17 passenger manifest in alphabetical order as supplied by MAS

ALDER/JOHN	UNITED KINGDOM
ALLEN/CHRISTOPHER	NETHERLANDS
ALLEN/IAN	NETHERLANDS
ALLEN/JOHN	UNITED KINGDOM
ALLEN/JULIAN	NETHERLANDS
ANDERSON/STEPHEN LESLIE	UNITED KINGDOM
ANGHEL/ANDRE	CANADA
ANTHONYSAMY/MABEL	MALAYSIA
AVNON/ITHAMAR	NETHERLANDS
AYLEY/ROBERT	UNITED KINGDOM
BAAY/JOYCE	NETHERLANDS
BAKER/THERESA	AUSTRALIA
BAKER/WAYNE	AUSTRALIA
BAKKER/WILLEM	NETHERLANDS
BATS/ROWEN	NETHERLANDS
BELL/EMMA	AUSTRALIA
BINDA/NATASHJA	NETHERLANDS
BINTAMBI/MUHAMMAD AFRUZ	MALAYSIA
BINTAMBI/MUHAMMAD AFZAL	MALAYSIA
BINTITAMBI/MARSHA AZMEENA	MALAYSIA
BORGSTEEDE/HELEN	NETHERLANDS
BRAS/CATHARINA	NETHERLANDS
BROGHAMMER/WILHELMINA LOUISE	GERMAN
BROUWER/THERESE	NETHERLANDS
BROUWERS/ELISABETH	NETHERLANDS
CAMFFERMAN/ANTON	NETHERLANDS
CHARDOME/BENOIT	BELGIUM
CLANCY/CAROL	AUSTRALIA
CLANCY/MICHAEL	AUSTRALIA
CROLLA/REGIS	NETHERLANDS
CUIJPERS/EDITH	NETHERLANDS
DALSTRA/AUKE	NETHERLANDS
DALZIEL/CAMERON	UNITED KINGDOM
DANG/MINHCHAU	NETHERLANDS
DANG/QUOCDUY	NETHERLANDS
DAVISON/FRANCESCA	AUSTRALIA

DAVISON/LIAM	AUSTRALIA
DE BORST/ELSEMIEK	NETHERLANDS
DE BRUIN/BARBARA MARIA	NETHERLANDS
DE HAAN/JOHANNA	NETHERLANDS
DE JONG/ANNETJE	NETHERLANDS
DE KUIJER/PIM WILHELM	NETHERLANDS
DE LEEUW/SASKIA	NETHERLANDS
DERDEN/LILIANE	AUSTRALIA
DE RIDDER/ESTHER	NETHERLANDS
DE ROO/JOOP ALBERT	NETHERLANDS
DESADELEER/CHRISTIENE	NETHERLANDS
DE SCHUTTER/MARIA ADRIANA	NETHERLANDS
DE VOS/MAARTEN	NETHERLANDS
DE VRIES/AAFKE	NETHERLANDS
DEWA/SHALIZA ZAINI	MALAYSIA
DE WAAL/ESTHER	NETHERLANDS
DJODIKROMO/DONNY TOEKIRAN	NETHERLANDS
DYCZYNSKI/FATIMA	GERMAN
ENGELS/LISANNE LAURA	NETHERLANDS
ERNST/TAMARA	NETHERLANDS
ESSERS/EMMA	NETHERLANDS
ESSERS/PETER	NETHERLANDS
ESSERS/VALENTIJN	NETHERLANDS
FAN/SHUN PO	NETHERLANDS
FOO/MING LEE	MALAYSIA
FREDRIKSZ/BRYCE	NETHERLANDS
GAZALEE/ARIZA BINTI	MALAYSIA
GIANOTTEN/ANGELIQUE	NETHERLANDS
GOES/KAELA MAYA JAY	MALAYSIA
GOES/PAUL	NETHERLANDS
GRIPPELING/MARCO	NETHERLANDS
GROOTSCHOLTEN/WILHELMUS	NETHERLANDS
GUARD/JILL HELEN	AUSTRALIA
GUARD/ROGER WATSON	AUSTRALIA
GUNAWAN/DARRYL	PHILIPPINES
GUNAWAN/HADIONO	INDONESIA
GUNAWAN/IRENE	PHILIPPINES
GUNAWAN/SHERRYL	PHILIPPINES

HAKSE/ANNEMIEKE	NETHERLANDS
HALLY/DAVY JOSEPH GERARDUS	NETHERLANDS
HALLY/MEGAN	NETHERLANDS
HASTINI/YULI	INDONESIA
HEEMSKERK/GEERTRUIDA	NETHERLANDS
HEERKENS/LIDWINA	NETHERLANDS
HEMELRIJK/ROBIN	NETHERLANDS
HENDRY/MR	INDONESIA
HIJMANS/SUSAN	NETHERLANDS
HOARE/ANDREW	UNITED KINGDOM
HOARE/FRISO	NETHERLANDS
HOARE/JASPER	NETHERLANDS
HOONAKKER/KATHARINA	NETHERLANDS
HORDER/HOWARD	AUSTRALIA
HORDER/SUSAN	AUSTRALIA
HORNIKX/ASTRID	NETHERLANDS
HUIJBERS/PIETER JAN WILLEM	NETHERLANDS
HUIZEN/ARNOUD	NETHERLANDS
HUIZEN/YELENA/CLARICE	INDONESIA
HUNTJENS/MARIA	NETHERLANDS
IOPPA/OLGA	GERMAN
JANSSEN/CORNELIA	NETHERLANDS
JESURUN/KEVIN	NETHERLANDS
JHINKOE/RISHI	NETHERLANDS
JIEE/TAMBI BIN	MALAYSIA
JRETNAM/SUBASHNI	MALAYSIA
KAMSMA/MATTHEUS	NETHERLANDS
KAMSMA/QIUM	NETHERLANDS
KAPPEN/YVONNE	NETHERLANDS
KARDIA/VICKILINE KURNIATI	INDONESIA
KARNAILSINGH/KARAMJITSINGH	MALAYSIA
KEIJZER/KARLIJN	NETHERLANDS
KOOIJMANS/BARRY	NETHERLANDS
KOOIJMANS/ISA	NETHERLANDS
KOOIJMANS/MIRA	NETHERLANDS
KOTTE/OSCAR	NETHERLANDS
KOTTE/REMCO	NETHERLANDS
KROON/HENDRIK ROKUS	NETHERLANDS

LAHAYE/JOHANNES	NETHERLANDS
LAHENDA/GERDA LELIANA	INDONESIA
LAMBREGTS/HUBERTUS	NETHERLANDS
LANGE/JOSEPH	NETHERLANDS
LAUSCHET/GABRIELE	GERMAN
LEE/JIANHAN BENJAMIN	MALAYSIA
LEE/KIAH YEEN	MALAYSIA
LEE/MONA CHENG SIM	AUSTRALIA
LEE/WHY KEONG	AUSTRALIA
LIEW/YAU CHEE	MALAYSIA
LOH/YANHWA	NETHERLANDS
MAAS/HENRICUS	NETHERLANDS
MAHADY/EDEL	AUSTRALIA
MAHLER/EMIEL	NETHERLANDS
MARCKELBACH/LISA	NETHERLANDS
MARTENS/ELIZABETH	NETHERLANDS
MARTENS/SANDRA	NETHERLANDS
MASLIN/EVIE COCO ANNE	AUSTRALIA
MASLIN/MO ROBERT ANDERSON	AUSTRALIA
MASLIN/OTIS SAMUEL FREDERICK	AUSTRALIA
MASTENBROEK/TINA PAULINE	NETHERLANDS
MAYNE/RICHARD	UNITED KINGDOM
MDSALIM/MOHDALIBIN	MALAYSIA
MEIJER/INGRID	NETHERLANDS
MEIJER/SASCHA	NETHERLANDS
MENKE/GERARDUS	NETHERLANDS
MENKE/MARY	NEW ZEALAND
MEULEMAN/HANNAH SOPHIA	NETHERLANDS
MISRAN/ANELENE ROSTIJEM	NETHERLANDS
MOORS/AUGUSTINUS	NETHERLANDS
MULA/MELINGANAK	MALAYSIA
NELISSEN/JOHANNA	NETHERLANDS
NG/LYETI ELISABETH	MALAYSIA
NG/QINGZHENG	MALAYSIA
NG/SHIING	MALAYSIA
NGUYEN/NGOCMINH	NETHERLANDS
NIEBURG/TIM	NETHERLANDS
NIEVEEN/DAFNE	NETHERLANDS

NIEWOLD/TALLANDER FRANCISCUS	NETHERLANDS
NOOR/RAHIMMAH	MALAYSIA
NOREILDE/JAN	BELGIUM
NOREILDE/STEVEN	BELGIUM
NORRIS/NICOLL CHARLES ANDERSON	AUSTRALIA
NUESINK/JOLETTE	NETHERLANDS
OBRIEN/JACK SAMUEL	AUSTRALIA
OEHLERS/DAISY	NETHERLANDS
ORESHKIN/VICTOR	AUSTRALIA
OTTOCHIAN/JULIAN	NETHERLANDS
OTTOCHIAN/SERGIO	NETHERLANDS
PALM/LUBBERTA	NETHERLANDS
PANDUWINATA/MIGUEL G	NETHERLANDS
PANDUWINATA/SHAKA T	NETHERLANDS
PARLAN/HASNI HARDI BIN	MALAYSIA
PAULISSEN/JOHNNY	NETHERLANDS
PAULISSEN/MARTIN	NETHERLANDS
PAULISSEN/SRI	NETHERLANDS
PIJNENBURG/SJORS ADRIANUS	NETHERLANDS
PLOEG/ALEX	NETHERLANDS
PLOEG/ROBERT	NETHERLANDS
POCOCK/BENJAMIN	UNITED KINGDOM
PUNJABI/KAUSHALYA JAIRAMDAS	MALAYSIA
RAAP/HIELKJE	NETHERLANDS
RENKERS/JEROEN	NETHERLANDS
RENKERS/TIM	NETHERLANDS
RISAH/DAISY	NETHERLANDS
RIZK/ALBERT	AUSTRALIA
RIZK/MAREE	AUSTRALIA
RUIJTER/CATHARINA	NETHERLANDS
RYDER/ARJEN	AUSTRALIA
RYDER/YVONNE	AUSTRALIA
SCHANSMAN/QUINN	NETHERLANDS
SCHILDER/CORNELIS	NETHERLANDS
SCHUYESMANS/RIK	BELGIUM
SIDELIK/HELENA	AUSTRALIA
SITIAMIRAH/BINTIPARAWIRA	MALAYSIA
SIVAGNANAM/MATTHEW EZEKIAL	MALAYSIA

SIVAGNANAM/PAUL RAJASINGAM	MALAYSIA
SLOK/GARY	NETHERLANDS
SMALLENBURG/CARLIJN	NETHERLANDS
SMALLENBURG/CHARLES	NETHERLANDS
SMALLENBURG/WERTHER	NETHERLANDS
SMOLDERS/MARIA	NETHERLANDS
SOETJIPTO/JANE ADI	INDONESIA
SOUREN/PETER	NETHERLANDS
SPECKEN/REINMAR	NETHERLANDS
STUIVER/CORNELIA	NETHERLANDS
SUJANA/WAYAN	INDONESIA
SUPARTINI/MRS	INDONESIA
SWEENEY/LIAM	UNITED KINGDOM
TAMBI/MUHAMMAD AFIF BIN	MALAYSIA
TAMTELAHITU/CHARLES ELIZA DAVID	NETHERLANDS
TAN/SIEW POH	MALAYSIA
TEOH/ELAINE	MALAYSIA
THEISTIASIH/YODRICUNDA	INDONESIA
THOMAS/GLENN RAYMOND	UNITED KINGDOM
TIERNAN/MARY	AUSTRALIA
TIMMERS/GERARDUS	NETHERLANDS
TOL/CORNELIA	NETHERLANDS
TOURNIER/HENDRIK JAN	NETHERLANDS
TRUGG/LIV	NETHERLANDS
TRUGG/REMCO	NETHERLANDS
TRUGG/TESS	NETHERLANDS
UIJTERLINDE/THAMSANQA	NETHERLANDS
VAN DE KRAATS/LORENZO	NETHERLANDS
VAN DE KRAATS/ROBERT JAN	NETHERLANDS
VAN DE MORTEL/JEROEN	NETHERLANDS
VAN DE MORTEL/MILIA	NETHERLANDS
VAN DEN HENDE/JOHANNES RUDOLFUS	NETHERLANDS
VAN DEN HENDE/MARGAUX LARISSA	NETHERLANDS
VAN DEN HENDE/MARNIX REDUAN	NETHERLANDS
VAN DEN HENDE/PIERS ADNAN	NETHERLANDS
VAN DEN SCHOOR/CHRISTINA ANNA ELISA	NETHERLANDS
VAN DER GRAAFF/LAURENS	NETHERLANDS
VAN DER LEIJ/JENNIFER	NETHERLANDS

VAN DER LINDE/MARK	NETHERLANDS
VAN DER LINDE/MEREL	NETHERLANDS
VAN DER LINDE/ROBERT	NETHERLANDS
VAN DER MEER/BENTE	NETHERLANDS
VAN DER MEER/FLEUR	NETHERLANDS
VAN DER MEER/SOPHIE	NETHERLANDS
VAN DER POEL/ERICUS	NETHERLANDS
VAN DER SANDE/PAULUS	NETHERLANDS
VAN DER SANDE/STEVEN	NETHERLANDS
VAN DER SANDE/TESSA	NETHERLANDS
VAN DER SAR/INGE	NETHERLANDS
VAN DERSTEEN/JAN	NETHERLANDS
VAN DER WEIDE/FRANK	NETHERLANDS
VAN DOORN/APRIL	NETHERLANDS
VAN DOORN/CAROLINE	NETHERLANDS
VAN DUIJN/GIJSBERT	NETHERLANDS
VAN ELDIJK/PETRONELLA	NETHERLANDS
VAN GEENE/RENE	NETHERLANDS
VAN HEIJNINGEN/ERIK PETER	NETHERLANDS
VAN HEIJNINGEN/ZEGER LEONARD	NETHERLANDS
VAN KEULEN/ALLARD	NETHERLANDS
VAN KEULEN/JEROEN	NETHERLANDS
VAN KEULEN/ROBERT	NETHERLANDS
VAN LANGEVELD/PETRA	NETHERLANDS
VAN LUIK/KLAAS WILLEM	NETHERLANDS
VAN MENS/LUCIE PAULA MARIA	NETHERLANDS
VAN MUIJLWIJK/ADINDA LARASATI PUTRI	NETHERLANDS
VAN MUIJLWIJK/EMILE	NETHERLANDS
VAN NIELEN/STEFAN F W	NETHERLANDS
VAN TONGEREN/JACQUELINE	NETHERLANDS
VAN VELDHUIZEN/ANTHONIUS	NETHERLANDS
VAN VELDHUIZEN/PIJKE	NETHERLANDS
VAN VELDHUIZEN/QUINT	NETHERLANDS
VAN VREESWIJK/HUUB	NETHERLANDS
VAN WIGGEN/WINNEKE	NETHERLANDS
VAN ZIJTVELD/FREDERIQUE	NETHERLANDS
VAN ZIJTVELD /ROBERTJAN	NETHERLANDS
VERHAEGH/KIM ELISA PETRONELLA	NETHERLANDS

VERMEULEN/MARIE	NETHERLANDS
VLEESENBEEK/ERIK	NETHERLANDS
VOORHAM/CORNELIA	NETHERLANDS
VORSSELMAN/WOUTER	NETHERLANDS
VRANCKX/ELINE	NETHERLANDS
WAGEMANS/HENDRIK	NETHERLANDS
WALS/AMEL	NETHERLANDS
WALS/BRETT	NETHERLANDS
WALS/JEROEN	NETHERLANDS
WALS/JINTE	NETHERLANDS
WALS/SOLENN	NETHERLANDS
WELS/LEONARDUS	NETHERLANDS
WELS/SEM	NETHERLANDS
WESTERVELD/INEKE	NETHERLANDS
WIARTINI/KETUT	INDONESIA
WITTEVEEN/MARIT	NETHERLANDS
WITTEVEEN/WILLEM	NETHERLANDS
YURIANI/NINIK	INDONESIA
ZANTKUIJL/DESIREE	NETHERLANDS

Acknowledgements

To write this book I have read thousands of newspaper articles, watched many heart-wrenching and revealing documentaries, read through lengthy investigation reports, and have spoken to a number of people.

This has not been an easy story to tell. While writing, my days were often clouded by tears, anger, disbelief and shame but there was also awe and admiration for people, who despite the unbelievable loss they had suffered, regained the courage to stand up and face life again. They will grieve for the rest of their lives, but they will not let hatred win.

Thank you once again to Richard Walsh, for reading and editing the first draft, for his probing queries and for all the days he supported me when doubt and lack of confidence took hold. His direction has been invaluable.

Thank you Rebecca Kaiser, who once again managed to turn all my bits and bobs into an actual book, for her support and patience. And all the other staff at Allen & Unwin who helped along the way. Thank you to my copyeditor Simone Ford who meticulously went through the whole manuscript and asked erudite questions that made me rethink some aspects of the story.

Thank you to Bob, Kasper and Jialu, without your love and support there would be no book.

Notes

As well as the material listed in the references, the following sources informed chapters.

Chapter 1

Correspondence with Renuka Manisha Virangna Birbal.

Chapter 2

Peter Byrne, 'From prison to president', *Kiev Post,* 11 February 2010, <www.kyivpost.com/article/content/ukraine-politics/from-prison-to-president-59338.html>.

Richard E. Berg-Andersson, 'The view from the brink: The "Ukraine Crisis" now casts a shadow over Election 2014', *The Green Papers*, 6 March 2014, <www.thegreenpapers.com/PCom/?20140306-0>.

The Ukraine Crisis Timeline, <http://ukraine.csis.org/>.

'Ukraine court boosts powers of President Yanukovych', *BBC News*, 1 October 2010, <www.bbc.com/news/world-europe-11451447>.

'Ukrainian PM attacked by egg thrower', *ABC News*, 25 September 2004, <www.abc.net.au/news/2004-09-25/ukrainian-pm-attacked-by-egg-thrower/557906>.

'The Orange Revolution and the Yushchenko presidency', *Encyclopedia Britannica*, <www.britannica.com/place/Ukraine/The-Orange-Revolution-and-the-Yushchenko-presidency>.

Chapter 3

'Firdaus' dream to be a dad cut short', *The Star*, 3 September 2014, <www.thestar.com.my/news/nation/2014/09/03/firdaus-dream-to-be-a-dad-cut-short-first-officers-wife-is-expecting-their-first-baby/>.

Chai Hung Yin, 'Flight attendants found love on MH17 years ago', *TNP*, 20 July 2014, <www.tnp.sg/news/flight-attendants-found-love-mh17-years-ago>.

Chapter 4

Elizabeth Piper, 'Special Report: Why Ukraine spurned the EU and embraced Russia', *Reuters*, 19 December 2013, <www.reuters.com/article/us-ukraine-russia-deal-special-report-idUSBRE9BI0DZ20131219>.

Michael B Kelley, 'Ukraine Just Made A "Civilization Defining" Decision—And It Picked Russia Over The West', *Business Insider*, 21 November 2013, <www.businessinsider.com/ukraine-wont-sign-eu-agreement-2013-11?international=true&r=US&IR=T>.

Oksana Grytsenko, 'Yanukovych confirms refusal to sign deal with EU', *Kyiv Post*, 26 November 2013, <www.kyivpost.com/article/content/ukraine-politics/yanukovych-confirms-refusal-to-sign-deal-with-eu-332493.html>.

Gabriel Gatehouse, 'The untold story of the Maidan massacre', *BBC News*, 20 February 2016, <www.bbc.com/news/magazine-31359021>.

Borislaw Bilash II, 'Euromaidan protests: The revolution of dignity', *Euromaidan Press*, 20 February 2016, <http://euromaidanpress.com/2016/02/20/the-story-of-ukraine-starting-from-euromaidan/2/>.

Nina Schuyffel, 'Kritiek Medvedev op bezoek ministers demonstratie Kiev', *Trouw,* 6 December 2013, <www.trouw.nl/home/kritiek-medvedev-op-bezoek-ministers-demonstratie-kiev~aedeb8a4/>.

'Kerry's Statement on Ukraine', *The New York Times*, 10 December 2013, <www.nytimes.com/2013/12/11/world/europe/kerrys-statement-on-ukraine.html>.

Chapter 5

Andy Dolan, Michael Seamark and Jason Groves, 'British victims MH17 revealed', *Daily Mail*, 18 July 2014, <www.dailymail.co.uk/news/article-2697082/Twins-dear-brother-I-love-Agony-sister-British-UN-worker-Flight-MH17-crash-victims.html>.

Anna Leask, 'MH17 widow's vow to her two boys', *News Mail*, 29 September 2014, <www.news-mail.com.au/news/mh17-widows-vow-her-two-boys/2402116/>.

Keiran Southern, 'MH17 Tragedy: Liam Sweeney and John Alder nominated for Mirror Football Fan of the Year', *Chronicle Live*, 21 April 2015, <www.chroniclelive.co.uk/news/north-east-news/mh17-tragedy-liam-sweeney-john-9090684>.

'MH17 crash: Tributes paid to Briton Robert Ayley', *BBC News*, 19 July 2014, <www.bbc.com/news/uk-28385567>.

Natalie Savino, 'Sunbury MH17 victims Albert and Maree Rizk to be honoured one year after tragic Malaysian Airlines crash', *Hume Leader*, 9 July 2015, <www.heraldsun.com.au/leader/north-west/sunbury-mh17-victims-albert-and-maree-rizk-to-be-honoured-one-year-after-tragic-malaysian-airlines-crash/news-story>.

Louise Cheer, 'Inseparable couple: Family of MH17 victims Mary and Gerry Menke pay tribute to the "devoted parents" and "doting grandparents"', *Daily Mail*, 25 July 2014, <www.dailymail.co.uk/news/article-2705603/MH17-victims-Mary-Gerry-Menkes-family-say-inseparable.html>.

Chapter 6

'Fighting continues in gov't controlled town of Krasny Liman', *CCTV*, 20 June 2014, <http://english.cntv.cn/2014/06/20/VIDE1403222043696558.shtml>.

Oksana Grytsenko and Shaun Walker, 'Kiev becomes a battle zone as Ukraine protests turn fatal', *The Guardian*, 22 January 2014, <www.theguardian.com/world/2014/jan/22/ukraine-opposition-leaders-meet-president-protests-fatal>.

Enjoli Liston and Charlotte McDonald-Gibson, 'Ukraine protests: Demonstrators stand firm despite resignation of prime minister Mykola Azarov', *Independent*, 28 January 2014, <www.independent.co.uk/news/world/europe/ukraine-protesters-stand-firm-despite-resignation-of-prime-minister-mykola-azarov-9091381.html>.

Chapter 7

Ingrid Harms, 'Obitury, Joep Lange (1954 – 2014)', <www.vn.nl/joep-lange-1954-2014/>.

'Inmemoriam Pim de Kuijer D66', <https://66.nl/in-memoriam-pim-de-kuijer/>.

Edward Malnick, Tom Brooks-Pollock, Lily Willis and Simon Johnson, 'Flight MH17: Ex BBC man Glenn Thomas and former RAF team leader among British victims', *The Telegraph*, 18 July 2014, <www.telegraph.co.uk/news/worldnews/europe/ukraine/10977536/Flight-MH17-Ex-BBC-man-Glenn-Thomas-and-former-RAF-team-leader-among-British-victims.html>.

Chapter 8

John Simpson, 'Russia's Crimea plan detailed, secret and successful', *BBC News*, 9 March 2014, <www.bbc.com/news/world-europe-26644082>.

Simon Shuster, 'Gunmen seize parliament in Ukraine's Russian stronghold', *Time*, 27 February 2014, <time.com/10149/gunmen-seize-parliament-in-ukraines-russian-stronghold/>.

Alan Yuhas and Raya Jalabi, 'Ukraine's revolution and Russia's occupation of Crimea: how we got here', *The Guardian*, 5 March 2014, <www.theguardian.com/world/2014/mar/05/ukraine-russia-explainer>.

Sophie Pinkham, 'How annexing Crimea allowed Putin to claim he had made Russia great again', *The Guardian*, 22 March 2017, <www.theguardian.com/commentisfree/2017/mar/22/annexing-crimea-putin-make-russia-great-again>.

The Kremlin, 'Agreement on the accession of the Republic of Crimea to the Russian Federation signed', <en.kremlin.ru/events/president/news/20604>.

Alan Yuhas, 'Ukraine crisis: an essential guide to everything that's happened so far', *The Guardian*, 13 April 2014, <www.theguardian.com/world/2014/apr/11/ukraine-russia-crimea-sanctions-us-eu-guide-explainer>.

Will Englund, 'Kremlin says Crimea is now officially part of Russia after treaty signing, Putin speech', *The Washington Post*, 18 March 2014, <www.washingtonpost.com/world/russias-putin-prepares-to-annex-crimea/2014/03/18/933183b2-654e-45ce-920e4d18c0ffec73_story.html?utm_term=.ae606e553622>.

Noah Sneidermarch, 'Mindful of past, many Tatars fear a Russian future', *The New York Times*, 13 March 2014, <www.nytimes.com/2014/03/14/world/europe/crimean-tatars-on-guard-against-joining-russia.html>.

Alissa de Carbonnel and Alessandra Prentice, 'Armed men seize two airports in Ukraine's Crimea, Yanukovich reappears', *Reuters*, 28 February 2014, <www.reuters.com/article/uk-ukraine/armed-men-seize-two-airports-in-ukraines-crimea-yanukovich-reappears-idUKBREA1H0EM20140228>.

Harriet Salem and Shaun Walker, 'Russian armoured vehicles on the move in Crimea', *The Guardian*, 28 February 2014, <www.theguardian.com/world/2014/feb/28/gunmen-crimean-airports-ukraine>.

'Timeline Political crisis in Ukraine', *Aljazeera*, 20 September 2014, <www.aljazeera.com/news/europe/2014/03/timeline-ukraine-political-crisis-201431143722854652.html>.

Chapter 9

Neil Walker, 'Mt Eliza couple lost in MH17 disaster', *The News*, 20 July 2014, <mpnews.com.au/2014/07/20/mt-eliza-couple-lost-in-mh17-disaster/>.

Erel Straathof, 'Darryl (19) vierde het leven vol overgave tot vlucht MH17', *Het Parool*, 21 July 2014, <www.parool.nl/amsterdam/darryl-19-vierde-het-leven-vol-overgave-tot-vlucht-mh17~a3692780/>.

'RIP: Cameron Dalziel', *Sea Rescue South Africa*, 18 July 2014, <www.nsri.org.za/2014/07/rip-cameron-dalziel/>.

'For many on board, flight held promise of new beginnings', *The Japan Times*, 24 July 2014, <www.japantimes.co.jp/news/2014/07/24/world/a-kiss-a-prayer-last-hours-of-the-mh17-plane-crash-victims/>.

Cindy Wockner, 'Living nightmare for Dutch grandparents of three Victorian children who died on Malaysia Airlines flight', *News.com.au*, 26 July 2014, <www.news.com.au/travel/travel-updates/incidents/mh17-living-nightmare-for-dutch-grandparents-of-three-victorian-children-who-died-on-malaysia-airlines-flight/news-story/332a>.

Chapter 10

'East Ukraine separatists seek union with Russia', *BBC News*, 12 May 2014, <www.bbc.com/news/world-europe-27369980>.

Julian Borger and Alec Luhn, 'Ukraine's acting president calls for action against pro-Russian separatists', *The Guardian*, 23 April 2014, <www.theguardian.com/world/2014/apr/22/ukraine-acting-president-calls-relaunch-anti-terror-operation>.

'Ukraine rebels hold referendums in Donetsk and Luhansk', *BBC News*, 11 May 2014, <www.bbc.com/news/world-europe-27360146>.

Daan Heijink, 'Wat gebeurt er precies in Oost-Oekraïne?', *NU*, 15 April 2014, <www.nu.nl/weekend/3752262/gebeurt-er-precies-in-oost-oekraine-.html>.

Philippus Zandstra, 'Oekraïne herovert vliegveld Kramatorsk en omsingelt Slavjansk', *NRC*, 15 April 2014, <www.nrc.nl/nieuws/2014/04/15/oekraine-leger-voert-speciale-operatie-uit-in-kramatorsk-bestormt-vliegveld-slavjansk-a1425741>.

Max Delany, 'Mysterious Russian fixer heads Ukraine rebel state', *The Times of Israel*, 18 May 2014, <www.timesofisrael.com/mysterious-russian-fixer-heads-ukraine-rebel-state>.

Andrew Higgins, 'In Ukraine, Russia plays a weighted word game', *The New York Times*, 16 April 2014, <www.nytimes.com/2014/04/17/world/europe/in-ukraine-russia-plays-a-weighted-word-game.html?_r=0>.

РИА Новости Украина, <rian.com.ua/analytics/20140303/340429692.html>.

'Geen uitstel referendum Donetsk', <nos.nl/artikel/645344-geen-uitstel-referendum-donetsk.html>.

Shaun Walker, Oksana Grytsenko and Howard Amos, 'Ukraine: pro-Russia separatists set for victory in eastern region referendum', *The Guardian*, 12 May 2014, <www.theguardian.com/world/2014/may/11/eastern-ukraine-referendum-donetsk-luhansk>.

Simon Denyer and Anna Nemstova, 'Eastern Ukrainians vote for self-rule in referendum opposed by West', *The Washington Post*, 11 May 2014, <www.washingtonpost.com/world/europe/ukraines-rebels-say-they-are-seeking-a-mandate-not-independence-in-referendum/2014/05/11/ac02688a-d8dc-11e3-aae8-c2d44bd79778_story.html?utm_term=.94356315e9ed>.

Olexiy Goncharenko, *Voorzitter van de Odessa Regional Council*, 16 October 2014, <blogs.pravda.com.ua/authors/goncharenko/534e20581d582/>.

Shaun Walker, 'An audience with Ukraine rebel chief Igor Bezler, the Demon of Donetsk', *The Guardian*, 29 July 2014, <www.

theguardian.com/world/2014/jul/29/-sp-ukraine-rebel-igor-bezler-interview-demon>.

Germain Moyon, 'Pro-Russian Gubarev, a symbol of east Ukraine separatism', *Digital Journal*, 9 March 2014, <www.digitaljournal.com/news/world/pro-russian-gubarev-a-symbol-of-east-ukraine-separatism/article/375337>.

'Luhansk People's Republic appoints Russian lobbyist to head Council of Ministers', *The Moscow Times*, 4 July 2014, <themoscowtimes.com/news/luhansk-peoples-republic-appoints-russian-lobbyist-to-head-council-of-ministers-37040>.

'First head of Russian-backed "Luhansk People's republic" Bolotov reported dead', *Euromaidan Press*, 28 January 2017, <euromaidanpress.com/2017/01/28/luhansk-donbas-ukraine-russia-bolotov-plotnitskiy/>.

'Latest news from the OSCE Special Monitoring Mission to Ukraine (SMM), based on information received until 18:00 hrs, 2 June (Kyiv time)', *OSCE*, <www.osce.org/ukraine-smm/119479>.

'Ukraine crisis: Military plane shot down in Luhansk', *BBC News*, 14 June 2014, <www.bbc.com/news/world-europe-27845313>.

Andrew E. Kramer, 'Separatists down military transport jet, killing 49 in Eastern Ukraine', *The New York Times*, 14 June 2014, <www.nytimes.com/2014/06/15/world/europe/ukraine.html>.

'In de greep van Poetin [In the grips of Putin]', *NPO*, 9 March 2014, <www.npo.nl/in-de-greep-van-poetin/09-03-2014/WO_KRO_794073>.

Harriet Salem, 'Who's who in the Donetsk People's Republic', *Vice*, 2 July 2014, <news.vice.com/article/whos-who-in-the-donetsk-peoples-republic>.

Chapter 11

'De Slachtoffers van Vlucht MH17', *de Volkskrant*, redactie 25 July 2014, <www.volkskrant.nl/nieuws-achtergrond/de-slachtoffers-van-vlucht-mh17~bf09e09e/>.

Marleen van Wesel, 'De wolken van Laurens', *Mare*, 26 May 2016, <www.mareonline.nl/archive/2016/05/25/de-wolken-van-laurens>.
'VU herdenkt slachtoffers MH17', Vrije Universiteit Amsterdam, <www.vu.nl/nl/nieuws-agenda/nieuws/2014/jul-sep>.
Lauren Hayes and Simon Day, 'Former Queenstown man on MH17', *Stuff*, 21 July 2014, <www.stuff.co.nz/national/10288814/Former-Queenstown-man-on-MH17>.
'In memoriam: vlucht MH17,' *Humo*, 22 December 2014, <www.humo.be/humo-archief/314291/in-memoriam-vlucht-mh17>.

Chapter 12

'Fighting continues in gov't controlled town of Krasny Liman', *CCTV*, 20 June 2014, <english.cntv.cn/2014/06/20/VIDE1403222043696558.shtml>.
David Stern, 'Ukraine's President Petro Poroshenko declares ceasefire', *BBC News*, 20 June 2014, <www.bbc.com/news/world-europe-27948335>.
Roland Oliphant and agencies, 'Ukraine army helicopter "shot down by pro-Russian rebels" less than 24 hours after ceasefire', *The Telegraph*, 24 June 2014, <www.telegraph.co.uk/news/worldnews/europe/ukraine/10923253/Ukraine-army-helicopter-shot-down-by-pro-Russian-rebels-less-than-24-hours-after-ceasefire.html>.
Steven Pifer, 'Poroshenko signs EU–Ukraine Association agreement', *Brookings*, 27 June 2014, <www.brookings.edu/blog/up-front/2014/06/27/poroshenko-signs-eu-ukraine-association-agreement/>.
Andrew Higgins and David M. Herszenhornjune, 'Defying Russia, Ukraine signs E.U. trade pact', *The New York Times*, 27 June 2014, <www.nytimes.com/2014/06/28/world/europe/ukraine-signs-trade-agreement-with-european-union.html>.
'Ukraine crisis: Separatists frustrated Russian support for insurgency dwindles Kyiv says separatists, Russia refusing to meet for

ceasefire talks', *CBC News*, 10 July 2014, <www.cbc.ca/m/touch/world/story/1.2703505>.

Jaroslav Koshiw, 'Donetsk separatists in dispute—Khodakovsky vs Strelkov', *Open Democracy*, 11 August 2014, <www.opendemocracy.net/od-russia/jaroslav-koshiw/donetsk-separatists-in-dispute–khodakovsky-vs-strelkov>.

'Ukraine separatists admit Russian fighters are among their ranks', *CBS News*, 28 May 2014, <www.cbsnews.com/news/russian-citizens-no-longer-hiding-among-ukraine-insurgents/>.

Charles Recknagel and Merhat Sharipzhan, 'Donetsk separatists dig in for street fighting', 17 July 2014, <www.rferl.org/a/ukraine-donetsk-separatists-dig-in/25460807.html>.

Richard Balmforth and Natalia Zinets, 'Ukraine jets pound rebels after deadly missile attack', *Reuters*, 12 July 2014, <www.reuters.com/article/us-ukraine-crisis/ukraine-jets-pound-rebels-after-deadly-missile-attack-idUSKBN0FH09720140712>.

'Ukraine crisis: Bridges destroyed outside Donetsk', *BBC News*, 7 July 2014, <www.bbc.com/news/world-europe-28191833>.

Peter Leonard, 'Ukraine says military transport plane shot down in east; blames Russia', *Global News*, 14 July 2014, <globalnews.ca/news/1449254/ukraine-military-plane-shot-down-along-russian-border/>.

'Ukraine forces clash with separatists at Donetsk airport', *BBC News*, 10 July 2014, <www.bbc.com/news/world-europe-28255174>.

Victoria Butenko, 'Ukraine forces take control of Donetsk airport, military spokesman says', *CNN*, 21 July 2014, <edition.cnn.com/2014/07/21/world/europe/ukraine-crisis-donetsk/index.html>.

Quintin Van Zyl, 'Ukraine crisis: why is there such a fierce battle for Donetsk airport?', *The Telegraph*, 22 January 2015, <www.telegraph.co.uk/news/worldnews/europe/ukraine/11363058/Ukraine-crisis-why-is-there-such-a-fierce-battle-for-Donetsk-airport.html>.

Jaroslav Koshiw, 'Donetsk separatists in dispute—Khodakovsky vs Strelkov', *Open Democracy*, 11 August 2014, <www.opendemocracy.net/od-russia/jaroslav-koshiw/donetsk-separatists-in-dispute%E2%80%93khodakovsky-vs-strelkov>.

Chapter 13

Kees Graafland, 'Ouders naar rampplek MH17: 'Onze dochter leeft nog', 24 July 2014, <www.ad.nl/buitenland/ouders-naar-rampplek-mh17-onze-dochter-leeft-nog~af6a96fb/>.

Malika Sevil, 'Achter dat mooie gezicht van Karlijn (25) ging een briljant brein schuil', *Het Parool*, 23 July 2014, <www.parool.nl/amsterdam/-achter-dat-mooie-gezicht-van-karlijn-25-ging-een-briljant-brein-schuil~a3696187/>.

Suzanne Mulder, 'Zijn laatste woorden', 15 July 2015, <www.rijnmond.nl/nieuws/131489/Zijn-laatste-woorden-waren-Daar-ga-ik>.

Ania Steere, 'Passenger on doomed flight MH17 "joked about the flight disappearing"', *Daily Mail*, 17 July 2014, <www.dailymail.co.uk/news/article-2696555/Malaysia-Airlines-MH17-passenger-Cor-Pan-joked-plane-disappearing.html>.

Chapter 14

'MH17 crash, 17 juli 2014', <www.onderzoeksraad.nl/nl/page/3546/mh17-crash-17-juli-2014>.

Anton Zverev, 'Bodies rained down on Ukraine village after plane disaster', *Reuters*, 18 July 2014, <www.reuters.com/article/us-ukraine-crisis-bodies/bodies-rained-down-on-ukraine-village-after-plane-disaster-idUSKBN0FN1JJ20140718?utm_>.

Chapter 15

Elsbeth Stoker and Wil Thijssen, 'Topman Malaysia Airlines "Ik was kwade boodschapper MH17"', *de Volkskrant*, 13 July 2015,

<www.volkskrant.nl/nieuws-achtergrond/topman-malaysia-airlines-ik-was-kwade-boodschapper-mh17--bce69724/>.

'Persconferentie premier Rutte en minister Timmermans over vlucht MH17 16.00 uur', 18 July 2014, <nos.nl/video/676578-persconferentie-premier-rutte-en-minister-timmermans-over-vlucht-mh17-16-00-uur.html>.

Charlotte McDonald-Gibson, 'Anguish in Amsterdam as families of Flight MH17 passengers arrive at airport', *Time*, 17 July 2014, <www.time.com/3002907/malaysia-airlines-ukraine-crash-families-amsterdam/>.

Chapter 16

Matt Kodama, 'Buk SAMs and the downing of MH17', *Recorded Future*, 23 July 2014, <www.recordedfuture.com/buk-sam-mh17-investigation/>.

The Bellingcat MH17 Investigation Team, 'Origin of the separatists' Buk: A Bellingcat investigation', 8 November 2014, <www.bellingcat.com/news/uk-and-europe/2014/11/08/origin-of-the-separatists-buk-a-bellingcat-investigation/>.

'Ukraine claims fighter plane shot down by Russian missile', *The Guardian*, 17 July 2014, <www.theguardian.com/world/2014/jul/17/ukraine-claims-plane-shot-by-russian-missile>.

Pastoor Geudens, 'Stefan was met het ramptoestel op weg naar maleisie', 4 August 2014, <grandioos.wordpress.com/2014/08/04/stefan-was-met-het-ramptoestel-op-weg-naar-maleisie/>.

'Malaysian airline shot down by "Buk" missile system, verified in possession of pro-Russian militants', *Euromaidan Press*, 17 July 2014, <euromaidanpress.com/2014/07/17/malaysian-airline-shot-down-by-buk-missile-system-verified-in-possession-of-pro-russian-militants/>.

Yuras Karmanau, 'There's increasing evidence that pro-Russian rebels shot down the plane', *Business Insider*, 25 July 2014, <www.businessinsider.com/mh17-story-2014-7?international=true&r=US&IR=T>.

Chapter 17

Charlotte McDonald-Gibson, 'Malaysia Airlines flight MH17 crash: Cruel wait continues for victims' families awaiting truth', *Independent*, 18 July 2014, <www.independent.co.uk/news/world/europe/malaysia-airlines-flight-mh17-crash-cruel-wait-continues-for-victims-families-awaiting-truth-9614123.html>.

The White House, 'President Obama speaks on Malaysia Airlines Flight MH17, Russia and Ukraine, and the situation in Gaza,' 18 July 2014, <obamawhitehouse.archives.gov/blog/2014/07/18/president-obama-speaks-malaysia-airlines-flight-mh17-russia-and-ukraine-and-situatio>.

'Logboek Oekraiense bergingsmissie slachtoffers MH17', <www.rtlnieuws.nl/nieuws/binnenland/logboek-oekraiense-bergingsmissie-slachtoffers-mh17>.

Niels Klaassen and Cyril Rosman, 'Nederland sprak wel met de rebellen', *BN DeStem*, 12 December 2014, <www.bndestem.nl/overig/mh17 nederland-sprak-wcl-met-de-rebellen~a4a8b036/>.

'De wond van MH17 gaat opnieuw open', *NRC*, 7 January 2015, <www.nrc.nl/nieuws/2015/07/01/de-wond-van-mh17-gaat-opnieuw-open-1511216-a392592>.

'Dutch Mother: "Mr Putin, Send My Children Home"', *Sky News*, 20 July 2014, <news.sky.com/story/dutch-mother-mr-putin-send-my-children-home-10396093>.

Chapter 18

'MH17: Australian flags to be flown at half-mast as nation mourns victims', *The Guardian*, 19 Jul 2014, <www.theguardian.com/world/2014/jul/19/mh17-australian-flags-flown-half-mast>.

Australian Government Department of Defence, 'Bringing home the victims of the flight MH17 disaster', <www.defence.gov.au/annualreports/14-15/features/feature_bringing-home-the-victims-of-the-flight-mh17-disaster.asp>.

Harriet Alexander, 'MH17: Holland comes to mournful standstill as victims of Malaysia Airlines begin journey home', *The Telegraph*, 23 July 2014, <www.telegraph.co.uk/news/worldnews/europe/netherlands/10987146/MH17-Holland-comes-to-mournful-standstill-as-victims-of-Malaysia-Airlines-begin-journey-home.html>.

Vince Chadwick and Nick Miller, 'Planes carrying MH17 victims land in the Netherlands', *The Sydney Morning Herald*, 24 July 2014, <www.smh.com.au/world/planes-carrying-mh17-victims-land-in-the-netherlands-20140724-zw7hq.html>.

Richard Spillett, 'Bodies of Malaysian MH17 victims arrive back home more than a month after the jet was shot down over eastern Ukraine', *Daily Mail*, 22 August 2014, <www.dailymail.co.uk/news/article-2731508/Bodies-Malaysian-MH17-victims-arrive-home-month-jet-shot-eastern-Ukraine.html>.

Shannon Teoh, 'Malaysia's MH17 victims back on home soil as national mourning begins', *The Straits Times*, 22 August 2014, <www.straitstimes.com/asia/se-asia/malaysias-mh17-victims-back-on-home-soil-as-national-mourning-begins>.

'Bringing them home', AFP *Platypus Magazine*, October 2016, <www.austlii.edu.au/au/journals/AUFPPlatypus/2016/15.pdf>.

Chapter 19

Shaun Walker and Harriet Salem, 'Black Boxes handed over', *The Guardian*, 22 July 2014, <www.theguardian.com/world/2014/jul/22/mh17-black-boxes-handed-over-pro-russia-rebels>.

'Belgische nabestaanden MH17 boos op regering', 22 July 2016, <www.ad.nl/buitenland/belgische-nabestaanden-mh17-boos-op-regering~a31bcf5c/>.

Maarten van Dun, 'Oekraïne: "Trein vertrekt om 19:00 uur naar Charkov"', *Het Parool*, 21 July 2014, <www.parool.nl/buitenland/oekraine-trein-vertrekt-om-19-00-uur-naar-charkov~a3692818/>.

Chapter 20

James Massola and Lisa Cox, 'Tony Abbott vows to "shirtfront" Vladimir Putin over MH17 tragedy', *The Sydney Morning Herald*, 13 October 2014, <www.smh.com.au/politics/federal/tony-abbott-vows-to-shirtfront-vladimir-putin-over-mh17-tragedy-20141013-115cm3.html>.

Peter Cluskey, 'Eight trucks carrying MH17 wreckage arrive in Netherlands', *The Irish Times*, 10 December 2014, <www.irishtimes.com/news/world/europe/eight-trucks-carrying-mh17-wreckage-arrive-in-netherlands-1.2032028>.

Netherlands Public Prosecution Service, 'Presentation preliminary results criminal investigation MH17', 28 September 2016, <www.om.nl/onderwerpen/mh17-crash/?pager_page=2>.

Steve Lillebuen, 'Remains of more MH17 victims arrive in Australia', *The Sydney Morning Herald*, 11 September 2014, <www.smh.com.au/national/remains-of-more-mh17-victims-arrive-in-australia-20140911-10fmfj.html>.

'Nabestaanden bekijken wrakstukken', 7 March 2015, <www.ad.nl/buitenland/533-nabestaanden-bekijken-wrakstukken-mh17~ab5c5395/>.

Chapter 21

Charles Miranda, 'MH17: How Dutch investigators pieced together the shot-down plane from wreckage in Ukraine', *News.com.au*, 16 October 2015, <www.news.com.au/travel/travel-updates/incidents/mh17-how-dutch-investigators-pieced-together-the-shotdown-plane-from-wreckage-in-ukraine/news-story/bd1980e50ea5a5ce720724fc1a0850fd>.

Kamerstuk 33997, <https://zoek.officielebekendmakingen.nl/dossier/33997>.

Hanna Daych, 'Dutch fear MH17 attackers get "amnesty" in Ukraine accord', *NL Times*, 12 February 2015, <nltimes.nl/2015/02/12/dutch-fear-mh17-attackers-get-amnesty-ukraine-accord>.

'Hastily signed Minsk agreement forgot the perpetrators of MH17', *Euractiv*, 13 February 2015, <www.euractiv.com/section/europe-s-east/news/hastily-signed-minsk-agreement-forgot-the-perpetrators-of-mh17/>.

United Nations Press Release, 'Security Council fails to adopt resolution on tribunal for Malaysia Airlines crash', 29 July 2015, <www.un.org/press/en/2015/sc11990.doc.htm>.

'Russia's Air Transport Agency urges US to make public satellite data on MH17 crash', *TASS*, 9 February 2016, <tass.com/politics/855451>.

Marcel Haenen, 'Er is geen satellietbeeld van raket', *NRC*, 20 December 2014, <www.nrc.nl/nieuws/2014/12/20/er-is-geen-satellietbeeld-van-raket-1452559-a864809>.

Chapter 22

Frank Thunnissen, 'Werk Burgerdetective Omstreden', 28 January 2016, <www.ed.nl/default/werk-burgerdetective-omstreden~ac48b681/>.

'Daders MH17 volgens Bellingcat', *RTL Nieuws*, 24 February 2016, <www.rtlnieuws.nl/nieuws/buitenland/daders-mh17-volgens-bellingcat-3x211>.

Arjen Schreuder, 'De vrees voor een Doofpot', *NRC*, 1 March 2016, <www.nrc.nl/nieuws/2016/03/01/de-vrees-voor-een-doofpot-bekruipt-nabestaanden-m-1596166-a873591>.

'Dutch MPs slam secrecy, question lack of evidence in MH17 investigation', *RT*, 3 March 2016, <www.rt.com/news/334358-dutch-question-mh17-investigation/#.VtfgRuMX2wU.twitter>.

Wilmer Heck, 'Ik vertrouw de Oekraieners totaal niet', *NRC*, 31 May 2016, <www.nrc.nl/nieuws/2016/05/31/ik-vertrouw-de-oekraieners-totaal-niet-1624856-a1315548>.

Luke Harding and Alec Luhn, 'MH17: Buk missile finding sets Russia and west at loggerheads', *The Guardian*, 28 September 2016, <www.theguardian.com/world/2016/sep/28/flight-mh17-shot-down-by-missile-brought-in-from-russia-ukraine-malaysia-airlines>.

Netherlands Public Prosecution Service, 'JIT: Flight MH17 was shot down by a BUK missile from a farmland near Pervomaiskyi', 28 September 2016, <www.om.nl/@96068/jit-flight-mh17-shot/>.

Amy Maguire, 'Lockerbie experience is no model for effective prosecution of MH17 bombers', *ABC News*, 5 October 2016, <www.abc.net.au/news/2016-10-05/lockerbie-no-model-for-the-effective-prosecution-of-mh17/7904644?pfmredir=sm>.

Chapter 23

'ICJ says it won't impose measures against Russia in case brought by Kyiv', *Radio Free Europe*, 19 April 2017, <www.rferl.org/a/icj-to-issue-ruling-on-ukraine-case-against-russia/28438420.html>.

International Court of Justice, 17 January 2017, <www.icj-cij.org/files/case-related/166/19310.pdf>.

Wilmer Heck, 'Niet alles was opgeruimd, dus nam ik die MH17-resten mee', *NRC*, 13 January 2017, <www.nrc.nl/nieuws/2017/01/13/niet-alles-was-opgeruimd-dus-nam-ik-die-mh17-resten-mee-6178691-a1541104>.

Bellingcat Investigation team, 'The role of Sergey Dubinsky in the downing of MH17', 2 March 2017, <www.bellingcat.com/news/uk-and-europe/2017/03/02/the-role-of-sergey-dubinsky-in-the-downing-of-mh17/>.

'Russen staan klaar om te helpen ontcijferen', 18 February 2017, <ria.ru/mh17/20170218/1488288474.html>.

The Hon. Julie Bishop, Department of Foreign Affairs, media release, <foreignminister.gov.au/releases/Pages/2017/jb_mr_170921.aspx?w=tb1CaGpkPX%2FlS0K%2Bg9ZKEg%3D%3D>.

Chapter 24

Will Stewart, 'Fighter pilot blamed by Russia', *Mirror*, 9 April 2018, <www.mirror.co.uk/news/uk-news/fighter-pilot-blamed-russia-shooting-12331172>.

Rudy Bouwma, 'MH17: "Luchtverkeersleider Kiev" ontmaskerd hij blijkt een fantast', *Nos*, 14 March 2018, <nos.nl/nieuwsuur/artikel/2222351-mh17-luchtverkeersleider-kiev-ontmaskerd-hij-blijkt-een-fantast.html>.

Frank Jackman, 'Conflict zones', 19 April 2016, Flight Safety Foundation, <flightsafety.org/asw-article/conflict-zones/>.

Flight Safety Foundation, 'DSB launches investigation', 22 March 2018,<flightsafety.org/dutch-safety-board-launches-investigation-into-flight-over-conflict-zones/>.

Government of the Netherlands, 'MH17: The Netherlands and Australia hold Russia responsible', 25 May 2018, <www.government.nl/latest/news/2018/05/25/mh17-the-netherlands-and-australia-hold-russia-responsible>.

'An open letter to the Russian people from the families of the victims in the downing of MH17', 18 May 2018, <www.novayagazeta.ru/articles/2018/05/22/76563-an-open-letter-to-the-russian-people>.

Jon Henley, 'Visual guide: how Dutch intelligence thwarted a Russian hacking operation', *The Guardian*, 4 October 2018, <www.theguardian.com/world/2018/oct/04/visual-guide-how-dutch-intelligence-thwarted-a-russian-hacking-operation>.

References

Investigation reports

Bellingcat, 'MH17', <www.bellingcat.com/tag/mh17/>.

Dutch Safety Board, 'MH17 crash', <www.onderzoeksraad.nl/nl/page/3546/mh17-crash-17-juli-2014>.

Government of the Netherlands, 'MH17 incident', <www.government.nl/topics/mh17-incident>.

Openbaar Ministerie, 'Joint Investigation Team's reaction to OVV report', <www.om.nl/onderwerpen/mh17-crash/@91208/joint-investigation-0/>.

Openbaar Ministerie, 'MH17 crash: Criminal investigation MH17', <www.om.nl/onderwerpen/mh17-crash/#>.

Books

Annyssa Bellal (ed.), *The War Report: Armed Conflict in 2014*, Oxford University Press, Oxford, 2015.

Elsevier, *Fatale Vlucht MH17*, E van Luit, Amsterdam, 2014.

Julie Fedor, Andriy Portnov and Andreas Umland (eds), *Journal of Soviet and Post-Soviet Politics and Society*, vol. 1, no. 1, ibidem Press, Stuttgart, 2015.

Documentaries

BNN/VARA Zembla, *Jacht op de MH17-daders*, 7 March [2018].

KRO Brandpunt Reporter, *MH17*, 30 October 2014.

KRO/NCRV, *MH17, het onderzoek*, 13 October 2015.

KRO/NCRV Brandpunt Reporter, *MH17: Vliegen boven oorlogsgebied*, 28 June 2015.

MAX, *Rouwen en leven na de MH17*, 16 July 2017.

Michiel van Erp, *MH17: Het verdriet van Nederland*, Vara, 16 July 2015.

NOS Monument MH17, 17 July 2017.

NOS, *NOS Journaal: Rapport MH17*, 13 October 2015.

YouTube videos

112.UA International, *MH17 case: Australia and the Netherlands officially charge Russia with downing the je*t, 25 May 2018, <www.youtube.com/watch?v=8TZZPSLjoqI>.

ABC News (Australia), *Aus. Foreign Minister Julie Bishop on MH17*, 18 July 2014, <www.youtube.com/watch?v=3QtE_TK9PEw>.

ABC News (Australia), *Julie Bishop addresses UN Security Council on MH17*, 21 July 2014, <www.youtube.com/watch?v=ekI4KLK idXw>.

ABC News (Australia), *MH17: Abbott announces Operation Bring Them Home*, 22 July 2014, <www.youtube.com/watch?v= yuXHMciIvII>.

ABC News (Australia), *MH17: High-ranking Russian officer identified as suspect*, 26 May 2018, <www.youtube.com/ watch?v=okXyyndKJwQ>.

euronews (in English), *MH17: 'Russia can't wash its hands of this' —Australia PM Abbott*, 20 July 2014, <www.youtube.com/ watch?v=IB2Yudbbvrk>.

Politie, *JIT MH17 press meeting MH17*, 24 May 2018, <www. youtube.com/watch?v=fqdW3_0pPr4>.

Politie, *JIT MH17 witness appeal about 53rd brigade*, 24 May 2018, <www.youtube.com/watch?v=rhyd875Qtlg>.

Sky News, *Moment rebels realised shot down MH17 was passenger plane*, 17 July 2015, <www.youtube.com/watch?v=-gPJUDOnMfg>.

The Star Online, *Australia holds memorial for MH17 victims*, 17 July 2015, <www.youtube.com/watch?v=y4hrQYWdCwM>.